Souls Made Great Through Love and Adversity

THE FILM WORK OF FRANK BORZAGE

by

FREDERICK LAMSTER

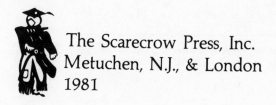

The Scarecrow Press, Inc.
Metuchen, N.J., & London
1981

Library of Congress Cataloging in Publication Data

Lamster, Frederick, 1954-
  "Souls made great through love and adversity"

  Bibliography: p.
  Filmography: p.
  Includes index.
  1. Borzage, Frank. I. Title.
PN1998.A3B6135   791.43'0233'0924   80-28441
ISBN 0-8108-1404-8

To Mom, for Sunday mornings
To Ira and Gail, for Sunday afternoons
To Grandpa, because everything is all right
To Rachel and Stephanie, for love

and

To Pops, just because.

CONTENTS

ACKNOWLEDGMENTS

The actual writing of a book is done by an author alone, yet the researching and support necessary are provided by so many others. I would like to thank Michael Silverman, Charles Nichols, and Bruce Rosenberg for their continued support. Thanks also to Deanna Durbin, Janet Gaynor, Burgess Meredith, Irving Stone, and the late Barbara Britton for answering letters and providing personal recollections; to John Belton, whose article "Souls Made Great Through Love and Adversity" suggested the title for this book, for his work and help; to the Museum of Modern Art, UCLA Film Center, American Film Institute, Wisconsin Center for Film and Theatre Research, Library of Congress, and Academy of Motion Picture Arts and Sciences for films, stills, scripts, and information; and to my friends David Miller, Peter Balakian, Susan Donaldson, Mel Donalson, Chris Nicoll, Jan Emerson, Helen Kebabian, Rheta Martin, Paul and Nancy Fees, Patricia Caldwell, Ezra and Riki Greenspan, Terry Spaise, Rosaleen Melone, Nancy Jasper, Theodore and Norma Knight, Sandy Honigsfeld, and Deborah G. Dunn for being there.

I would like to thank the following sources for allowing me permission to quote from their material: Methuen and Co. Ltd. of London (for quotations from Victorian Melodrama, by James L. Smith); Terry Curtis Fox (for quotations from his article "Three Comrades"); Gary Morris of Bright Lights (for quotations from parts one and two of Robert Smith's article "The Films of Frank Borzage"); Hutchinson Publishing Group Limited of London (for quotations from English Melodrama, by Michael Booth); Screen Magazine and Philip Rosen (for quotations from "Difference and Displacement in SEVENTH HEAVEN"); David Kehr (for quotations from "Moonrise"); John Belton (for quotations from his articles "Souls Made Great Through Love and Adversity" and "I've Always Loved You"); Fred Camper (for quotations from his articles "Man's Castle," "The Shining Hour," and "Disputed Passage"); Yale University Press (for quotations from Peter Brooks's The Melodramatic Imagination); University of California Press (for quotations from Fred Camper's "Disputed Passage"); Penn State Press of University Park (for quotations from The World of Melodrama, by Frank Rahill). Finally, I would like to thank A. S. Barnes/Tantivity for quotes taken from The Hollywood Professionals, vol. III, by John Belton and the University of Chicago Press for use of material reprinted from Melodrama Unveiled, by David Grimsted.

And, finally, to acknowledge a great director--FRANK BORZAGE.

Puff: Now then, for soft music.

Sneer: Pray, what's that for?

Puff: It shows that Tilburnia is coming--
        nothing introduces your heroine like soft music.

Sheridan, The Critic (1779)

The general attitude in Hollywood, and out of it too, is to
try to escape this essential dualism: Making movies must
be either a business or art, rather than both. For most
people in executive positions it is a business, where, according to the folklore, "for a nickel you get a dollar."
The goal is profits, large and quick ones.... For the artist there is another traditional goal. He tries to give his
interpretation a segment of experience he has either known
or observed, which he wants to communicate to others
[Hortense Powdermaker, Hollywood, The Dream Factory
(Boston: Little, Brown, 1950), pp. 25-26].

Ever since Andre Bazin set forth his auteur theory critics
from Andrew Sarris to Richard Corliss have debated its veracity or,
in looking for a better word, its plausibility. Exactly who gets
credit, either positive or negative, for the finished product, the
"movie"? Should the critics praise the director or the writer, the
actor or the cinematographer? And why praise only one and not all?

To evaluate auteurism, that theory which a number of French
critics who wrote for Cahiers du Cinema set forth in the late 1950s,
is no easy task. No matter how much we may want to find one person to praise or pummel, it is impossible. Film is, after all, a
cooperative art form, perhaps the only cooperative art form. A director neither writes a film nor does the actual "shooting." Then
why claim that the director is the "auteur," the author, of a film?
Why study all of a director's work in search of visual and thematic
continuities?

Perhaps the best way to work out this problem is to begin by
looking at the studio system as it existed in America from the mid-
to late 1920s. After the confusion of coming to Hollywood had settled, and after the major studios--Metro-Goldwyn-Mayer, Paramount,
Warner Brothers, Universal, and Fox--had consolidated into a set
structure, film came to be seen as being as much a business as an
art form. Actually, to those living during those times, it was all
business. The debate was not over the artistic merit of a film; it
was over the salability of a product.

The best example is Metro-Goldwyn-Mayer. Like the other
major studios, M-G-M was created through a series of mergers; by
1932 this studio, like the others, had developed an internal structure
that could compete with any American corporation. Not only was the

studio a horizontal monopoly (in which production and distribution
were West Coast concerns, and financing an East Coast concern),
but it was a vertical monopoly as well. Within the gates of this
single studio, and the other large studios to a similar degree, was
a roster of producers, directors, actors, writers, and cameramen
immediately "on-call" for work. Under Irving Thalberg, M-G-M
vice-president in charge of production, most film projects could be
carried to completion in a matter of weeks. This system became
even more highly structured and efficient when the corporation was
broken up into separate production units. Under this more complex
system producers were given a "set" of directors, stars, and writers whom they could use to fashion new products. Hunt Stromberg
"handled" the Joan Crawford pictures, a function later taken over by
Joseph Mankiewicz. Al Lewin had control over "such sophisticated
jobs as THE GUARDSMAN and PRIVATE LIVES." (Metro-Goldwyn-
Mayer," Fortune 6 [December 1932], pp. 51-52). Larry Wein-
garten, Bernie Hyman, Paul Bern, and Harry Rapf each had a
production company set up under the aegis of M-G-M and, more
precisely, under the watchful eye of both Irving Thalberg and
Louis B. Mayer. The producers and directors may have changed,
but the structure did not. And the same can be said of the
other major and minor studios. It was just as true for Frank
Capra at Columbia; Ernst Lubitsch and Mitchell Leisen at Paramount;
Michael Curtiz, Raoul Walsh, and William Wyler at Warner Brothers;
and Gregory LaCava, Val Lewton, and Orson Welles at RKO.

How, then, can any critic claim that there is any single
"auteur" or artist within this business structure? The answer to
this must be found in the second part of this Preface's epigraph.
Film is not just a business. It is an art form as well. Why the
director is this artist, and not the producer or the writer, is because
it is the director who gives the film its complete vision. It is the
director who not only supervises all who are on the set, but who de-
termines how to shoot a scene, how to say the words, and how it is
all to "come out." Writers had neither the freedom nor the respect
that directors received in the studio system. Producers from Thalberg and Mayer down, while concerned with the outcome of the product, did not supervise its every step. This was the job of the director, and it is in this that we find the "authorship" of a film.

Before the studio system developed into its "modern" form it
was the director whose single-minded devotion and artistry created
a product. We still look at the films of D. W. Griffith, Thomas
Ince, Cecil B. De Mille, Erich von Stroheim, and Charlie Chaplin
as "the films of" Griffith or Ince or De Mille or von Stroheim or
Chaplin. Throughout the period beginning in 1908, when Griffith
first directed THE ADVENTURES OF DOLLY, and lasting through
the 1920s, there was no real question as to the director's primacy.
Yet while this primacy may have declined with the use of the star
system the director's centrality did not. And even under the super-
structure of the studio system itself there was a great deal of freedom to be found. The studio system was present to decrease the
time and expense of production. It did not necessarily decrease

creativity. It was a structure that made available to the artist all
of the tools he or she could possibly need. After the coming of
sound, in particular, the director became central in making all of
the elements cohere. In doing so, he put a personal mark, more
than any other, on the finished product.

While numerous auteur studies have been done of those directors considered "great" by whatever evaluation process a critic sets
forth, what auteurist criticism is really doing is forcing film scholars to go back and to look at previously ignored films and film artists. In this way critics and scholars are attempting to get a clearer
sense of film, and of those who created the product we view.

INTRODUCTION:
MELODRAMA IN FICTION AND FILM

The most persistent criticism of Frank Borzage is his reliance upon the outdated conventions of melodrama. Yet the cinema
seemed ideally suited to the precepts of melodrama, and from its
earliest days film was recognized as the ideal medium "for action
and spectacle; intercutting created new forms of suspense."[1] The
western, in particular, proved an excellent vehicle for the style. The
implication of simplicity, the reduction of all conflict to a struggle
between good and evil, and the externalization of all conflict reinforced the conception of melodrama being synonymous with intellectual simplemindedness and naivete.

Melodramatic structure, according to such critics as Peter
Brooks, is one of "bipolar contrast and clash."[2] The world is the
place of battle between good and evil, and melodramatic situations
become those of extremes, of "either/or"[3] and of "all-or-nothing."[4]
In such a Manichean world there is no middle ground, no place for
compromise, no gray in a world of moral black and white. Two
value systems compete for existence, and all else, including character, is subsumed within the framework. Identity and values are
not so much sought as tested and reaffirmed, and positive and negative ideals are set against each other so that an ethical system may
be validated. Some basic definitions of melodrama by leading literary critics reinforce this idea of "wholes," of ideal good and absolute evil set in contrapuntal existence.

> ... we can note that we find there [in melodramatic works]
> an intense emotional and ethical drama based on the Mani-
> chaeistic struggle of good and evil.... The polarization of
> good and evil works toward revealing their presence and
> operation as real forces in the world. [5]

> Melodrama is a form of dynamic composition in prose
> partaking of the nature of tragedy, comedy, pantomime and
> spectacle, and intended for a popular audience.... It is
> conventionally moral and humanitarian in point of view and
> sentimental and optimistic in temper, concluding its fable
> happily with virtue rewarded after many trials and vice
> punished. [6]

> Ideologically, melodrama insists upon the ultimate good-
> ness of man; its single dramatic aim is to demonstrate the
> triumph of good over evil.... The catastrophe of melo-

1

> drama finds virtue rewarded and wickedness punished ...
> and its final appeal is to the relief that we experience when
> virtue escapes intact. [7]
>
> ... Its structure was seldom thoughtfully worked out. Its
> ideals were truisms, the more commonplace and widely ac-
> cepted the better. Its avowed purpose was moral; and to
> abet this it set up ridiculous opposites of purity and pollu-
> tion, innocence and guilt, with natural and poetic justice,
> granting the victory to the righteous. All this divorced the
> melodrama from any realistic tradition.... [8]
>
> Essentially, melodrama is a simplistic idealization of
> human experience dramatically presented. For its audience
> melodrama was both an escape from real life and a drama-
> tization of it as it ought to be; uncomplicated, easy to un-
> derstand.... [9]

All of these statements point to a definition of melodrama that
will prove itself different from that of film melodrama. Melodrama,
as a literary form, is "primarily concerned with situation and plot,"[10]
relegating character development and complexity to a place of secondary importance. It is a drama of linear movement, which emphasizes
not so much what happens to the innocent hero and heroine, but that
they, and the good that they represent, do ultimately triumph over
evil. Melodrama aims at an ordering of the social system and attempts to bridge the gap "between different moral states."[11] Evil
is presented as a real and powerful adversary to the good within the
world of the drama, a constant menace to the existing moral (or
Judeo-Christian) order. Melodrama sets out to depict this conflict
and to signify through it the ultimate triumph of good. Melodrama
becomes

> not only a moralistic drama but the drama of morality:
> it strives to find, to articulate, to demonstrate, to "prove"
> the existence of a moral universe which, though put into
> question, masked by villainy and perversions of judgment,
> does exist and can be made to assert its presence and its
> categorical force among men. [12]

What occurs is a drama of confrontation, complete with coup
de théâtre and deus ex machina, one in which two opposed moral states
come to blows. The stock characters--the noble and good hero, the
suffering and sacrificing heroine, and the evil villain--are manipu-
lated by the dramatist and, by implication, outside forces. The
struggles and the "race against the clock"[13] take on a larger significance and become more than simply the struggles of a small group
of people in a particular place and time: melodrama strives for universal meaning.

Melodrama, being topical, has its roots in the anxieties of a
particular time. Be it the anxiety of freedom in an era of socio-
religious change and breakdown or a larger anxiety concerning the

failure of the moral universe, melodrama becomes "an expression
of ... involvement with ... a way of feeling and of dramatizing
[with] conviction ... the antagonism between two ways of life"[14]--
an exorcism as well as an expression of social fears and fantasies.[15]
The characters express, "directly and indirectly, their moral judgments of the world,"[16] and their feelings, ideas, and values are not
only tested but discussed and dissected as "tactile models held out
for all to see and handle."[17] Social repression and convention are
removed in the search for understanding we see articulated in the
drama. Melodrama conceptualizes and in its search for solutions
allows both the characters and the audience a catharsis.[18]

Whether it be, as Robert Heilman terms it, a "melodrama of
triumph," a "melodrama of defeat," or a "melodrama of protest,"
the drama is of primary importance, not the characters.[19] What is
important about the characters is not so much their personality or
their deeds, nor the struggle and the hardships they endure. What
is important is the achievement or reachievement of some semblance
of order in their, and by implication, the larger universal, moral
order. Virtue is rewarded not so much by material gains, or even
by the eventual erotic union of the hero and the heroine at the end
of the drama, but by its recognition and its reaffirmed place within
the moral order of the universe.[20] Evil, in the guise of the villain,
is again subdued. Its once-imminent triumph is halted and its emergence into an all-powerful design is circumvented.

In the typical case, ... melodramatic structure moves
from the presentation of virtue-as-innocence to the introduction of menace or obstacle, which places virtue in a
situation of extreme peril. For the greater part of the
play, evil appears to reign triumphant, controlling the
structure of events, dictating the moral coordinates of reality. Virtue, expulsed, eclipsed, apparently fallen, cannot effectively articulate the cause of the right.... Its
recovery will depend upon recognition of error by those
set in the position of judges which itself depends on the
recognition of evil.... This clarification of signs--first
of evil, then of virtue--is the necessary precondition for
the re-establishment of the heroine.... The play ends with
public recognition of where virtue and evil reside, and the
eradication of one as the reward of the other.[21]

This eradication, however, is true for this particular situation and
time only. Melodrama is a drama of the temporal present; evil will
surely raise its head again in the context of another situation in another drama. This is the major conflict contained within the genre--
it strives for universalism while being firmly and clearly anchored
in the present.

While the melodramatic situation is recognized by most critics
as being "topical," the characters within that mode of drama may be
recognized as types. In tragedy the major character is seen as internally divided, but in melodrama the characters are "whole," lacking

psychological or emotional schisms.   In melodrama it is not a reordering of the self that is sought so much as the "reordering of
one's relations with others, with the world of people and things; not
the knowledge of self but the maintenance of self, in its assumption
of wholeness, until the conflicts are won or lost. "[22] The characters
within melodrama are either more saintly than the saints or more
evil than the devil himself.   In this way literary melodrama avoids
the basic "moral ambiguity"[23] presented within tragedy and presents
sin more as a "product of character than of situation and society. "[24]
The search for a social reordering becomes one acted out within the
context of familial and small-group relationships; an ideal world in
which morality and not accident rule is substituted for the "real"
world, which is ruled more by accident than according to any overall design.[25]   Maintaining the present social and moral codes is
given primary emphasis, and, in contrast to tragedy, character is
relegated to a secondary place of importance.

        Whereas in tragedy virtue and evil are seen as being equal
parts of a single, albeit divided, personality, in melodrama these
same values are externalized and personalized in opposing characters.
Tragedy is predicated upon the "divided whole" idea and studies self-
knowledge.   Not only do the protagonists try to understand their
deeds, but they seek to understand the conflicting values behind their
actions or lack of them.[26]   Whether the internal division be one of
"imperative" (duty) as opposed to "impulse" (desire)[27] or that of
"unruly passion" as opposed to "moral ordinance, "[28] what is implied
is a choice.   Tragedy further implies some greater knowledge than
the simple intuitive knowledge of the characters in melodrama, and
that self-knowledge is closely tied to internal strength.[29] Suffering,
in tragedy, implies self-awareness and not the self-pity of melodrama.   It is not external forces as seen in opposing characters (the
hero and the villain) that do battle, but two sides of the tragic hero's
consciousness.   Thus tragedy, by originating within the self, deals
more with the individual than with the society.   Tragedy needs no
externalized villain.   The end of the tragic drama brings with it "a
clear vision of spiritual realities--of man recognizing the self in his
constant struggle between damnation and salvation. "[30]   No such "resolution" occurs in melodrama.   The "self-confrontation"[31] of tragedy
yields in melodrama to the concept of villainy outwitted.   Tragedy
and melodrama "deal in different heroes"[32] and, by extension, in
"different structures of experience. "[33]

        The hero, in melodrama, does not seek to understand himself
and his actions so much as to protect (and, in the process, to win)
virtue, in the guise of the heroine, while at least temporarily de-
stroying evil.

        Between the villain and the heroine, morally and often
        physically, stood the hero.   His mediating role differed.
        Often he was primarily a shield, fending off the thrusts
        of the villain.   Occasionally he was the pawn over whom
        the forces of good and evil, the heroine and the villain
        struggled.   Particularly if the hero and heroine were

married was he likely to be the center of this moral tug-of-war. 34

The hero in melodrama is the representation of all that is strong, good, and ideal within society and, by implication, the greater universe. He is both the perfect match for the heroine and the obvious antagonist for the villain. Being the pawn or centerpiece in the fight between the villain and the heroine, the melodramatic hero gains some stature, but lacks the insight and struggle of the tragic hero. His struggle is not self-inflicted, and his suffering is for the most part undeserved. His end finds him not in a state of "existential despair, stoic resignation or Christian fortitude"35 but reunited with a reordered and rational system.

Idealistic social and religious concepts like salvation, redemption, and purity were "affixed to the heroine: [an] 'angel woman' ... a guardian angel, meant to guide, protect, and solace...."36 It is she who echoes the faith in heaven and in heavenly justice that the hero struggles to achieve and that stands at the back of the play itself. She is, furthermore, central to the drama both in her place as "keeper of the home" and as the prize that is fought for by both the hero and the villain. She and the hero together represent and embody a greater wholeness in their connection with the spiritual, which they are powerless, for much of the drama, to defend adequately.

Directly opposed to the noble hero and the angelic heroine is the black-hearted villain. The villain becomes not only the personification of evil but a representation of the continued fall from the Edenic state itself. It is he who seeks to shatter virtue and to destroy (often by sexual corruption) its actual existence through subterfuge and machination. It is, however, within the villain that most of the intelligence of the play resides. He is crafty and devious, often taking on the very attributes of the devil. His end is usually, if not always, defeat and destruction at the hands of morality and "good." His evil must be destroyed because it is more than just an immediate or transitory development. The evil represented by the villain is the key to the larger and greater "terrors of a hostile universe"37 as well as the powerful opponent of worldly virtue.

This whole idea of universalism is central to the growth pattern in Borzage's career as a director of melodrama. Borzagean melodrama--and, by extension, the larger genre of film melodrama--reverses some of the components of literary melodrama. Not only does it concentrate on character rather than on plot or situation, but in adding visual and aural elements, it evolves more complex levels of sensory and symbolic meaning. As with literary melodrama, the story is used as the structure through which the problems of the characters and of the greater society are acted out. Yet more so than in literary melodrama, however, direct implications of "something greater" or something more universal become more important than what is seen as being immediate. Visual and aural signs found within the individual film and within the corpus of film melodrama reinforce this sense.

Because it had to rely on piano accompaniment for punctu-
ation, all silent film drama ... is "melodramatic." It
meant that directors had to develop an extremely subtle
and yet precise formal language (of lighting, staging decor,
acting, close-up, montage and camera movement), because
they were deliberately looking for ways to compensate for
the expressiveness, range of inflection and tonality, rhyth-
mic emphasis and tension normally present in the spoken
word. [38]

From the first time that a piano accompanied movement on celluloid,
melodrama, in a larger and more general sense, presented itself.
It was retooled and refined over the nest sixty or seventy years by
masters from Griffith and Ince to Borzage, John Ford, Vincente
Minnelli, Max Ophuls, and Douglas Sirk.

Borzage's earliest films, in which he was often found acting
as well as directing, were westerns. This film genre most clearly
expressed melodramatic preconceptions and most clearly maintained
the structure of stage melodrama. Moral judgments were clearcut,
with evil residing in the villain, who often dressed in black, or,
more prominently in later years, the savage Indian. Good resided
in the hero and the heroine, a couple much like their literary or
stage counterparts. The hero acted "positively, as a morally free
agent, on the changing situations where and when they presented
themselves ... always through direct action ... [and] in an unre-
lentingly linear course." [39] Evils and conflicts were completely externalized, and the actions taken against such negative forces were
direct and decisive (e.g., gunfights). With social upheavals and
spiritual crises personalized and acted upon, the private fears and
emotional upsets of the viewing audience were, by extension, laid
to rest as well. Very much like the nineteenth-century literary
and stage melodrama, the western film melodrama explained social
flux and the attempted reordering of existence into some rational
and logical pattern. It not only stressed the alignment of newer
sections of the nation with the older and more established sections,
but generally reaffirmed American ideals of government and the
principle of strong and individualized action as a civilizing force.

Later film melodrama takes this even farther. In Borzage's
work it is commonplace to find an individual or a small, tightly-knit
group set against some larger, disruptive force. Whether it be
war, as in A FAREWELL TO ARMS (1932) and NO GREATER GLORY
(1934); depression, as in MAN'S CASTLE (1933) and LITTLE MAN,
WHAT NOW? (1934); or Fascism, as in THREE COMRADES (1938),
THE MORTAL STORM (1940), and TILL WE MEET AGAIN (1944),
neither the individual nor the outer state of chaos is of primary importance. The central concern is the characters' growing self-
knowledge and ability to transcend the immediate surroundings and
to become aligned with something larger and more universal.

The male-female relationship is used as the central point of
the story, as is the movement from "the specific material and emo-

tional commitments to an acceptance of the universe"[40] that accompanies the growth within that relationship. The major characters exist outside of the actual or material world and within their own spiritual and emotional sphere, which even physical separation and death cannot destroy. Borzage allows for the "co-existence of several moral and spiritual systems."[41] The characters--the childlike and emotionally innocent hero who becomes capable of understanding and, therefore, love and the sacrificial and self-aware heroine who devotes herself to something greater than herself--"make a trial of one [spiritual state] by contrasting it with another, providing the catalyst for his [Borzage's] characters' growth out of one order and the emergence into another, transcendent one."[42] The characters give each other and the objects surrounding them--for instance, the stove in MAN'S CASTLE and the dressing table in LITTLE MAN, WHAT NOW?--a spiritual reality previously denied. Physical space is often disregarded, as in SONG O' MY HEART (1930), or lacks any "deterministic reality,"[43] as in HIS BUTLER'S SISTER (1943). The same happens to time, which is given a nonphysical and nonbinding character. It is not enough, as it is in literary or stage melodrama, for the reordering of the present to be achieved. Within Borzagean melodrama this is only the first step to the protagonists' later and complete alignment with the outer world of spiritual forces.

Borzage is more interested in describing these "states of grace" and the movement of characters within them than the "processes by which they are achieved. This places Borzage's dramatic structure far away from the melodramatic norm, since very little weight is placed upon individual action."[44] No single act becomes decisive, nor does any single moral decision. Backgrounds take on a spiritual more than material quality,[45] and dogmatic ideals and beliefs are downplayed against the purely spiritual nature of humanity and the world. This is reinforced by the single plane of depth within the frame itself. Lighting, in Borzage films,

> unifies frames into a single level of depth, and characters
> do not derive their spirituality from single objects or from
> specific parts of the frame and the succession of frames
> around it (i. e. editing).[46]

The evenness of tone within the frame creates an equally weightless background and foreground, in which objects do not exert physical force on individuals.[47] There is no conflict between the foreground and the background as there is in Griffith, and the conflict between the characters and the environment takes on a spiritual more than material aspect.[48] Images, such as the flickering light in MANNEQUIN (1938) and the Bible in STRANGE CARGO (1940), function "as metaphors for larger transcendent issues."[49]

In a sense, the silent cinema "was the culmination of melodrama"[50] in its creation of a total world of both fantasy and desire.[51] Technically, the silent camera proved itself adept at the "demands of melodrama,"[52] as it was ideal for showing action to the fullest advantage (through cross-cutting and parallel action, in particular) as well as for building suspense and eliciting audience reaction. [53] Griffith, making full use of the close-up for both individuals and objects, drew the audience into closer involvement with the drama, just as his cuts to battlefields in BIRTH OF A NATION (1915) and his cuts between separate stories in INTOLERANCE (1916) tied both the audience and the characters to something beyond the individual experience. Griffith and Ince, and the legions of film directors whom they influenced, tapped the "crude power of melodrama while subtly reconstituting the elements. "[54] In doing so they reduced the obvious sentimentality of melodrama while retaining its dramatic strength. As recognized in the work of Borzage, the emphasis tended to rest upon the characters' responses to the situations before them and not just to the situations themselves. Stronger and more fully developed characters brought believability and strength to the weak or hackneyed plots.

Film melodrama, Borzage's in particular, developed into a much more subtle art. In his earliest films, and especially in the pre-1920 westerns (like THE PITCH O' CHANCE (1915), THE GUN WOMAN (1917), and UNTIL THEY GET ME (1917), Borzage plays upon different aspects of character, tying it to the larger, non-Manichean issues of good versus evil and of civilization as opposed to wilderness. The themes set forth and studied within these films are picked up in the later works, and many of the ideas concerning love, desire, security, and faith are tested and retested throughout his career. His themes are not only the obviously melodramatic ones of simplistic situations so much as they are reflective of larger moral concerns. In THE PITCH O' CHANCE the heroine is left with the dilemma of choosing between her love for the bad man and the security offered by the noble hero, with the home and children he promises. In THE GUN WOMAN the "Tigress" rises above her disillusioning love affair and moves on to a higher spiritual level as well as to a higher level of understanding about herself and her true desires. Not surprisingly, she reaches this decision as she reaches the top of a mountain overlooking both the hometown she is leaving permanently as well as the town in which she has left her dead thieving lover.

In the later silent films Borzage develops these themes to an even finer degree and evolves to an almost philosophical level the idea of multiple spheres in which different characters exist. In films such as SEVENTH HEAVEN (1927), STREET ANGEL (1928), and THE RIVER (1928) individuals unspeakingly come to some understanding of themselves and, in doing so, of their connection with the greater moral and religious universe of which they are a part. This becomes the moment of transcendence. Diane and Chico in SEVENTH HEAVEN transcend time after Chico's return from the dead in the same way that the love of Angela and Gino in STREET ANGEL takes on religious overtones through the symbol of the madonna portrait and in the same way that Rosalee uses her love as a transmittable force to revive the frozen Allen John in THE RIVER. In this period Borzage further develops his idea of the true or

spiritual love between a man and woman as representative of the
understanding necessary to move up into a higher spiritual world.
The melodramas of this period go beyond the Manichean terms of
literary melodrama and supersede the reliance upon stage melodrama plot conventions found in Borzage's earlier work. These master-
pieces move in to an analysis of individuals and the spiritual growth
within and between them.

This idea of spiritualization is played upon in many ways in
the later Borzage works as well. In the early years of the sound
era Borzage further refines the theme of the individual couple set
against the immediacy of the chaotic outer and, symbolically, internal world. Lammchen and Hans in LITTLE MAN, WHAT NOW?
(1934) grow together during their times of adversity and, in doing
so, grow into a greater understanding. They escape the Depression
and the decadence of their Germany after the birth-in-the-manger
of their child, the symbol for life and its continuity. The pregnant
Trina and the once-wandering Bill do the same in MAN'S CASTLE
(1933) by "hopping a freight" for a new start and a new life. The
spirituality of their lives is reinforced as the camera reveals them
in a manger-like place, the straw-covered boxcar, from an extremely high-angle. In all of these films the characters' religiosity grows
from within as well as between, and the characters move to a higher
spiritual realm together. It is not a dogmatic or doctrinaire religion
that changes them and allows them symbolically and literally to move
on, but a naturalistic and humanitarian one.

> ... Borzage's characters do not run away from their cha-
> otic, troubled backgrounds as much as they grow out of
> them spiritually. Borzage so totally transforms them that
> it becomes impossible for his surviving characters to re-
> turn to their former lives. ... [They find] liberation from
> the weight of their own bodies and chaotic backgrounds. [73]

It is in the later 1930s, in such films as THE GREEN LIGHT
(1937), THREE COMRADES (1938), THE SHINING HOUR (1938),
DISPUTED PASSAGE (1939), and STRANGE CARGO (1940), that this
theme is enlarged and expressed through a more obvious sense of
religious mysticism and symbolism--the ritualistic murder outside
of the church in THREE COMRADES and the conversion endings of
THE GREEN LIGHT and DISPUTED PASSAGE--as opposed to the
more muted Catholicism of the earlier works.

In the 1940s and 1950s Borzage moves out of this increasingly
mystical realm and returns to a more secular religious sense. In
TILL WE MEET AGAIN (1944) a nun learns the true nature of God
and of religion only after she is forced to experience life outside of
the convent and only after she learns to understand herself and her
unity with humankind. In I'VE ALWAYS LOVED YOU (1947) it is
only when Myra finally breaks Goronoff's hold upon her during the
second concert sequence that she can find peace with George and
her daughter on their farm. The fullest attempt at personalization
within a film, however, and the fullest study of an individual and

and his learning process comes in MOONRISE (1949). Here we are presented with a melodrama that concerns itself not only with the story of an individual's understanding and coming to terms with the past, but with his learning to live in the present. More important is that here the landscape completely reflects the state of the character's mind throughout, and his final emergence into the sunlight reflects his final escape from the dark and strangling hold of the past.

What we recognize through all of this is the growth, development, and refinement of an idea--the study of men and women within the context of their immediate adversities and their entrance into a larger universal ideal. Borzage's melodramas center on character development, the growth of a man or woman out of the immediate, out of isolation, and into an understanding of some more divine self, part of a larger spiritual nexus.

Borzage's melodrama is a study of growth, and while this is presented as a linear process (A yields to B yields to C), it is without any real beginning or end, as the characters are only unconsciously awaiting the moment of their rebirth. Borzage's universe is cyclical, with all events and individuals tied together and with all emotional and spatial separations between individuals bridged only through understanding and love. The immediate world and the immediate problems of society take on a lesser importance, being relegated to a place below that of the realignment with the larger spiritual belief system. The technique of using black or white stock-character types, of last-minute rescues and of races against the clock, as well as the fight against defeat and disaster or the fight for some tangible victory, take on a lesser degree of importance as the spiritual nature of the characters within the drama becomes the basic focus.

NOTES

[1]David Morse, "Aspects of Melodrama," Monogram 4 (1972), p. 16.
[2]Peter Brooks, The Melodramatic Imagination (New Haven: Yale University Press, 1976), p. 36.
[3]Ibid., p. 36.
[4]Ibid.
[5]Ibid., p. 13.
[6]Frank Rahill, The World of Melodrama (University Park: Pennsylvania State University Press, 1967), p. xiv.
[7]Leo B. Levy, Versions of Melodrama: A Study of the Fiction and Drama of Henry James (Berkeley: University of California Press, 1957), p. 2.
[8]David Grimsted, Melodrama Unveiled: American Theater and Culture, 1800-1850 (Chicago: University of Chicago Press, 1968), p. 234.

[9]Michael Booth, English Melodrama (London: Herbert Jenkins, 1965), p. 9.
[10]Rahill, p. xiv.
[11]Levy, p. 3.
[12]Brooks, p. 20.
[13]Ibid., p. 31.
[14]Levy, p. 28.
[15]James L. Smith, Victorian Melodrama: Seven English, French and American Melodramas (London: Methuen, 1976), p. xiv.
[16]Brooks, p. 37.
[17]Ibid., p. 41.
[18]James L. Smith, Melodrama (London: Methuen, 1973), pp. 9-10.
[19]Robert Bechtold Heilman, The Iceman, the Arsonist and the Troubled Agent: Tragedy and Melodrama on the Modern Stage (Seattle: University of Washington Press, 1973), p. 85.
[20]Brooks, p. 32.
[21]Ibid., pp. 31-32.
[22]Heilman, p. 86.
[23]Grimsted, p. 222.
[24]Ibid.
[25]Smith, Victorian Melodrama, p. xv.
[26]Heilman, p. 251.
[27]Ibid., p. 10.
[28]Ibid., pp. 10-11.
[29]Ibid., p. 15.
[30]Heilman, p. 162.
[31]Ibid., p. 239.
[32]Smith, Melodrama, p. 65.
[33]Ibid.
[34]Grimsted, pp. 179-180.
[35]Smith, Melodrama, p. 64.
[36]Grimsted, p. 173.
[37]Smith, Victorian Melodrama, p. xv.
[38]Thomas Elsaesser, "Tales of Sound and Fury: Observations on the Family Melodrama," Monogram 4 (1972), p. 6.
[39]Ibid., p. 9.
[40]Robert Smith, "The Films of Frank Borzage" (part 1), Bright Lights I, 2 (Spring 1975), p. 5.
[41]John Belton, The Hollywood Professionals: Howard Hawks, Frank Borzage and Edgar Ulmer vol. 3 (New York: Tantivity, 1974), p. 128.
[42]Ibid., p. 128.
[43]Ibid., p. 127.
[44]Terry Curtis Fox, "Three Comrades," Focus! 9 (Spring-Summer 1973), p. 32.
[45]Belton, p. 123.
[46]John Belton, "Souls Made Great Through Love and Adversity," Focus! 9 (Spring-Summer 1975), p. 21.
[47]Belton, Hollywood Professionals, p. 124.
[48]Ibid.
[49]Belton, "Souls Made Great," p. 20.

[50]Morse, p. 16.
[51]Ibid.
[52]Ibid.
[53]Ibid.
[54]Ibid. , p. 17.

1. THE EARLY SILENT PERIOD

Part One: The Westerns

Ten films exist from Borzage's early silent period, three of which are westerns. These three films give a glimpse of Borzage the storyteller "more than the free creator."[1] Yet in them we can see some of the stylistic devices of the later films as well as themes that are more fully developed later. The whole idea of the "moral dilemma," of the choice between opposites that implies a given choice of lifestyles, is especially apparent throughout. Yet, most of all, this period proves to be one of stylistic and thematic experimentation for Borzage. The somewhat uneven quality that results has to do as much with the materials that the director starts with as it has unquestionably to do with the attempt to copy other leading directors of his day, such as Ince and De Mille.

There is some controversy over exactly which film was Borzage's first directorial assignment. It is supposed that after working as a leading action in Thomas Ince's westerns Borzage moved into directing most probably in 1915. It was only natural that the training that he had received from Ince should lead him into directing westerns first. Ince was, after all, a leading pioneer in the development of this genre. Furthermore, the western allowed Borzage to explore the basic ideas of good and evil, civilization and wilderness, and the concepts of free will, choice, knowledge, and growth.

Borzage's first feature, only a part of which exists today, was THE PITCH O' CHANCE (1915). This is the story of a gambler, Kentuck; a tenderfoot, Rocky Scott, who "bets on everything, anything, or nothing at all"; and the two women who become the center of their conflict: Nan, who "sort of belongs to Kentuck," and Kate, a dancehall girl who wants Kentuck for her own. Each character is introduced at the start with an iris-in, an intertitle, and an iris-out. We first meet Rocky Scott sitting out-of-doors by a well, rolling a cigarette. In the next shot we meet Kentuck, dressed in a dark coat and vest, his dark eyes accentuated and a long cigar in his mouth. Nan, the simple girl, is introduced next, followed by Kate. Kate is costumed in a white dress covered with rhinestones and a black-and-white shawl. The two women, representing two obvious types, the good woman versus the scheming whore, are rarely seen next to each other, and then only when Kentuck stands between them. Often, as in the opening shot of the

13

actual drama, as Kate enters from the right and moves toward Kentuck, in the center, Nan exits to the left at a corresponding rhythm.
In the second cut to the saloon, as Nan enters from the left, Kate
stops hugging Kentuck's shoulders and exits right.

Into this seemingly placid scene rides Rocky--a rowdy gambler
who is as irreverent toward his trade as Kentuck is serious. Rocky
bets at the bar on where a fly will land, while Kentuck sits at his
table, playing poker as Nan watches over him. Rocky next moves
over to the table, positioning himself above Nan, thus setting the
drama in action by visually and thematically presenting the premier
conflict: Rocky versus Kentuck, with Nan as the pawn played between them.

Rocky attempts to win Nan over with his charm; failing that, he returns to the bar. At this point Kate returns, setting the second
drama into action. Nan and Kate face each other, visually stress-
ing their opposition, as Kate says (on an intertitle): "You're only
afraid of him--I love him." Nan replies: "I ... know it."

Falling into Kate's arms for a moment, Nan soon rouses herself and the two face forward toward Kentuck, the center of their
attention. Rocky, in the meantime, has returned to the table and
is gambling with Kentuck. The drama now proceeds into open conflict.

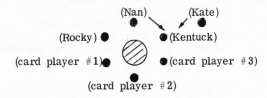

Rocky begins to win and bets more and more recklessly.
Finally he proposes to play out one hand of poker for all of the money as well as for possession of Nan. The placement of the characters foretells the outcome of the game, as Rocky and Nan both face
right, in opposition to Kentuck and to Kate, who both face left. Kentuck agrees, and while Nan faints, Kate proceeds to fix the cards.
As the game proceeds Rocky and Kentuck sit facing each other as
Kate moves fluidly between them. In doing so she visually reinforces her role as "director" of the drama. As expected, Rocky
wins, and he and Nan exit left.

Rocky and Nan return to her home to pick up her things.
They enter the (symbolically) dark cabin, and Nan lights a lamp.
She also reaches for her rifle to shoot Rocky and thus end her di-
lemma. Yet the drama cannot be resolved by this simple act; losing

her courage, she collapses crying on the bed, just as she earlier
collapsed and cried on Kate's shoulder. Kate's previous statement
("You're only afraid of him") is proved false, as Nan's love for Kentuck becomes obvious. Furthermore, through these statements and
events we are assured that Kate's deed will be found out. The other
part of Kate's remark is proven false as well, ("I love him") as we
recognize that hers is a selfish rather than a selfless love and,
therefore, doomed to a short and unreciprocated duration. As if
to reinforce this visually, Borzage cuts back to the bar, where Kate
stands behind Kentuck and looks left, as Kentuck dazedly looks away
from her and off to the left, the direction that Nan and Rocky took
to exit (// ˍKentuck ˍKate).

Nan and Rocky leave the cabin and start off on the road leading out of town and, symbolically, out of the past. They camp just
outside of town, lighting a fire in the dark, an image parallel to the
one in the cabin earlier. Nan, lit by the Rembrandt tones of the
fire, cries while Rocky, holding her hand, attempts to comfort her.
There is then a cut to Kate attempting to comfort Kentuck. The two
shots in juxtaposition deny any possible fruition of the Rocky-and-Nan
or Kate-and-Kentuck unions. As if to reinforce this idea further,
Rocky crosses around the fire, just as Kate did the gambling table,
gives Nan his guns (a gesture that she does not acknowledge), and
returns to his side of the frame. The two sit facing each other,
her rejection understood even though never verbalized, the fire between them representative of the emotional barrier that exists between them as well.

Reel two opens with Kate again attempting to comfort a drunk-
en Kentuck and Kentuck rejecting her advances and, by extension,
her love. He next goes to the table, picks up the cards, recognizes
the fraud and decides to go after Nan and bring her back. Borzage
cuts to Nan and an intertitle through which she tells Rocky of her
wish to return to Kentuck. The resolutions of Kentuck and Nan come
at the same moment, creating a tie between them previously not recognized, or not there. As Kentuck returns to Nan's cabin this idea
is further reinforced as he rejects Kate (now in street clothes similar to the ones Nan wears) and her entreaties once again.

Rocky decides to allow Nan to return to Kentuck ("I've done
you enough harm"). She returns to the cabin to find Kentuck, who
is about to go after Rocky, whom he believes to have fixed the cards.
Because of his kindness, Nan rides off to warn Rocky of the approaching danger. She does so, but Rocky's only response is to
stand and fight ("He says I cheated, eh! If ye see him, tell him
I'm ridin' down to meet him"). As in the opening scenes, Nan is
again forced into a position of being between the two men. When
she warns Rocky of the approaching fight he faces right and she left
(Rocky→ ˍNan). When she returns to Kentuck to deliver Rocky's
message she faces right and Kentuck left (Nan→ ˍKentuck), again
visually underscoring the opposition of the two men and her centrality.

As a traveling pan shot of the road follows their movements, Kentuck chases Rocky and Rocky finally shoots and wounds Kentuck. Borzage cuts to Nan leaving the cabin as Rocky carries the wounded Kentuck into town; she is "burning her bridges behind her." Tired of being between the two and tired of the life she is forced to lead, she opted for escape. As she does so, Rocky returns to town and, in guilt, gives the money that he won previously in the crooked poker game to Kate for Kentuck and Nan ("I can't never use that pile after the way it was played.... They'll need it"). He will give up Nan to Kentuck, it appears, sacrificing his present happiness for something that is outside of self-gratification, in contrast to the unreformed Kate. Yet once he rides away he discovers Nan crying, grasps her hands, again in close-up, and almost as a last hope, proposes to her. The visual and thematic parallels to the campfire scene are striking. Here, as in the earlier previous scene, Nan must refuse Rocky. The fragment of the film ends with Nan's two daydreams. First, she sees herself in a dimly lit dancehall with Kate and a crowd of wild drinkers. Then, looking directly at Rocky, she imagines herself in a homey, well-lit kitchen, with two children. Nan faces right toward Rocky both in the fantasy and at the moment of the proposal--a reversal of her earlier position when she warned him about Kentuck. Thus she becomes trapped as she was in the opening scenes, and his offer of love and protection for the future is undercut by its stifling quality. (1) Rocky→ ←Nan + (2) Nan→ ←Rocky = (3) Rocky→ ←Nan→ ←Rocky.

The drama is complicated because of this and because, throughout the previous part of the film, we see Kentuck's hold over Nan. Kentuck's hold is not one of evil, however, but one of love. Since the connection between Nan and Rocky is undercut throughout the earlier part of the film, the gunfight is undercut as a climax, much as the fire sequence is undercut in importance in the later THE SHINING HOUR (1938). Nan does not ever really move into alignment with Rocky, even though she does love what he offers and believes in his value system. While it appears that together they can move out of the external wilderness that they live in and into the peace of the home (civilization as fantasy) this exists only in fantasy and not as an immediately viable reality. She cannot yet attain stability and civilization--the problem cannot resolve itself that quickly and that easily. The "ending" is too ambiguous, not being the catharsis promised at the end of melodrama. From what has occurred before all of this--Nan's unspoken rejection of Rocky, Kentuck's open refusal of Kate (and, therefore, of a completely one-sided relationship without any promise of growth), as well as the visual ties between Nan and Kentuck created throughout--it is probable that we will find Nan returning to Kentuck, physically healing and morally reforming him and the two of them creating and building a life as opposed to just as existence out of the raw materials of the wilderness. Nan aligns herself to the eventuality of peace and security, just as, in a larger sense, the West, which is represented in Kentuck and Nan, must slowly align itself with established American principles. Nan does not reject Rocky's principles outright--she still yearns for the cabin, the children, and the settled home life that Rocky offers. Nan only rejects Rocky as the avenue through

which to achieve these things. This achievement is to be a slow process, and Nan's probable refusal of Rocky spiritually reaffirms this.

The film plays upon melodramatic conventions--the black-and-white morality, the externalization of evil, the final catharsis--yet they are not as clearcut and simple as they appear to be. Borzage extends these melodramatic conventions, especially through the inclusion of the idea of spiritual growth, thus removing some of the naivete often found within the genre. Throughout the film camera movement and visual setup undercut as well as reinforce the drama in a planned manner, and character placement, in particular, is never random.

The basic story line of THE PITCH O' CHANCE is used again in THE GUN WOMAN (1918), yet here the characters and the story are more fully developed and the results of the moral dilemma bring about a new and greater self-awareness.

This second film begins with a quotation from "The Ballad of Reading Gaol":

> Some love too little, some too long,
> Some sell and others buy,
> Some do the deed with many tears
> And some without a sigh:
> For each man kills the thing he loves,
> Yet each man does not die.

The ambiguous quality of the passage is reflected in the film. It is only in the resolution of the action that this ambiguity disappears.

The film is set in "gold country," where "life [was] lived raw" and where desire directed actions. Into this area come the bandit, "The Collector," and Ed Brady, the Boston tenderfoot--the bandit being representative of the wilderness of the uncivilized West; the tenderfoot, of civilization, manners, and morality. Between these two is "The Tigress," proprietor of the "Devil's Kitchen" saloon. She is dimly lit and often seen through a haze of cigarette smoke, a parallel to the bandit, who is masked. As a contrast, the tenderfoot is always brightly lit. This is extended even farther. The powerless sheriff walks in and out of the shadows, his face occasionally lit by a match. He is representative of the law, on the one hand, and its powerless place in the West, on the other. As if to reinforce his powerlessness, the Tigress blows smoke in his face as if to make him disappear. Borzage extends this image of light and smoke to tell the audience that the Collector is the stranger who arrives in town just after the tenderfoot. When the Collector robs the stage, he is shown in close-up, his features masked. He lights a match, however, and draws on his cigarette. Later, when in the town, the Stranger lights a match before a reward poster for the Collector. Again, this is in close-up, paralleling the earlier gesture. He unmasks himself not only through this gesture by holding

the match before his own face, but before the face on the poster as
well.   His two sides are, in this way, revealed to the audience without any verbal assurance through titles.

The Tigress is more a creature, or a man, than a woman,
wearing animal skins, buying drinks for the boys, smoking cigarettes,
and galvanizing action.   When the Stranger, whom we know to be the
Collector, enters the town, however, her attraction to him is immediate.   Both puff on their cigarettes and look directly at each
other, finally sitting at a dimly lit table together.   This action, ex-
ceedingly unusual for her, is further emphasized because just at this
moment news comes to her of the suicide of Ed Bennett, a man the
Tigress refused to marry.   At this point Borzage cuts to the Stranger fingering his glass suggestively as he stares at the Tigress.
The action of the drama is set.   What remains is the playing out
of events and the results of this attraction.

Borzage cuts to the Tigress out in the sunshine, in street
clothes.   She has left her jungle costume and the saloon for a new
medium--one that love has made her desire.   She looks shy and
loving, totally trusting in the stranger she has suddenly grown to
love.   As if to symbolize this, she offers him the money that he
needs for his business venture.   He announces that he must go, upset that he must leave her "alone and unprotected."   At first she
laughs, and only after a moment of careful thought does she become
serious and agree.

Just as all of this is occurring, Borzage cuts to the Boston
tenderfoot volunteering to become a deputy and to apprehend the Collector.   The easterner believes that he can catch the bandit (and,
by extension, help to civilize the West).   Those within the town see
him only as a disrupter.   Already the larger conflicts of East versus
West, and civilization versus wilderness, are recognized as intruding
upon the course of the individual, oppositions set up by cutting between the tenderfoot and the Tigress-Stranger.   Not only is the tenderfoot destined to go after the Collector and to interfere with the
course of the lovers' affair, but he is destined to change the town
itself.   By juxtaposed shots we see his course and that of the Collector to be in direct confrontation.

The two sides of the Tigress continue to act as the central
point of the drama.   She plans for the future with the Collector, offering gifts of her love, money to start a business, and a partnership between them.   Yet their relationship is undercut both visually
and thematically because of the source of the money--prostitution,
gambling, and drinking.   Thus the beauty of her love rests upon a
corrupt foundation and is doomed to failure, a fact reinforced when
the Stranger goes off to open an even more lavish and corrupt saloon in another boom town.   They give each other, in exchange, two
gifts that promise a future.   She gives him "unclean" money to make
a new life while he places an engagement ring, which we know to
be stolen, on her finger.   At this same time we notice that the tenderfoot-deputy is obviously "falling" for the female aspect of the

Tigress, as visually stressed through his increasingly close proxim-
ity to her within frames and in his long glances.   Here again a point
of conflict between the two men is stressed and ensured, with the
Tigress placed between them and bound to be hurt by them both.
The deputy even takes her for walks in the woods as the Collector
did, thus allowing her once again to escape her present and to act
out her dream in her fantasy world of the woodlands.

The drama takes its strong narrative turn with news of a gold
strike in another town, Bravos.   The once-quiet settlement becomes
another lawless boom town with all of the vices of the frontier.   This
movement farther west drains off the population of the "Devil's Kitch-
en" and of the town itself.   The deputy proposes to take the Tigress
away, but she dreams only of the Stranger and exits rear frame to
her upstairs room and to her dreams.   These dreams are undercut,
as is her whole belief in the Stranger, by a cut to the Stranger's
new saloon--a grander, slicker, and more corrupt palace than that
owned by the Tigress.   When she finally does go to join the Stranger
he offers to "do the right thing by you"--to give her a percentage of
the business, informing her that he never promised marriage at all.
Her love is still stronger than her anger, and although she threatens
to shoot him, she eventually reneges, much as Nan did in THE PITCH
O' CHANCE.   Their relationship is reduced to a purely economic
one, however, as the Tigress demands the return of her loan within
thirty days.

Again confirmed in her suspicions about men and about the
futility and weakness of love, the Tigress returns to the safety of
her home turf.   When the deputy finds her discarded engagement
ring and goes to her apartment she can only sneer and say, "Now
I suppose you want to protect me!," thereby repudiating the Collector's earlier promise.   In truth, he has only come to complete the
destruction of her dream world, as he tells her that the ring has
been identified as one stolen by the Collector during the earlier stage-
coach robbery.   The Stranger whom she loved is now positively identified as the Collector, verbally support for what the audience learned
earlier through the two parallel match-lighting scenes.   She asks the
chance for the Collector to make good on his debt to her first, declaring that "he is mine by every law save the law made by man."
Her request is granted, as it must be.   Her claim on him, based
on emotion, is stronger than the claim that the law has upon the
criminal.   She must punish the Collector as a cathartic process of
her own, in order to free herself from his hold.   It is she who
must become a "collector," therefore, and the name now becomes
ironic when used as the name of the Stranger.

The Tigress returns to Bravos to find the Collector and to
collect her debt.   Dressed like Annie Oakley in buckskins and carrying pistols, she takes on the persona of the avenger.   Her sexless-
ness is reinforced by her entry through the gentlemen's entrance.
Once inside, she shoots down lamps, demands her money or ownership of the saloon, and, as the hellish angel of fury she has become, sets the saloon on fire.   As if to undercut the last two lines

of the Reading Gaol ballad ("For each man kills the thing he loves, /
Yet each man does not die"), she then shoots the Collector, kneeling
by his lifeless body for a moment only and then walking away. She
has made her peace with him and, more importantly, with her own
conflicting desires.

With new resolution, she can now escape the past and look
forward to the future and to starting anew. The saloon burns, becoming a "pyre of the past" as she rides into the hills. The deputy
follows and the two meet on a hilltop, where he formally proposes.
She being free of the hold of the Stranger, the audience would expect
her to accept his offer, just as one would originally have expected
Nan to accept Rocky, yet she refuses ("I do love you as a friend,
but my heart's back there"). They separate, riding off in opposite
directions, leaving only the western landscape behind them. The
price paid for love and for the self-awareness it brings has been
great, but through this greater self- and, by extension, spiritual
and world, understanding, the Tigress escapes this part of her life
and continues her progression into the future. In killing the Collector and burning his saloon she has externalized and exorcised the
evil and the contradictions within herself and has spiritually grown
out of her present sphere. As if to underscore this, she rides away
from both her town and from Bravos, just as in later films--MAN'S
CASTLE (1933) and LITTLE MAN, WHAT NOW? (1934), in particular--
the characters leave their spiritually outgrown environments for newer ones in which they can settle and begin again.

THE GUN WOMAN overtly plays upon the theme of spiritual
regeneration and growth as well as employing the melodramatic
themes of good and evil, and civilization as opposed to wilderness.
In contrast to the characters in the later Borzage films, however,
the Tigress goes off alone, sadder but more unified spiritually. In
some ways she is more a tragic than a melodramatic heroine, especially as the end of the film finds her dual nature unified. She has,
as seen in the ending of the film, and in the conclusion of her affair with the Collector, exorcised the beast within and has been made
"whole" for the first time, having moved from a self-reliant pose to
real self-reliance. She can, therefore, turn down the marriage proposal that the tenderfoot-deputy offers. Only now can she "see"
clearly and not through the curtain of smoke that she looked through
when the drama began, and only now can she find some hope of
peace in the future, as visually underscored through her place on
top of the mountain looking out at the horizon at the end of the film.
Offered the chance once again to share her life, she declines in fa-
vor of remaining alone. The tenderfoot, acting as the immediate
agent of her change through his role as carrier of knowledge, brings
her the sadness connected with the recognition of truth. By extension, bringing civilization to the town (Boston civilizing the West),
he brings pain as well as the knowledge of "traditional" customs and
modes of behavior. His knowledge forces her final actions as much
as the words and actions of the Collector. No quick resolution to
her pain, such as marriage to the tenderfoot, is possible, as the
regeneration of her spirit will be achieved slowly and alone.

The same idea of regeneration is played upon in UNTIL THEY GET ME, a film that Borzage made in 1917. Here Borzage attempts to interweave two narratives--the unity of two characters, as well as an individual unity.

UNTIL THEY GET ME is set in Canada in 1885. Borzage again introduces the story with an iris-out; this time, however, it is an iris-out directly upon the action: a man furiously riding a horse over a western landscape. He encounters a group of men lounging beneath a tree, pleads with them for the purchase of one of their horses, breaks a jug accidentally, and is forced to kill one of the men in self-defense. From this moment on the man, Kirby, becomes a hunted fugitive and the first narrative is set in motion.

We are next introduced to Richard Selwyn, a mounted police-man. Selwyn joins with the dead man's friends, and a traditional chase ensues. The chase becomes more significant in that it be-comes symbolic of the personal journey Selwyn undertakes as well. As if to underscore his incorporation within this group, Borzage groups Selwyn in the center of several frames with two of the dead man's comrades. Selwyn takes on the burden of justice and, in his capacity as law-enforcer, becomes the representative of society and of the punishment demanded by that society.

Kirby, riding a white horse symbolic of the purity of his motives, returns to his ranch, "an outpost of civilization." The white horse and the settlement in the wilderness visually undercut the idea of Kirby as a brutal killer and reinforce the idea that there is a justifiable reason behind the actions he has taken, a reason made evident in the orange-tinted scene that follows. Kirby's wife, urgently in need of a doctor's aid, has died in childbirth, leaving their newborn son with her Indian servant, Toopani. The viewer is tied to Selwyn at this point, because just as we learn all of this, Selwyn enters the ranch house and learns this as well. The audi-ence shares his sympathy, and, by extension, becomes identified with Selwyn and with the internal and moral struggles he is forced to face because of what he sees during this moment of recognition. The rest of the film centers upon Selwyn's journey--his attempt to catch Kirby, who had escaped through a rear door, and what this does to Selwyn's life. He becomes a man torn between his own de-sires and sympathies and his devotion to duty, justice, law, and civilization.

The tie between Kirby and Selwyn is underscored in the sec-ond narrative of the film. Kirby vows to return and see his son every year on the boy's birthday. The narrative next picks up one year later on a ranch in the north country. Here we meet Margy, a pretty orphan dressed like a boy, mistreated and overworked by her adoptive parents. Kirby, hiding in the family barn, hopes to steal a horse so as to ride to his son, a parallel to the opening scene of the drama. Margy helps him steal the horse so that she can go with him and escape her own hell, a parallel to the structure of the later SEVENTH HEAVEN (1927). Kirby takes her along but

tells her to go to the Mounties for protection.   Once she is set free
from her constricting environment, as seen in her stroll through the
sunlit woods, and once Kirby leaves her, Margy, now transformed
(as indicated by her dress), meets Selwyn and is taken to his post,
another "outpost of civilization," for refuge. This event ties Selwyn
and Kirby even closer.   Margy protects Kirby by refusing to admit
to any knowledge of his whereabouts and, in doing so, becomes the
tie between the two narratives.   This is weakly presented, however,
and Margy's knowledge of Kirby's plan does not become as immediate
a point of conflict between Margy and Selwyn as it should.   The love
between Margy and Selwyn grows unheeded, and her knowledge becomes more a means of resolving the dramatic conflict than a point
of moral contention.

     Margy is welcomed by the troop, and in the four years that
pass, she becomes an integral part of post life, adding brightness
to the desolation and wilderness around the fort.   She grows into
womanhood as well, her final transformation recognized at the central Christmas Eve scene, where Margy appears in a long, fitted
white gown.   The gown symbolizes not only her purity, in its whiteness, but her initiation into womanhood, in that it accentuates her
figure as well.   The reactions of the troop reflect upon her obvious
change.   Selwyn too sees her differently, and after this the two are
found spending more and more time alone.   This culminates with a
scene of the two sitting outside in the sun, an image used throughout THE GUN WOMAN.   Yet Selwyn cannot completely give himself
to Margy and the peace that she offers.   He refuses to propose until
he catches Kirby and pacifies both his sense of duty (his conscience)
and the law.   He shows Margy a picture of Kirby that he carries
with him, like the picture of a lover that one holds next to his
heart.   Margy "slips" and tells what she knows of Kirby.   Selwyn,
torn between duty and Margy's vow to Kirby, inevitably chooses duty.
Margy, angered by all of this, first looks away from Selwyn and,
at his final refusal to leave Kirby alone, turns and walks off, giving
up Selwyn.   She too chooses duty over love.

     Resolution of the drama swiftly follows, as the oppositions
(Kirby versus Selwyn with Margy between them) have been clearly
defined.   Selwyn rides off to capture Kirby, and Margy rides off to
warn him.   Borzage cuts to Margy standing amidst "bar" shadows
on the door of Kirby's cabin, a visual reflection of her part in the
"web" of the situation.   Kirby shows up at his ranch at the appointed
time but, physically and emotionally worn out, gives himself up to
Selwyn and to the law.   His capitulation to society is completed in
the surrender of his son to Selwyn so that the boy may be raised
by the troop.   His duty fulfilled, Selwyn returns to the post and re-
signs his commission, giving up his pistols, the sign of his authority.   It is Margy who reverses his actions, picking up the pistols
and returning them to him.   Recognizing the importance of duty,
she can effect a reconciliation.   In returning his guns and, therefore, his identity, she accepts the importance of Selwyn's beliefs
and those of his moral order.   She accepts the code of law, order,
and duty that he follows.   Both she and Selwyn are now free to

realize the nature of their love and to accept it freely. Margy leads
Selwyn out of the shadows and into the sunshine, symbolically leading
him into their new and mutual sphere. The two face each other and
kiss, thus ending the drama. Duty has been vindicated as a basis
of belief and action, as much by Kirby's easy surrender as by Margy's final actions, as has love. Love provides the understanding
necessary to resolve the dilemma in which Margy and Selwyn finally
find themselves. Kirby's easy capitulation to law and society undercuts Margy's earlier denial of Selwyn. Margy's acceptance of Selwyn and of his beliefs unifies them and makes them both "whole" as
well as interdependent.

In the three western films Borzage plays with the idea of regeneration and knowledge and relies heavily upon the journey motif.
The three films each deal with both spiritual and intellectual growth
and with the obstacles that impede that growth. While in THE PITCH
O' CHANCE the idea of growth is underplayed when set against a
greater good/evil and civilization/wilderness constructs, it is present
in Nan's internal struggle and in her choice to leave the good man
and the promise of home and security that he offers for that of struggle and hardship and the greater fulfillment that this offers. In THE
GUN WOMAN and in UNTIL THEY GET ME, however, the journey
toward self-awareness, knowledge, and regeneration is much more
clearly defined. THE GUN WOMAN is a story of spiritual awakening as much as one of love and loss. UNTIL THEY GET ME, while
flawed in its faulty double-narrative construction, shares this focus,
as well as the concern with the conflict between duty and external
obligations and individual desires and internal forces.

All three films play upon the conceptions of melodrama, such
as black-and-white moral divisions and the externalization of evil,
in particular, and extend them so as to concentrate more on character than on situation. As character development becomes increasingly important, so does the conflict within the individual, as opposed
to between two individuals, each representing some self-contained
belief. Morality becomes not so much the structural premise as
something that the individual-in-the-middle--such as Nan, the Tigress,
and Selwyn, in these films--questions, changes, and only after a
struggle accepts. Seeking a course for their lives, the characters
find some type of spiritual awareness that leads to their movement
into a new sphere of existence and understanding. It is this idea,
predicated so early in his career, that becomes perhaps the most
essential tenet of almost all other Borzage films, especially those
of the later silent and of the 1930-1940 sound periods.

Part Two: The "Society" Dramas

The remaining seven films still in existence from this early
silent period are "society" dramas. These films concentrate on the

plight of individuals within some microcosmic society, such as the
town in LAZYBONES (1925), or within some highly structured individual part of the social hierarchy, such as the upper-class British
of THE CIRCLE (1924). In these films Borzage looks at social cus-
tom and social hypocrisy and, of greater importance, love as a spiritual force and marriage as an ultimate reflection of an individual's
"heaven" or "hell."

LIFE'S HARMONY (1916) combines both the themes and
the settings of the western films with the questions of the later works. 2
This simple drama is the story of an aging organist, Josiah Pringle;
his adopted daughter, Faith; and her love for the new church organist, Gordon Howard. After Josiah, church organist for some twenty
years, misses a note while playing a hymn, the church elders decide that it is time to get a younger man. As in later Borzage
films, what is immediately noticeable are the grouping shots throughout. Pringle is constantly surrounded by his family: while at the
church, returning home after the service, when he learns of his
dismissal, at the dinner scenes, and at the resolution of the drama.
This protective group is often contrasted with opposing looser groups,
such as the church elders. This idea is further used to contrast
and compare Pringle with Gordon Howard. We see Pringle and a
group of his women music students gathered around the piano and
later see a parallel shot of these same students gathered around
Gordon, albeit with much less benign and innocent expressions on
their faces. This idea is picked up in the almost-Freudian treatment of Faith and her relationship to both Josiah and Gordon.

Psychoanalysis "has a clear relevance to melodrama"[3] both
in its emphasis on conflict and in the excessive behavior stressed
throughout. [4] The ego, superego, and id of Freudian psychology are
equated with the black-and-white morality conflicts of melodrama.
Furthermore, the melodramatic battle of virtue and evil becomes
the psychoanalytic "drama of recognition"[5] as is "the cure of souls"[6]
sought in both. In LIFE'S HARMONY the "drama of recognition" is
incorporated into the whole of the drama and especially in the more
melodramatic segment of the plot found in the latter half. The central action of the drama takes on more obvious Freudian overtones
in the similarity of the relationship of Faith and Pringle to that of
Faith and Gordon. The resolution of the action becomes, then,
equated with both the catharsis of melodrama and that sought through
psychoanalysis as well as an understanding of the interrelationship
of the ego, superego, and id.

Faith is the spiritual support of Pringle in the same way that
Pringle is her financial support and the axis of the scope of her actions. Her role prefigures many of Borzage's later heroines as her
support takes on a much more crucial aspect in the drama. When
the leader of the elders tells him of his dismissal Pringle holds his
chest in pain. It is Faith who supports him, her physical support
of the weakened Josiah representative of the emotional support she
provides him throughout the rest of the drama.

The parallel between Pringle and Gordon is continued, and
Faith's attraction to the younger man is prefigured in her attachment
to the older. Not only are the two men both organists and not only
are they grouped similarly, such as when each gives a lesson at the
organ, but scenes of Gordon entering the church, surrounded by elders, are followed by those of Pringle entering surrounded by his
family. At the end of the service this is underscored when Faith
walks out with Josiah's maiden sister, his obvious spiritual mate,
as Josiah and Gordon follow. The tie created, like the one existing
between Faith and Josiah, becomes one of child and parent. Soon
after, Gordon saves Faith from an attacker, and Faith brings him
home and leads him into the Pringle family unit. Not only does
Gordon play the organ for the group, but he joins them at dinner.
Here he is placed across from Josiah and to the left of Faith, who
is at the head of the table, a position that reinforces her central
spiritual and familial roles in the drama. As in the western films,
the next shots depicting the growing love of Faith and Gordon take
place outside in the bright sunshine of the woods. Borzage even cuts
to a shot of two doves cooing in a tree and then returns to one of
Gordon hugging Faith after she puts a flower in his lapel.

In the shots of the family that follow, Gordon becomes a fully
integrated figure within this unit, and the realignment of the family
begins to take shape. Gordon and Josiah work on Josiah's invention
while Faith and her aunt sit together in the parlor. There are cuts
between the two groups in which a "reduction" takes place. Once
Gordon helps Josiah perfect his discovery there is a family shot of
the four characters in which Gordon stands between Faith, on the
left, and Josiah, on the right, with Josiah's sister positioned on Josiah's left (Faith/Gordon/Josiah/Aunt). The next shot of the group
contains only three of the characters, the aunt not being shown. The
final shot is one of Gordon and Faith only. At this point Faith, in
her white dress, leads Gordon out the door and kisses him for the
first time, creating a feeling of a symbolic marriage existing between the two, and then returns to the house and to her father.

The plot now takes on more obvious melodramatic aspects.
After several weeks no word is heard from Gordon, who has gone
to register Josiah's invention with the patent office. A picture in
the newspaper of an embezzler who looks surprisingly like Gordon
raises the possibility that he himself is an embezzler. Furthermore,
without the money needed to support his family, Josiah must return
Faith to the orphanage. Faith, finding the dejected Josiah in the
darkened church, leads him, symbolically, out into the sunshine,
realizes that she cannot change the situation, and accepts her fate.
Again she sits by Josiah, this time caressing him as she cries.
She kneels before him and the two cry as they discuss the evidence
that implicates Gordon as an embezzler. Just as they are about to
leave, Gordon returns with a check for $20,000 and saves the day.
This reunification is visually supported within the frame as well.
Gordon stands in the doorway and in the sunlight while Josiah and
Faith stand within the darkened parlor of the cabin.

Gordon→ // →Josiah, Faith
(light→)   (→dark)

Gordon explains that his absence was due to a loss of memory after
being hit by falling bricks and explains that the embezzler seen in
the newspaper is his deceased brother. A shot of Gordon holding
Faith follows, as does one that places Josiah beside his sister. The
final scene opens with a group shot of the four at the church as Faith
leads Josiah to the organ. The last shot is of Josiah alone and re-
vitalized, playing the organ with an ecstatic/religious look on his
face, only his face lit. Faith and Gordon thus become the active
and spiritual forces that renew Josiah's strength. The last scene
implies a transcendence by Josiah, one achieved through the love of
Faith and the actions of Gordon. The relationship of these two younger characters not only realigns the family unit, but returns the father
to a reverential and almost nonphysical state.

     Borzage continued to stress the metaphysical and sacrificial
aspects of the love relationship throughout this period, looking at
different types of relationships, such as the love of husband and
wife, sacrificial love, and love between parent and child. In the
fragment of THE Nth COMMANDMENT (1923) and in THE CIRCLE
(1924) a woman is blinded by what she thinks is love, only learning
what true (i. e., spiritual) love is just before it is too late. In SE-
CRETS (1924) the power of a wife's love draws an aged and dying
man back to life, a play upon the Orpheus myth. In LAZYBONES
(1925) the loss of a child breaks the spirit of a woman who is pushed
into a marriage that she does not want. In THE FIRST YEAR (1926)
a child solidifies a relationship that is failing due to internal and external pressures. In this latter film the spiritual strength of the
marriage is recognized only at the very last moment.

     THE Nth COMMANDMENT is the most overtly spiritual of
Borzage's existing early films. Consisting of only a one-reel fragment of the original length (7, 339 feet), the film opens with the same
conflict faced by Nan in THE PITCH O' CHANCE. In this case it
is Sara, a corset-department salesclerk, who must choose between
Harry Smith, an "Everyman" figure, the clerk who loves her, and
Jimmy, the music-department clerk to whom she is physically attracted. Sara learns the value and importance of love and, from
what little is known of the ending, gives herself to Harry, who is
dying of consumption, a theme picked up later in THREE COMRADES
(1938).

     The film opens in a department store, the editing creating a
montage of separate shots of the people and the activities found within it. In contrast to the opening of the later film STREET ANGEL
(1928), here the sequence consists of separate shots, thus presenting
the store not as a single or continuous unity but as an area of in-
difference and extreme individuality. The customers within the store
exist alone, not within any larger spiritual or emotional sphere. The
department store, as opposed to the city of Naples as it is seen in
STREET ANGEL, is not an area in which people's lives interact on

anything other than a surface level, nor is it an entity in the sense
that any one action really effects the greater whole. The conflict
that develops between Sara, Jimmy, and Harry, and the resolution
that follows are of primary importance, not the larger world in which
the three move. Despite the existence of separate spheres of being,
it is this smaller area of focus that supports the opening title credit:

> Whoever you are, sooner or later in your life
> comes a situation which no one of the Ten
> Commandments seems to cover.
> It is the Nth Commandment you follow then, the
> unwritten commandment to serve, to suffer,
> to sacrifice for what you love and cherish.
> This is the story of one heart which followed
> this highest law of all.

Harry is a simple man deeply in love with Sara. Sara is a
woman more attracted to a showy exterior (in this case, Jimmy) and
more easily influenced by her materialistic friends (i. e., Angie) than
she is able to recognize and follow her deepest feelings. From the
start of the film conflicts arise. Harry wishes to go to the park so
that he can propose, while Sara, under the influence of Angie, opts
for the excitement and the crowd of the rollerskating rink. Sara
falls sway to Angie's materialism, failing to see the greater importance of the love and devotion that Harry can give her in contrast
to the immediate excitement and gratification that Jimmy offers.
Harry fails to recognize the attraction between Jimmy and Sara,
which the juxtaposition of cuts points out to the viewer. At the
skating rink, just as earlier at work, Jimmy walks into Sara's frame
and stands with her, the two facing Harry (S/J→ ←H). In the larger
visual context of the next shot Sara and Harry are separated from
all of the others and tied to each other. In this shot we watch all
of the skaters skate around Harry and Sara. The mass of other
skaters do this skating at the edges of the rink and, therefore, at
the edges of the frame, those edges being almost dark enough to
completely conceal them. In the central circle of light are Harry
and Sara and skating around them is Jimmy.

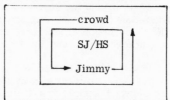

The levels of the drama are set before us in this single shot,
Harry and Sara being emotionally and visually tied to each other with
Jimmy in their immediate sphere. The larger mass of people exist outside of the three and are fairly indistinct, an image used again
at the end of HIS BUTLER'S SISTER (1943). As if to underscore
what is to follow, Harry, thrown off balance by Jimmy's tricks and
taunts, falls to the floor, an adumbration of his later weakened phy-

sical condition, while Sara stares back and forth, torn between helping Harry up and, thereby staying with him, and skating off with
Jimmy. Borzage then cuts between separate shots of the three--Jimmy
laughing, Sara on the floor looking first at Jimmy and then at Harry,
and Harry struggling to rise--separating them visually and, symbolically, "freeing" Sara to make her decision. The cutting serves to
tie the three in the same way that Borzage used later in a similar
cutting pattern in the wedding scene of THE SHINING HOUR (1938).
Through this shot the transformation that occurs within the action of
the drama is predicated. At first, Sara and Harry both face Jimmy:

Next, Jimmy helps Sara to her feet and the two stand above Harry
and face him:

In the final shot the camera moves back as Sara and Jimmy join the
larger crowd continuously circling them, Harry remaining alone and
outcast on the floor, central in the frame just as he is central to
the action of the drama. Sara and Jimmy skate away as Harry rises
alone, falls once again, and finally skates off to the left, against the
movement of all of the other skaters, including Sara and Jimmy, who
skate from left to right.

Within this short piece the thematic conflict of the plot is
completely set before the viewer. The visual level acts to reinforce
this as well as to strengthen the image of Harry's isolation. In this
roller-skating sequence Borzage places the three major characters
within a world and spiritual sphere of their own as if to reinforce
the earlier department-store shots, which created a sense of the
separate worlds or spheres of the customers. Yet we are forced
to recognize the immediate drama as a part of some larger entity,
which is both immediate, as reinforced through the mass of skaters
dimly surrounding the three major characters, and more spiritual,
as reinforced by the epigraph that opens the film.

In many ways this opening situation and especially the larger
idea of an individual previously without intuitive knowledge or some
greater understanding slowly learning first to find and finally to accept what is "right" is picked up in THE CIRCLE (1924). Made
one year after THE Nth COMMANDMENT, THE CIRCLE plays upon
the questions of intuitive knowledge, of understanding, and (albeit
less successfully) of appearance as opposed to reality. In this latter
film the outward trappings of setting and class are completely different from those in films that have come before.

THE CIRCLE is a reflection of De Mille's influence upon the

American cinema of the 1920s. The story, based on a play by Somerset Maugham, is one of the upper class, in this case the British
nobility, and the film is much more obviously a "society drama"
than a romantic or spiritual one. The spiritual undercurrent present
in some of the earlier films is not present in this piece. Yet once
again the visual narrative is strongly used to undercut the action of
the drama. There is a great deal more sincerity here, however,
as well as a great deal more feeling than is to be found in such De
Mille films as THE CHEAT (1915), DON'T CHANGE YOUR HUSBAND
(1919), and WHY CHANGE YOUR WIFE? (1920).

The two narrative portions of the film deal with two love tri-
angles, the first concerning Lord Cheney, Catherine Cheney, and
Hugh Porteus, and the second concerning Arnold Cheney, Elizabeth
Cheney, and Teddy Luton. In the first part of the drama the elder
Lord Cheney loses his wife, Catherine, to his closest friend, Hugh
Porteus. Catherine seeks the excitement and "true" love that Hugh
offers more than the position and the security offered by her husband. Leaving her son, Arnold, behind, Lady Catherine and Hugh
ride off into the misty street, leaving the past behind them as well.
The second part of the narrative is set thirty years later. Arnold,
now grown up and married, is in the same situation that his father
was in before him. His wife, Elizabeth, is contemplating an elopement with Teddy Luton just as Catherine did with Hugh, and she in-
vites Catherine and Hugh to the Cheney estate to see if their "stolen"
happiness and their love has lasted through the years.

Arnold and Elizabeth are visually played off against each
other, as Arnold comes to represent his father's generation and the
beliefs of that generation and, in doing so, widens the gap that already exists between himself and his wife. Elizabeth is a product
of a more modern age, seeking the thrills and excitements that life
offers. She, symbolically, opens the drapes while Arnold closes
them as if to keep out the present. Elizabeth cannot accept the idea
that their home is to be kept "like a tomb" nor can she consider
locking out the world as Arnold does (a hope that Hannah desperately
clings to in THE SHINING HOUR [1938]). Arnold is visually tied to
his father throughout, overseeing things and looking through doorways,
just as his father was pictured doing in the earlier part of the film.
The tie between Arnold and his father is broken only in their different reactions to the news of Catherine's visit. Arnold paces back
and forth, further opposed to the static reactions of Elizabeth and
Teddy. Lord Cheney only wonders whether or not his former wife
is still as beautiful as she once was, lauding her for being one who
"loved and dared."

All of the guests, including Elizabeth's friend, Alice, gather
around Lord Cheney as he receives the news of the visit. Elizabeth
stands beside Teddy on Lord Cheney's left, and Arnold stands on
Lord Cheney's right, placed in opposition to Teddy.

Alice   Elizabeth
 \   /
Arnold→Lord Cheney◄—Teddy

Throughout the scene Lord Cheney, who had been about to go to Scotland to hunt, holds his rifle. As all of the others leave and as Teddy takes the gun away from Lord Cheney's chair Lord Cheney calls Elizabeth over. He puts her on his lap, signifying his position as father, while locking her tightly in his arms as he talks of Catherine. He also talks of Teddy, comparing him to Hugh Porteus ("I had a friend of just his kind. "). At this point there is a close-up of Lord Cheney toying with Elizabeth's wedding ring, thus strengthening the viewer's recognition of his insight or intuition concerning the situation ("the circle of generations").

Lady Catherine now enters and immediately mistakes the dashing Teddy for her son. Hugh stands off to the side and oversees the proceedings nervously. Lord Cheney re-enters and stands back, overseeing the drama calmly, as if knowing that the situation rests in his hands. His position within the frame further symbolizes his role in the drama to follow. He enters Hugh's frame and shakes Hugh's hand, predicating an uneasy truce and removing the emphasis from the older generation and their past conflict. The next shots are grouping shots: Catherine standing between Arnold and Elizabeth, and Lord Cheney standing between Catherine and Hugh. These shots play off against each other and underscore the ambiguity of just what is to happen. Catherine, either actively or passively, is either to tie Arnold and Elizabeth or she will (indirectly) be the cause of their final separation. Being in the same position as Lord Cheney, between a husband and wife, emphasizes her importance. The shots of Elizabeth and Teddy that follow as well as that of Arnold alone tie these five characters and the two generations as well as the two pieces of the narrative into one whole.

The next scene occurs at the dinner table. Elizabeth sits at the head with Arnold opposite her. To her right sits Hugh, Alice, and Lord Cheney, who is, therefore, next to his son. On her left are Teddy and Catherine. The oppositions and ties of the drama are, through this, visually underscored once again. Elizabeth sits directly opposite Arnold as if in confrontation, with Teddy close by on her left. Catherine sits opposite Lord Cheney, the two tied by their past relationship as well as in a confrontation stance, with Hugh outside of the immediate action just as he is outside of the immediate events of the drama.

The ambiguity of the outcome is played upon in the parlor sequence that follows. Here Hugh, Catherine, Teddy, and Elizabeth sit at a card table while Arnold and Lord Cheney oversee the unfolding situation and stand directly above Elizabeth.

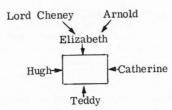

Soon after, Arnold leaves the room, therefore leaving his father to
oversee the drama alone. Throughout the scene Hugh and Catherine
argue, and Hugh finally tells Lord Cheney, in exasperation, that he
has "had it sweet" all of these years, thereby admitting that life with
Catherine has not been all that he expected it to be. Yet this admission is undercut in the next sequence, strengthening the ambiguity
present throughout. Elizabeth, looking through an old photograph al-
bum, finds a picture of the young and once-beautiful Catherine taken
when she was married to Lord Cheney. Catherine, now old and pow-
dered, laments her lost youth. Elizabeth leaves for a moment and
Hugh enters. Instead of his usual gruffness, however, Hugh comforts Catherine ("You are as lovely as ever") as Catherine leans
upon his shoulder. The tenderness missing in the earlier scenes is
finally recognized, as is the love that they still share.

   Borzage follows this with a cut to Lord Cheney advising Arnold on how to handle the situation before him, telling him that, with
gentleness, all will work out. Once again the ambiguity of the drama
is faced, as this too is undercut at the same moment. Elizabeth re-
enters the living room to find Catherine and Hugh sitting together and
asks if their love has lasted throughout the years. With Hugh's af-
firmation she leaves the room ready to take action and to leave Arnold for a life with Teddy. Brought to Arnold by Lord Cheney, she
turns away from him as he tells her of his love for her and runs
out of the room. She runs directly to Teddy, demanding reassurance
of his everlasting love. In a scene to be expected of De Mille, she
asks what he would do if someone took her from him. He declares
that he would "blacken her eye and close the other" and she smilingly
calls him a brute and kisses him passionately in happy response.

   Elizabeth tells Catherine of her plans while Teddy waits for
her by the staircase in a pose similar to that which Hugh took thirty
years earlier. The couple exit out to the yard and into a cab in a
series of shots parallel to Hugh and Catherine's escape. This time,
however, history does not repeat itself, because Arnold is found in
the driver's seat of the car. He finally stops the car, blackens one
of Teddy's eyes and closes the other, and pushes Elizabeth into the
car. He drives off with Elizabeth screaming. Arnold returns her
to the house, where, as she enters, she meets Catherine, who tells
her how glad she is that Elizabeth has decided not to leave Arnold.
At this moment Arnold descends the stairs and the two women face
him. This is reduced to a shot of Arnold facing Elizabeth, the two
placed in separate frames. Arnold tells her that it is "time to re-
tire," and for the first time she enters into his frame and they pro-
ceed upstairs. Elizabeth enters her room with Arnold following and
stretching his arms symbolically, and there is a final cut to Hugh
and Lord Cheney in the living room laughing, each thinking that they
have outsmarted the other with their "inside knowledge" of the drama
that has just taken place.

   THE CIRCLE lacks the intense quality of LIFE'S HARMONY
and THE Nth COMMANDMENT, being much more a frivolous society
drama than an overridingly spiritual one. While it deals with the
family, it is far less the drama of realignment that LIFE'S HARMONY

is and far less a drama of spiritual love than THE Nth COMMAND-
MENT. Borzage is somewhat out of his element here in his obvious
copying of De Mille and the De Mille themes of this period. The
drama is more interesting because of the way the visual narrative
is used to reinforce the narrative ambiguity, an idea and technique
more fully realized in the structure of MAN'S CASTLE (1933). The
drama is an episodic one, in which pairs of episodes (such as the
dining-room scene and the parlor scene, the two living-room scenes,
and the two elopement scenes) are played against each other and
where one scene is used to undercut another. What becomes more
interesting than the character parallels (Catherine/Elizabeth, Arnold/
Lord Cheney, and Teddy/Hugh) are the situations. It is situation
and plot that become more important than character development,
and the characters are reduced to types rather than developed into
full personalities. Borzage's lack of interest is obvious, especially
in the final scenes. None of the characters is invested with an
"otherworldliness" such as exists in THE Nth COMMANDMENT, nor
does the love relationship take on the deeper significance that it has
in some of the earlier films and especially in the films of the late
twenties and the thirties. THE CIRCLE is a filmed play, and Borzage is forced to rely almost completely upon the original text of
Maugham's drama. Very little Borzagean self-expression is ascer-
tained. In SECRETS (1924) this lack completely disappears.

        SECRETS is a much more traditional melodrama than THE
CIRCLE. THE CIRCLE lacks most of the characteristics of film
melodrama and is more a morality play than a spiritual examination. It is a drama of upper-class life, morality, and games rather
than a study of forces such as good versus evil, vice set against
virtue, or of spiritual questioning and discovery. SECRETS is much
more a part of the spiritual framework that becomes so important
in Borzage's later work.

        The film opens at the deathbed of an elderly man and relies
upon flashbacks to fill in the story. The film almost becomes a
prayer in both feeling and structure, a call by a wife for her husband's return to life. The family, gathered around the bedside, exits one by one, leaving the woman alone with her husband, her diary, and her thoughts. Sitting in a chair just outside of the door,
she falls asleep, and there is a fade-in to a young girl writing in
her diary. A long take of her face leads into another flashback of
a rich young girl preparing for a party amidst all of her finery.
What follows must be pieced together, since the surviving print of
the film is incomplete, out of sequence, and has Yugoslavian inter-
titles.

        Mary Marlowe is in love with someone of whom her parents
do not approve. Because she will not renounce him she must face
the anger and punishment of her parents and family. Refusing to
change her mind, she is locked in her room alone. She blows out
all of the candles and, in some of Borzage's most beautifully photo-
graphed shots, walks to the balcony, opens the French doors, and
looks out to where her lover awaits. Subverting the Romeo and

Secrets

Juliet theme, Borzage has her lover climb up to her, and they kiss, lit only by the moon.   Once he enters the room she relights the candles, thereby reintegrating herself into life, and he kneels before her and kisses her hands while she looks up at the sky.   Introducing this religious motif not only gives their love a spiritual quality but ensures its success against parental (i. e. , earthly) opposition.   As if casting off her family and her past, Mary removes her finery and escapes in her petticoat.   In contrast to the couples in THE CIRCLE, however, this pair escapes on a bicycle and not in a carriage or car, again emphasizing what Mary is leaving behind in running off with John.

The next sequence takes place in a frontier ranch, an isolated outpost of civilization like that in UNTIL THEY GET ME.   Mary is found standing by the hearth with her baby.   Two riders, John and the doctor, approach and enter, all three gathering around the hearth and the crib, the symbols of the home, the husband and wife facing the doctor and the baby.   The doctor and the husband support Mary in the same manner that Faith supported Josiah in LIFE'S HARMONY as the news of the baby's imminent death is announced.   Mary then kneels by the crib, again reinforcing the spiritual and religious motifs, where she is joined by her husband.   As the two gather around the crib to create a scene of muted sadness there is a cut to a wild mob approaching and then attacking the house.   Mary, although completely distraught, inspires her husband and refuses to let him simply give up, displaying a trait central to most later Brozagean heroines.   She instills courage in her mate even while disaster threatens, like Angela in STREET ANGEL (1928), Lammchen in LITTLE MAN, WHAT NOW? (1934), Pat in THREE COMRADES (1938), Jessie in MANNEQUIN (1938), Olivia in THE SHINING HOUR (1938), Audrey in DISPUTED PASSAGE (1939), and Freya in THE MORTAL STORM (1940).

While her husband fights, Mary returns to her child only to find that the child is dead.   Even though she is stunned, however, instead of collapsing she joins her husband and fights off the invaders.   The one man she kills falls, symbolically, before the hearth fire.   At this point the law arrives and the mob is forced away. Again the forces of civilization defeat the chaos of the wilderness. Mary stands and smiles jubilantly, but suddenly she remembers her dead child and walks slowly into the child's room, now a tomb, alone.

While this sequence closely follows the thematic and narrative structure of UNTIL THEY GET ME, what follows returns to the setting of the first flashback.   It is now some fifteen or twenty years later.   Mary is now a wealthy woman, surrounded by her four children and her parents.   Her happiness is undercut, however, because her husband is having an affair.   The "other woman" enters, and she and Mary confront each other (Mary→ ←woman).   As if representing the emotional support offered by her family, in the next shot Mary is surrounded by her mother and father (mom/dad/Mary→ ←woman).   Her mother and father leave, only to be replaced by

her eldest son. At this point John enters, positioned in the center
of the frame, a parallel to his position within the action, between
the two women who now face him. He goes directly to Mary, touching her hand just as he did in an earlier sequence when the two
learned of the baby's approaching death. He angrily grabs the other
woman, who then stalks out, as Mary attempts to calm him. As he
explains she walks around the room and listens. The two are in
separate frames throughout, and often as John is about to reach for
Mary he clasps his own hands instead. Finally he does reach for
her, and she rises and enters his frame. He kneels to her, reinforcing the idea of the spirituality of their union, and holds her
hands. The reconciliation is completed.

The action fades back to the "present" and to the aged and
sleeping Mary. As she awakens she hears her husband call for her.
The final shot is of her march through the double doors and into his
room for their reunion. Love has triumphed over death, and her
movement across to him becomes a journey across all space and
time, a motif and image used in the final shot of HIS BUTLER'S
SISTER (1943). Mary has called John back to life (her action reminiscent of the Orpheus theme) and back to her, just as Trina calls
Bill back to her in MAN'S CASTLE (1933) and as Audrey calls Beav-
en back to life in DISPUTED PASSAGE (1939). Love transcends the
mortal nature of men and woman. The bond that it creates between
two people bridges time, place, illness, and death. In this early
film an important Borzage theme is obviously employed for the first
time, and the spiritual side of love, played upon in the earlier films,
is depicted strongly and its importance made clear. The extreme
melodramatic elements used in the westerns and touched upon in the
society dramas are in this film much more sublimated. Character
development and the influence of love upon the characters and their
actions are stressed. It is only a short step to Borzage's presentation of the idea of a movement into higher spiritual spheres, a theme
that is fully developed in SEVENTH HEAVEN (1927), STREET ANGEL
(1928), and THE RIVER (1928).

While in SECRETS Borzage first employs the idea of transcendence, in LAZYBONES (1925) he employs biblical imagery (the
Moses story) as a means of investing the narrative with religious
significance. The story becomes more than that of Steve Tuttle, a
lazy young man who sleeps all day and fails to "keep up" the farm
he and his mother own. Yet the major failure of the film is its
inconsistent use of, and its incompleteness as, parable.

Central to the development of the religious nature of the film
is the secondary narrative, that of Ruth (a name with biblical implications of fidelity), sister of Steve's beloved, Agnes. Ruth, we
learn through flashbacks, has without her mother's knowledge and
consent married a sailor who died at sea shortly thereafter. She
has had a child and knows that she cannot bring the child home because her family will not accept her story, as they believed Ruth
to be away at school. Desperate, Ruth climbs onto a bridge and,
in an action symbolic of her aloneness and her awareness that she

Lazybones

has taken a "wrong" direction, walks against the current of the river.   She throws herself into the current, leaving her child in a bas-
ket in the rushes.   Steve, a good Samaritan, saves her and agrees
to keep the child until Ruth can take the child home.

The child becomes a point of contention between Steve and
Agnes, visually as well as thematically.   When first in his frame,
she faces Steve.   As she tells him of her fears--the "talk" all of
this will bring--she and Steve are in separate frames.   When she
decides to leave him after convincing herself that the child is his,
a gate is between them.   The gate is broken, thus reflecting their
broken relationship.   Only Steve's mother believes his story, seeing
the truth in his eyes, much as Gino sees the truth in Angela's eyes
at the end of STREET ANGEL (1928).

The visual groupings that follow support a sense of Steve's
separation from Agnes and her family as well as reflecting Ruth's
continued and intense emotional tie to the child.   Steve, holding the
child, stands in the lower left of the frame, as Agnes and Ruth ride
by in a carriage with their mother and Elmer.   The baby, earlier
seen playing with a hat, waves at Ruth, who waves back while clutch-

ing a straw hat.   The other three in the carriage turn their backs
on Steve and the child.   Elmer, the mother's choice for Ruth's husband, is continually paired with the girls' mother, thereby reflecting
their mutual agreement.   The two girls are placed beside each other
and in a position of secondary importance in the back seat.

When Ruth finally confesses to her mother about the child,
her mother, placed in a separate frame throughout, refuses to accept the story, horsewhips her instead, and threatens to have the
child institutionalized if Ruth tells the story to anyone else.   This
is juxtaposed to the scene in which Steve finally breaks with Agnes
(she walks out of his frame) and decides to adopt the child as his
own.

Some years pass, and Ruth and Elmer are now married.   Elmer is a prosperous, well-fed, and well-groomed bank president.
Ruth, in direct contrast, has grown physically weaker, sitting idly
by the window staring after her "lost" child.   Her attempts to talk
to the child have been continually frustrated by her mother.

The process of Ruth's physical and emotional degeneration is
continued in the next sequence.   It is now 1915, ten years later,
and Ruth is dying.   Her mother still refuses to allow her to see
the child and to acknowledge it as her own.   It is Steve who fulfills
Ruth's last desire by bringing the child, Kitt, to her.   This is the
only scene of physical contact Ruth is given in the film.   She and
Steve, Kitt's spiritual parents, touch hands tenderly.   As she clutches
Kitt and is about to tell her the truth of their relationship, however,
she dies.   Steve explains to Kitt: "Death is a natural thing--folks
get tired and are called home."   Kitt prays for Ruth, she and Steve
standing before her body, their family finally united, even if only in
death.

Once this second narrative is "completed" the full focus of
the drama is turned to Steve.   It is now 1917, and Steve is going
to fight in France.   He leaves his mother and Kitt behind at the
broken gate.   Steve stands between the two women, reflecting his
centrality to the story as well as his familial tie to the women.
After a war montage Steve is shown returning home a hero.   Yet,
as if in comment upon the arrival of the twentieth century, he returns to find changes.   Most symbolically, the gate has been fixed
and the house repaired.   Steve has changed as well, his hair now
grayer, as has Kitt, who now appears in a white dress, symbolic
of her transformation into a woman.

Steve slowly falls in love with Kitt; he begins singing aloud
around the house and touches Kitt far more than before.   The possibility of a romantic relationship between the two is undercut by
visual parallels between Steve and Ruth.   Steve sits in a chair by
the window watching Kitt as Ruth did earlier.   His position as father
is reaffirmed in the way that his position as lover is undercut.   Yet
the parallel continues, and just as Kitt, now in love with a garage
mechanic named Dick, appeared in a dress earlier, Steve now dresses

in "city clothes," ostensibly to go to the town dance. As if to rein-
troduce Ruth's influence once again, the group--Steve, Kitt, Dick,
and Mrs. Tuttle--ride a hay wagon past Ruth's home, where Agnes
and her mother sit at the window and watch. The mother, now old,
sick, and dressed in black, as Ruth was before she died, is haunted
by visions of Ruth, who becomes an avenging angel. She finally tells
Agnes the reason for her guilt, sinks to the floor, and dies. Her
long-withheld confession becomes her last rite and allows her to die
in the hope of finding peace.

Steve decides to propose to Kitt, yet his decision is abruptly
changed when he overhears Dick and Kitt tell each other of their
love. The relationship of these two lovers subtly plays upon the
Agnes/Steve relationship of the earlier part of the film. When the
two marry there is a cut to Steve and Mrs. Tuttle alone in the foreground, and, in a cyclical fashion, the two are left as they were
before Kitt came to them. As if to reinforce this, the fade-out follows a shot of Steve again sleeping in a tree while fishing. Steve
throws a small fish back into the river, a symbol of life, just as
Kitt has been sent off into the world. Steve is, once again, left behind.

LAZYBONES plays upon this river image with far less subtlety
than a later Borzage film, THE RIVER (1928). In LAZYBONES the
images and the incorporation of biblical themes are decidedly simple,
whereas the later work is one of greater emotion, spirituality, and
eroticism. LAZYBONES centers on familial and romantic love and
physical and emotional growth, yet it attempts to go no further than
this. Borzage strives neither for complexity and depth nor for the
creation of some greater spiritual nature within the characters or
the situations. Without the power and the complexity of SECRETS,
the film is reduced to a too-simple narrative. There is even a lack
of visual complexity, and the grouping shots are ordinary, only the
window scenes mentioned earlier providing some complexity.

Even the minimal complexity and depth of LAZYBONES are
completely lacking in THE FIRST YEAR (1926). THE FIRST YEAR
is a simple marital drama in which the sanctity of both love and
marriage are reaffirmed and sealed with the promised birth of a
child, a device used much more effectively at the end of MAN'S
CASTLE (1933) and LITTLE MAN, WHAT NOW? (1934). The film
ridicules greed and dismisses worldly obstacles to love and happiness as comic situations to be treated with humor.

Tommy Tucker loves Grace Livingston. She seeks more than
love, however. Grace, like Sara Juke in THE Nth COMMANDMENT,
craves excitement, here in the person of Dick Loring. Tommy finally wins Grace by "grabbing her" and by "sweeping her off her
feet," again, a play on the ideas found in De Mille's society dramas. The two set up a traditional home, yet Grace becomes increasingly dissatisfied. She desires to see strange new places (a
theme carried out more fully in THEY HAD TO SEE PARIS [1929]),
no longer content to just sit at home in Josepher, Missouri.

After a slapstick shopping excursion, in which Tommy accidentally leaves Grace behind in the rain, and after a flat and tragicomic dinner party complete with a sterotypical black maid, Tommy's railroad deal falls through due to the manipulations of Dick Loring, and Grace leaves him and returns home. Tommy finally makes the $125, 000 deal and returns to "grab" Grace once again. At this point she cements the reconciliation by telling of her pregnancy, and the film ends with the prospect of a happy future for Tommy and Grace.

The premise of THE FIRST YEAR is that marriage should always begin with the second year, since the first is filled with adjustments and problems. Borzage uses stereotypical characters, like the earnest working man and the live-for-today woman, and stereotypical situations, such as the failed dinner party, relegating depth and emotion to a secondary place. The problem here is not only a weak script but an obviously bored director, uninspired by his material. This is a problem that will be faced again, since Borzage directed numerous "studio" films that held little appeal for him. The failure of THE FIRST YEAR and, to some extent, LAZY-BONES, will be seen again in some of Borzage's more trivial works of the 1930s (FLIRTATION WALK [1934] and STRANDED [1935]) and the 1940s (THE MAGNIFICENT DOLL [1945]). Only with SEVENTH HEAVEN (1927) did Borzage finally hit his stride and could fully express himself for the first time. It is from this point that we see consistent expressions of what became Borzage's most recognizable thematic and visual qualities.

This 1915-1926 period is one of experimentation. Its unevenness stems from Borzage's failure to express fully and clearly the beliefs so obvious in the later films or to develop a consistent thematic or melodramatic style. Perhaps it is the fault of the material, although there are recognizable elements in many of the films previously discussed, or perhaps it is a lack of cinematic sophistication in these early studio products. Whatever the reason, Borzage finally succeeds in creating and presenting a consistent vision only with SEVENTH HEAVEN and its "sequels, " STREET ANGEL (1928) and THE RIVER (1928).

Borzage's search for form reflects the changes within film-making and within the genre of melodrama itself. Throughout this period there is experimentation with melodramatic situations especially in the westerns but also in LIFE'S HARMONY and THE Nth COMMANDMENT, as well as an emphasis on character in such films as SECRETS and LAZYBONES. But with SEVENTH HEAVEN, STREET ANGEL, and THE RIVER Borzage centers the story on the individuals, finally subordinating the plot and its inconsistencies to character growth, change, and transcendence. These become the major themes in the films that he directs during the next thirty years of his work. The groundwork is recognized in these early works just as clearly as is the influence of Borzage's early Ince training and in his dissatisfaction with themes popularized by other leading directors of the period, such as De Mille.

NOTES

[1]Burt Shapiro, "Desire, Gun Woman, Stage Door Canteen, " Focus! 9 (Spring-Summer 1975), p. 34.

[2]A second pre-1918 film that bridges both of these categories. In NUGGET JIM'S PARDNER (1916) Hal, the son of wealthy business-man, goes west after his father disowns him because of his dissolute ways. His regeneration, like those that occur in the "conversion" films of the late 1930s, becomes the force that leads to a group re-generation.

Nugget Jim, a prospector, leads Hal to a river, where Hal learns to pan for gold and where he is, symbolically, baptized into a purer life. His change ultimately influences Jim and Jim's daugh-ter, Madge, as well. Hall brings Madge out of the darkness of the saloon and into the sunlight, where her anger seems almost to dis-appear and where she regains her lost purity. Furthermore, from this point on until the end of the film she appears only in white. Jim is locked in a dark closet by the two and is allowed out to join Hal and Madge at the table only when his violent nature is chastened. When Hal's father writes and asks Hal to return, Hal boards a train but soon after jumps off and returns to Madge, who loves him, to Jim, and to the unit that the three have created. The three have be-come "whole" only in their interdependence, and Hal's return is a reaffirmation of this fact.

In this film society is presented as a virtual "hotbed of cor-ruption, " and the untamed nature of the western frontier becomes the testing place of the soul and the site of a general conversion. Unlike PITCH O' CHANCE and THE GUN WOMAN, there is no am-biguity here in regard to the value of the wilderness and to what one experiences there. Its wildness becomes its greatest moral as-set. Hal's journey, like that of Newell Paige in GREEN LIGHT (1937) and John Beaven in DISPUTED PASSAGE (1939), becomes a journey to moral awakening as well as one that leads him to love and to spiritual growth.

The use of contrasting dark and light in the film is a motif that appears throughout Borzage's work. It is important to a film like THAT'S MY MAN (1947), and its fullest expression is seen in the final scenes of SEVENTH HEAVEN (1927), A FAREWELL TO ARMS (1932), and THREE COMRADES (1938). This motif takes on moral implications of great scope and acts as a clue to the state of the characters' spiritual progress.

[3]Peter Brooks, The Melodramatic Imagination (New Haven: Yale University Press, 1976), p. 201.

[4]Ibid., p. 201.

[5]Ibid., pp. 201-202.

[6]Ibid.

2. THE LATER SILENT PERIOD

The period of experimentation ends with Borzage's work on SEVENTH HEAVEN (1927). Beginning with this film Borzage crystalizes a recognizable thematic and visual style. No longer does he rely upon the work of others, such as Ince's westerns and De Mille's "society dramas," to direct his own. With his work on SEVENTH HEAVEN Borzage fully breaks away from Griffith and Griffith's thematic and visual patterns. Whereas Griffith relied more on a strictly "physical vitality"[1] or upon characters with a pure "madonna-like innocence,"[2] Borzage's characters combine spiritual energy and purity with physical attractiveness and sensuality.

Borzage de-emphasizes the Griffith theme of family restitution, placing it behind the theme of individual salvation and internal order.[3] In doing so, he focuses upon character development much more than upon situation. Thus, while both directors saw melodrama as a viable way of viewing the world, they differed in their focus. Using such devices as even lighting or shallow focus, Borzage "reduces the power of the physical world."[4] Environment is subordinated to character, and the world external to the characters ("the real world") is "blurred over"[5] and softened just in the way that the sharp "moral conflicts diminish in centrality and the individual's spiritual development is explored."[6] Borzage thus stresses the essences that lie beyond the physical nature of things, the environment. The backgrounds, being visually de-emphasized, are de-emphasized thematically as well, and they "are there only to be transcended as the characters forge binds that go beyond time and space."[7]

In escaping the present or topical orientation of melodrama Borzage emphasizes moral and spiritual transcendence far more than reintegration within the existing social order. Physical reality as a subject is downplayed while the quest for purity within the soul is stressed. What becomes important is not so much war (as in SEVENTH HEAVEN [1927], A FAREWELL TO ARMS [1932], and THREE COMRADES [1938]) or depression (as in MAN'S CASTLE [1933] and LITTLE MAN, WHAT NOW? [1934]) as fact but the characters' spiritual growth that results. Borzage's melodramas do not pit characters against environment nor does he simply externalize good and evil as obvious polarities. Whereas this does appear in the earlier works, even there it is underplayed because of the larger implications. The moral polarities that bring about conflict in literary melodrama, and the conflict through which a cathartic resolution, such as the destruction of evil, is achieved, are, in Borzage's cinema, de-emphasized. In the films, and especially in those made

after 1927, several moral and spiritual systems coexist. [8] Their
juxtaposition provides the catalyst necessary "for his characters'
growth out of one system and emergence into another, more transcendent one. "[9]

It is interesting to note that both SEVENTH HEAVEN and
STREET ANGEL (1928) use the themes of the "angel-heroine"[10] and
the struggle for sanctification. Borzage and Griffith both work in
this mold, yet Borzage's immediate popularity outlasted that of Griffith, especially at this particular time. It is, however, as if the
two were consciously working against the social trends of this period. Molly Haskell relates in From Reverence to Rape that the 1920s
saw a split between the characterization of women as virgins, Borzage's general view, and as vamps, the view of such directors as
De Mille and, later, von Sternberg and Lubitsch. The popularity
of the two sets of directors reflects upon the tensions within the
American consciousness. It is almost as if Borzage, like Griffith
before him, was consciously working against the coming of the twentieth century by harkening back to a Victorian vision of women, in
particular, and of love, in general. Borzage's addition of ultimate
religious transcendence, while mystical, is extremely romantic. The
world of importance is the private world of the lovers. The outside
world exists not so much outside of their spheres of consciousness
as it exists as a device of realization and as an avenue to transcendence.

In the earliest films this juxtaposition of spiritual and temporal states--such as the civilization-wilderness dichotomy of THE
PITCH O' CHANCE and THE GUN WOMAN, family realignment in
LIFE'S HARMONY, and the representation of love as a spiritual
force in THE Nth COMMANDMENT and in SECRETS--is much less
complex. In the films made after 1926 this juxtaposition and the
idea of transcendence itself become the thematic, narrative, and
visual centers of most of Borzage's films. Transcendence becomes,
in fact, the reconciliation of the oppositions found within the text
of the film. This is central to an understanding of Borzage's stylistic "mark. " No longer is he an experimenter or an imitator. With
the release of SEVENTH HEAVEN Borzage becomes what can be
termed an "identifiable director, " if not an auteur.

SEVENTH HEAVEN is the love story of a Paris waif and a
sewercleaner, each of whom yearns for greater things. The film
opens with a "sewer shot, " which visually echoes the theme of the
intertitle: "There is a ladder of courage that leads from the sewer
to the stars. " The film centers on numerous interlocking philosophical oppositions (physical and spiritual, external and internal, logic
and the unexplainable) and cultural oppositions (atheism and religion,
war and peace, sexual independence and sexual union), which are
echoed in the visuals (ground and sky, low in frame and high in
frame, non-home environment and home environment), as well as
in the actual narrative. [11] Thus from the opening the characters
are thrust into a set of oppositions, which they must unify so that
they themselves may become "whole. "

Chico works in the sewers of Paris yet yearns for a job as a streetcleaner.   The greater complications of this and of these philosophical oppositions are immediately made apparent and serve to reinforce and visually strengthen the final transcendence of Chico and Diane.   In the first shot Chico's striving to "rise" is accentuated He is first seen looking up and out of a manhole cover, the sunlight cascading around him.   Chico calls himself a "remarkable fellow, " and his assumption of "wholeness" is supported by the simplicity of his two foremost desires: a job as streetcleaner and a good wife with blond hair.   Yet his "wholeness" is undercut throughout the narrative, and his self-containment eventually crumbles before narrative events and before the intrusion of important spiritual questions.

Borzage cuts from Chico to Diane, a poor waif dressed completely in black and living in a hovel with a cruel sister, Nana, who is addicted to absinthe and prone to whipping Diane at the slightest provocation.   In the immediate close-up of Diane that follows her face is brightly lit even though she covers herself with her shawl. A high-angle shot, a device that later comes to represent spirituality, follows her progress into a bar, where she pawns a locket to get enough money to buy the absinthe that her sister desires.

In the cut that follows, the priest, Father Chevillion, enters with news for the women.   Yet even before he can tell his story the sister undercuts him by telling him that "this is the wrong place to spout religion. "   This idea is played upon throughout, and Chico echoes it later.   The priest tells the women that their aunt and uncle have returned from the South Seas and want to take them in. All that the sister can do, however, is curse the priest and the "new hope" he brings.   When the aunt and uncle do arrive they are visually placed in opposition to the two women, just as the propriety and bourgeois attitudes they uphold are contrasted to the economic plight of the sisters.   Diane, refusing to lie about her fallen virtue, foregoes the "smell of home" and the easy way out of the slums that her relatives offer.   The aunt and uncle leave the girls behind, their moral sensibilities shocked and their "benevolent" attitudes changed to absolute moral condemnation.

Diane, chased into the street by a half-mad Nana, is only saved by the intervention of Chico.   Diane has already been visually tied to Chico by an action taken on her return from the bar.   As she walks back in the rain she stops and stares at a streetlight just as Chico stared out from the sewer.   Each, staring upward, is bathed in soft light, and their mutual desire to "rise" is echoed. Chico intervenes, holds Nana above the darkened opening, and threatens to drop Nana into the sewer if she does not stop abusing Diane--a threat that is important and symbolic in its opposition to the upward strivings of Diane and himself.

Once Nana leaves, Chico returns to the company of his two friends and sits centered within this contained unit.   This unit is symbolic of his own self-centeredness and his belief in his self-

Seventh Heaven

containment and total self-reliance. Diane is consciously placed
alone, sitting dazedly on the periphery, refusing Chico's offers of
food. Chico calls her a creature, declaring that she would be "better
off dead" and claiming that her trouble is that "you won't fight....
You're afraid. " As if consciously to separate himself from her,
he juxtaposes this statement to another ("I'm not afraid. That's why
I'm a remarkable fellow. "), which once again brings forward his
claim of "wholeness. "

> At this point the priest re-enters the narrative. He is

> > the character representing the institution of religion. In
> > the course of the film he illustrates many of the virtues
> > resulting from belief in the Bon Dieu, since he performs
> > good works, seemingly provides answers to prayers, and
> > comforts the dying. [12]

Chico and the priest appear to be in direct opposition, Chico being
the realist, or so he believes, and the priest representing the spiritual alone and upholding what Chico sees as human illusions. Chico
claims to have tested God twice, both times achieving no satisfaction.
He believes in a religion not of faith but of barter. He lit candles
twice, and prayed to no avail for a job as a streetcleaner and for
a wife with yellow hair. He gave God a chance, but God failed him
and, in essence, owes him ten francs, the cost of the candles. "In
response to Chico's twin prayers, ... the priest can supply only
Chico's streetwasher appointment. "[13] Throughout his tirade Diane
is within the frame, leading the audience to realize that she is to
be the wife Chico desires. The priest, in response to Chico's second request, gives Chico two religious medals, introduced "in an
inserted close-up that marks them as privileged signifiers"[14] and
the admonition that "they may help you someday. Who knows?"

> Up to this point the priest and the formal religion that he
represents have been thoroughly undercut. The result of his news
to the sisters is the beating that Diane receives and her desire to
commit suicide ("I can't go on living this way without hope. ").
Chico's realist philosophy and his atheism further undercut the
priest's code. Chico's desire for a wife, in particular, is displaced,
since all that he receives are the medals. The medals come to
displace the priest as well, since they are used later by the couple
to perform a marriage ceremony of their own devising.

> > On one level the medals displace Chico's future wife--the
> > answer to his prayers. On another level they also become
> > the place where the power to answer prayers resides. As
> > they progressively demonstrate that power they displace the
> > priest as its locus. For example, they replace the priest
> > in the argument against atheism: as Chico refuses Diane's
> > wish for a church wedding ("I am an atheist--I walk alone, "
> > he says), he sits on the medals which comically drive him
> > out of his posture of repose. And when the war breaks
> > out and the couple must marry without institutional support

of church or state, it is the medals which take the place
of those institutions and which the lovers drape around each
other's necks to sanctify the union. Most forcefully, during all the years that the two are separated by the war,
every day at 11:00 AM they gaze at the medals and "say"
to each other the magic litany which violates the physical
constraints of space by putting them in telepathic communication "Chico-Diane-Heaven."[15]

The medals displace the significance of the priest and, by extension,
the significance of formal religion. The medals become representative of the church and of the priest, but go beyond this to encompass
all of the spirituality that grows out of the couple's relationship. The
spirituality that resides within the medals becomes a signifier of the
spirituality of the characters, however, only after they are exchanged
during the wedding vows.

As Diane is about to get up and leave, Chico stands over her.
The two are under the streetlight, and through this image the two
are tied once again as they were visually during Chico's tirade. At
this point Chico tells the police who have come to arrest Diane that
"she's my wife," declaring what is later to become fact and supporting the visual cues. Chico himself does not understand the implications of his actions ("Why did I do that? Now I'm ruined"). Diane
can only thank him ("You have great heart"), kiss his hands, an
early sign of the spiritual and religious nature of their relationship,
and promise to leave after the police visit his home and check out
his claim.

Chico and Diane eventually go to Chico's apartment. It is
here that his yearnings are most vividly visualized and here that
the images of the opening scenes are expanded in significance. After
entering a dark hallway the couple go up seven flights of stairs to
his home far above the sewers, the street--reality. Diane is amazed,
calling the room "Heaven" as she turns around, staring at its con-
tents and its size. Chico exits through a large window, standing
upon a plank and surrounded by the roofs and the stars. He calls
Diane out to look at the streets below, but she refuses, much too
scared and unsure of herself. It is only when Chico takes her hand
and leads her out onto the ledge that she goes. Communicating the
rest of his philosophy of life, he tells her never to be afraid and
"never look down. Always look up."

The two re-enter the room and prepare for bed. Diane removes her black dress and stockings, wearing only a white nightgown that Chico gets for her, which serves as a symbol of her spiritual purity. He goes for water, ignoring a woman who flirts with
him at the faucet, as Diane gets into bed. When he returns he takes
a pillow and a cover and sleeps under the window arch, beneath the
stars and next to the bars that separate him from the outside world.
She stares up and out of the window, looking at the stars just as he
does, and visually the two are tied once again. By connecting their
actions and their emotions Borzage connects their unformed yet

developing yearnings and, in particular, their desire to grow or rise
more than to escape.

      Through a number of domestic scenes--Diane making Chico
coffee, helping him wind on his belt, and giving him a haircut--the
viewer is made to feel the growing love of these two. The effect
on Diane is most noticeable. Her courage and security grow, and,
after sitting by the window and looking first out at the street below,
representative of her past, and then up at the sky, representative of
her eventual spiritual transcendence, she walks slowly and unsteadily
onto the plank and stands alone outside of the window. She affirms
the growing spiritual nature of their relationship, telling Chico that
"God brought me to you" and kneeling before him, her close-ups
"shot against hazy, indeterminate backgrounds [that] call ... attention
to [her] spiritual qualities."[16] As if to symbolize their union and
its purity, Borzage has Chico enter with a white wedding dress.
While he cannot verbally tell her of his love, he moves into her
frame, his action replacing his words and affirming their union.
Once in the frame and facing Diane, Chico chants the three words
("Chico-Diane-Heaven") that come to symbolize their transcendence.
As if to reaffirm his refutation of the priest and of the dogmatic,
religion that the priest represents, he refuses a church wedding ("I
am an atheist--I walk alone"). This statement is undercut, however,
by his realization that he walks alone no longer. Just as he says
this he sits on the medals that the priest gave him earlier, jumping
up in surprise. Diane realizes the change love brings about as
well, and she walks out on the plank with a new sureness ("I'm not
afraid. I never will be again").

      At this point a mobilization order arrives. Chico, forced to
leave within the hour, must postpone the wedding until he returns.
Told the news as she stands wearing the wedding dress, Diane en-
capsulates both her former self and her present courage in her two
lines of dialogue. At first she claims, "I'm afraid," but after Chico's admonition always to look up and not down, she claims to be a
"remarkable fellow," echoing his words and his courage. Their
love, in which she draws courage from his strength, allows her to
escape her immediate fears and to believe in the future. As if to
symbolize her change and her imminent transcendence, Chico lifts
her into the air and carries her weightlessly around the room, a
scene that occurs with similar effect in A FAREWELL TO ARMS
(1932) just before Frederick must catch the train for his return to
the front.

      Chico too is changed, and he decides to give God "one more
chance," performing a wedding ceremony of his own, the religious
medals serving the function that the priest and the rings usually
serve. As each holds a medal, and Chico asks God to "make this
a true marriage," he places the medal around Diane's neck. She
does the same, and the two say their own vows. Shot from a high
angle, the wedding takes on a religious significance that underscores
the spiritual nature of the union. To Chico's simple vow ("I take
you, Diane, as my wife") Diane adds the word "forever." The vows

that the two exchange invest the medals with a natural spirituality instead of the dogmatic formalism that they previously held. Chico further vows to come to Diane every day at 11:00, at which time the two will renew their vow ("Diane-Chico-Heaven") and remain spiritually together. In this way they exchange the time, space, and distance of the immediate world for the closeness of their own spiritual world.

Diane gets a job in a munitions factory, which ties her to Chico, who is at war. There she meets Colonel Brissac, an amoral hedonist, who tells her that the traditions of the world are upside down and that she should allow him to "take care" of her. Her refusal ("We [she and Chico] are shoulder to shoulder. That's all that matters") becomes a refusal of the materialism and hedonism of the world outside the sphere that she and Chico inhabit.

The years pass, and finally the last major offensive begins. In the war montage that follows (similar to the one in A FAREWELL TO ARMS [1932]) Chico is wounded. Believing himself at the point of death, he returns his religious medal to Father Chevillion and returns Diane to herself[17] while symbolically giving his spirit to her as well. The horror of their separation, both present and future, is reinforced in Diane's reaction when the priest puts Chico's medal around her neck, intertwining it with her own. The medals, once signifiers of the growing spirituality of the relationship, now take on the full implications of externality and become pieces of metal without significance,[18] just as the spirituality that they originally upheld becomes representative of an empty and externalized God. Diane, believing herself to be "right back at the beginning again," negates all that has come before Chico's death ("he never came at all") and refuses the consolations of religion offered by the priest ("We must not question God's will ... "). Her belief in God now gone ("For four years I called this Heaven--prayed--I believed in God--I believed He would bring Chico back to me"), she strikes the priest repeatedly on his chest, striking out at divine injustice and at the world itself. At this moment there is a disturbing "flat cut"[19] to Chico fighting his way through the crowd celebrating the Armistice.

> This disruption [of spatial and narrative continuity] is doubled with more force by the highly significant cut which initiates the climactic alternating syntagm. There is no preparation in the narrative for Chico's return, and the first appearance of him back from the dead is not softened by an explanatory intertitle or even a dissolve. All that heralds his return is a brutal, flat cut which marks the transformation between one narrative event (sorrow at Chico's death) and another (Chico's return). The contradiction [is] between the triumph of the oppositional column headed by the spiritual.... Thus the difference between frames, which is normally effaced in the classical cinema, here stands for the difference between the two founding signifieds [physical and spiritual] of the text.[20]

Chico returns at precisely 11:00, thereby reinstating the spirituality
of their union as well as supporting the implications of justice and
order in the universe that Diane previously denied. "Chico, having
surrendered the material signifier of 'spirituality,' returns the signi-
fied, which does not disappear but rather becomes lodged in him."[21]
His words ("They thought I was dead, but I'll never die" and "God
is within me") restrengthen the belief in God and in spirituality that
were almost lost.

The last shot consolidates the physical and spiritual, and religious and humanistic, qualities of the relationship, and signifies its
transcendence. After the continual cross-cutting between the previous
scenes of Diane and the priest and of Chico in the crowd, there is a
long "culmination shot." Chico returns to Diane, and the two kneel
in each others' arms. The priest stands to the left and the window
opening to Paris is at rear center. "During this shot, a diegetically
unmotivated beam of light from the upper left comes and the frame
materialises into a strong downward left-right diagonal, blanking out
the wall and bathing the couple in a sanctifying light."[22] The couple
move beyond the immediate and into the spiritual, tied to God by the
light. The priest is crowded into the left corner, yet his presence
in the frame, in contrast to the materialist Brissac, is significant.
On the one hand he signifies the position of religion in the world of
lovers, yet by being left out of the actual beam of light his importance is undercut, as it has been throughout the film. The lovers
have transcended their immediate world as well as the set of beliefs
imposed by a formal and often untested religion. Theirs is an escape from dogma and an entrance into true understanding.

This idea of transcendence through some final realization is
presented just as strongly at the end of STREET ANGEL, a film that,
while playing upon virtually the same themes as SEVENTH HEAVEN,
is much more Germanic in style. The heavy mist at the start, the
darkness and shadows especially throughout the earliest scenes, and
the low-keyed lighting create an undercurrent of doom and entrapment
that is only removed within particular scenes, such as those of Angela
and Gino at home, and only completely escaped at the point of final
transcendence, at which the two characters become "whole" in their
interdependence and march into the fog together.

The film opens with a heavy mist, which reinforces a feeling
of gloom and depression as well as of an impersonal and "physically
and spiritually overwhelming world."[23] The opening "establishes the
film's atmosphere"[24]--a bustling city of people living within a contained entity. The individuals of the city are tied together in a single spiritual community through the use of the connective camera and
through the long opening tracking shot.

> Borzage captures a sense of discrete stories recurring in
> a continuous, all-encompassing environment. Though all
> the stories take place independently of one another, Bor-
> zage ties them all together into a simpler event by use of
> connective camera movement and editing. Though different

Street Angel

and separate from one another, they share a common setting and atmosphere. This sort of thing makes no sense
logically ... but it does work intuitively to define the in-
difference, sordidness and despair of the environment that
begins the film. [25]

This opening, combined with the opening intertitle ("Everywhere ... in
every town ... in every street ... we pass, unknowing, human souls
made great through love and adversity") sets the mood. [26] The camera wanders around a heavily misted Naples, passing a man getting
his shoes shined, policemen on rounds, a circus troupe, a priest
walking down a stone stairway, and a beggar girl asking for alms.
The track continues:

... past a man milking, past a fruit stand where a custo-
mer is haggling over a price with the fruitseller, to a knot
of women talking at the foot of a stairway, waiting to find
out what's going on inside an apartment. Finally, he [Bor-
zage] cuts into an apartment in which a doctor is telling
Angela [Janet Gaynor] that she must buy some medicine
in order to save her sick mother. [27]

Borzage creates a mood seemingly like that of the opening of

THE Nth COMMANDMENT. There are, however, substantial differences. In the earlier film the opening shots within the department
store are disconnected and therefore do not tie the customers together in any particular or shared sphere. The transcendence that results in that film becomes rather an escape from a particular situation than a transcendent release from an ontological condition. In
STREET ANGEL the city becomes an entity, and the camera, through
its tracking shot, follows along its streets and creates a web-like
feeling of interconnection. When Angela and Gino finally "rise" at
the end of the film they rise above more than their poverty, their
past, or their present reality. They rise from a lower spiritual
state to a more universal and spiritual one, from the world of loosely connected individuals to a spiritual sphere of their own.

On an immediate level STREET ANGEL "deals with that re-
current myth of the woman who prostitutes herself, ... endures dis-
grace, and is finally forgiven."[28] To save her mother Angela attempts to become a prostitute. Potential clients, however, pass her
by without the slightest degree of interest. Failing at this, she re-
sorts to theft, but she is caught and sentenced to a one-year term
in the workhouse. Escaping into the shadows, she returns home to
find her mother dead and the police close behind. She escapes out
of a window, an iconographic connection to SEVENTH HEAVEN, and
down a drainpipe, hiding in a broken bass drum and finally escaping
with some circus people.

While with the circus troupe she meets Gino, an itinerant
artist. After laughing about the foolishness of love she eventually
does fall in love with him, swayed by his soft manner and open
avowals ("Love is like measles--when it comes you can't stop it").
Gino attempts to paint Angela but complains that she "hides herself
... in a mask," not letting her soul shine out as it should. His
painting, once viewed, becomes recognized as his vision of what she
can be more than what she is now. Angela attests to this fact when
she finally views the work, claiming that she isn't really like that.
Gino's answer ("You are ... to me!") is the statement of his love.
After Angela's reply ("I wish I could be ... always") the two look
at each other, and for the first time Angela touches Gino's face,
her kiss interrupted by the intrusion of the circus owner.

Angela and Gino leave the circus troupe after Angela has an
accident and breaks her ankle. Standing on stilts, an image reflective of her precarious freedom, she falls when some policemen walk
by. The two decide to return to Naples, taking a boat and reiterat-
ing the journey motif created by the traveling pan of the opening, as
Gino whistles "Angelo Mia" ("God sent you to me"). This song, like
the "Chico-Diane-Heaven" vow of SEVENTH HEAVEN, serves to join
the two throughout the film, even when they are apart. Angela even
whistles the tune later while in prison, using it to keep Gino with
her.

Angela and Gino return to Naples, where Gino seeks commissions to support them. When none are found he sells the painting

of Angela so that the two can eat. The painting, however, continues
to exert an influence over the two just as the Bible does in STRANGE
CARGO (1940). Gino's portrait of Angela comes to represent more
than their love or the soul he sees within her; it becomes representative "of the abstract, transcendent nature of this relationship."[29]

> Even though it has been sold, the painting and its absence
> exert a powerful influence over the lovers. When Borzage
> cuts to shots of the bare wall where the painting was hung,
> the emptiness [and the ethereal glow of the white wall]
> conveys even more profoundly the painting's metaphysical
> significance: it, like their love, transcends material re-
> ality.[30]

As if to reinforce this, the art dealer to whom Gino sells the painting commissions another artist to forge it into a virginal madonna of
an Old Master.

> Several times during the film Borzage cuts back to the
> painting of Angela. As she herself becomes more and
> more completely changed by her love for Gino and her
> trials in the world, the painting slowly transformed into
> a madonna. When Angela, without Gino's knowledge, is
> taken back to jail after spending her last hour with him,
> Brozage cuts to a shot of the forger painting a halo over
> her head.[31]

The painting becomes the spiritual guardian of their relationship once they are separated. Angela, caught by the police once
again, is given one hour before the officers will return to arrest
her. Gino still knows nothing of her past, reinforcing the idea that
her life began only when her relationship with him brought out her
love and her soul. She re-enters their apartment, closing all of
the windows and drapes so as, as Angela says, "to shut our happiness in" and, in truth, to shut reality out. The two drink to the
future ("to tomorrow with you ... to our love ... our faith in each
other ... always"), the toast being more prophetic than either expects. Gino continues talking of their future, toasting the "glorious
world, " the children they are to have ("A girl ... a little rabbit ...
like you. A boy ... with funny big feet ... like me"), and of how
they are "going to climb ... higher and higher." Juxtaposed to this
and at Gino's back are the police who look through a crack in the
drapes. Once more toasting "our good fortune, " and reaffirming
their eternal togetherness, Angela leaves to meet the present reality
of her worldly fate. The two once more whistle to each other, and
as Angela exits with the policeman Borzage cuts to the forger putting
a halo over the madonna.

Angela is met in the workhouse by Lisetta in scenes filmed
in the heavy Germanic style of Murnau, the effect created by the
use of huge studio sets and extreme low-key lighting. Lisetta is
a prostitute and serves as Angela's negative counterpart throughout.
She calls Angela "a street angel, like me, " failing to realize Angela's

depth of soul. The look of satisfaction on the prostitute's face stems from the fact that Lisetta desired Gino in the way that evil desires to corrupt good, but was rebuffed by him as "impure." The contrast to Angela is underscored by a cut to three men studying the madonna and declaring it an authentic eighteenth-century masterpiece by Vianotti.

Released from the workhouse, Lisetta tells Gino the "truth" about Angela and her arrest for soliciting and robbery and Gino's sadness turns to anger. He laughs at himself and at his stupidity. Yet he still refuses Lisetta's consolation and the corruption that she once again offers. The cutting between Lisetta and Angela is continued, as is their thematic contrast.

We next see Angela staring into Gino's room, now filled with cobwebs and dust. He "went to the devil" after she left, the landlady announces. Angela then exits into the night. The next cut is to Lisetta, trying to caress Gino. He rebuffs her again, she mocks him, and he makes a final vow to paint women as they "really are"-- with the faces of angels and with souls "as black as hell." Lisetta tells him to go to the wharves for a model, as there are many such women there. Unwittingly, she is sending him back to Angela, and just as she says this there is a cut to Angela entering and wandering along the foggy wharves.

The importance of such shot juxtapositions continues in the scenes that follow. There are cuts between Angela walking on the wharf and Gino studying the whores along the wharf as well as of Angela sitting alone by a wall next to a plate of empty clamshells and Gino wandering past different groups. Gino walks from left to right, lighting matches and studying the faces of the women he meets. These cuts are juxtaposed to those of Angela walking from right to left, an outsider to the groups she passes. The two meet in mid-screen. Gino lights a match, recognizes her, and chases her through the fog, through this back part of the city, and, unknowingly, into a church.

He catches her and starts to strangle her on the altar when he accidentally knocks over a Bible, looks up and realizes where he is. With his hand still around her throat, Gino lifts his eyes and sees his transformed painting of Angela hanging above the altar. Borzage here cuts to a high angle shot of Gino and Angela from the position of the painting. [32]

Gino removes his hat and steps back in fear and reverence. He looks from the painting to Angela at his feet and makes his accusation ("To think I once painted you like that"). She looks up at the painting, paralleling his action. Her answer ("But I am like that still, look into my eyes") forces him to look at her for the first time. He looks directly into her eyes and sees the innocence in them just in the way that Mrs. Tuttle sees the truth in Steve's eyes in LAZYBONES. He lifts her up off the floor, embracing her in

the air, and, after a final shot of the painting, carries her home
through the fog, into their renewed state of togetherness and transcendent love.

The elevated state of their relationship is now formally tied
to the painting and to the force that the painting exerts.

> The religious atmosphere, coupled with the painting's trans-
> formation into a madonna, makes clear the quasi-religious
> nature of their new awareness of and need for one another.
> Through the painting, each redeems the other. Borzage's
> great dissolve from the painting to them eloquently equates
> the rebirth of their love with a greater, more mysterious
> spiritual regeneration. [33]

The painting joins the characters and interacts directly, in contrast
to the juxtaposed but separated earlier shots, with the characters.
It prevents Angela's death and becomes "the agent of their reunion.
The unlikely presence of the painting here is less absurd coincidence
that it is indicative of the mystical design of Borzage's universe. "[34]

Once again, as in SEVENTH HEAVEN, the lovers are united
and move out of their sphere and into a higher level of understanding. They achieve their transcendence through their connection with
some divine source and power. Their spiritual rejuvenation and rebirth opens them to each other and allows the relationship to escape
earthly problems and obstacles. The divine power of the painting is
an even stronger symbol of this than the religious medals used in
SEVENTH HEAVEN. The medals only held significance as long as
they were believed in by the carriers. When Chico's medal was returned to Diane by the priest its role as a meaningful signifier was
lost. The painting suffers no such fate. The transformation of the
work parallels Angela's transformation. Gino painted her soul. The
forger paints her transcendence. In the final shots, when Angela
and Gino are reunited, it is under the eye of the painting, now a
madonna hanging in the church. The power of the painting acts as
an external force that is always hovering over the lovers, whether
separated or together. There is no chance of Gino's returning Angela to herself as Chico does by returning the medal to Diane. Nor
is there a symbolic intermixing of the two as there is when the two
medals are joined around Diane's neck. The painting acts as both
the force of recognition and as the device of transcendence, joining
the lovers in a spiritual union much as the beam of light does at
the end of SEVENTH HEAVEN.

The immersion of Chico and Diane in the beam of light is
parallel to the walk into the fog that Gino and Angela take at the
end of STREET ANGEL. Both couples transcend their reality and
enter a sphere that has first been incorporated within their souls,
souls that have been "made great through love and adversity. " They
are changed within themselves and can become fully interdependent
and interconnected spiritual parts of a whole. They are not, like
characters in literary and stage melodrama, already whole, although

they often think they are. Nor are they characters as internally divided as are those found in tragedy. They are characters made
whole only through their connection with the soul of another. Love
and immortality found through it allows them to move beyond their
reality and into some religious or spiritual state of transcendence.
These films, and those that follow, become chronicles of the journeys that the characters make. In most of the films the journey is
unconscious. Yet by the final scenes, with a final recognition, the
implications of the journey are made clear to the viewer and, more
importantly, to the characters. The catharsis of stage and literary
melodrama is kept, but it is not so much evil expunged as love recognized and immediate reality transcended. The focus changes from
the outside world to that of the inner state of the lovers. The attacking forces become representative of the world to be transcended.
Their importance is not so much the fact of their existence as the
transcendence that they imply.

This transcendence almost always works from within to create
a bond that finally and irrevocably joins the lovers together. In Borzage's next film, THE RIVER (1928), this inner change becomes associated with the rebirth of innocence and the "thawing" of an almost-
dead soul. The film more fully and openly plays upon the themes of
innocence and regeneration, yet here the idea of a spiritual awakening
is tied to a sexual awakening as well.

THE RIVER is thematically Borzage's most complicated and
compelling silent work. Visually, it is interesting for its extreme
long shots, such as those of the train and of the work crews, and
for Borzage's tendency to "pose" Rosalee. Her lassitude and ennui
continually contrast with Allen John's activity and zest, both of which
stem from his innocent love for nature and from his willingness to
confront life. Almost from the first shots of the film contrasts are
evident. Allen John floats down the river toward the whirlpool. This
is in juxtaposition to an earlier shot of a barrel and some other de-
bris floating in the same manner. To float as close to the whirlpool
as possible without falling into its current is a game to Allen John,
just as life itself is. As he floats toward the shore there is a cut
to Rosalee, sitting on a rock with Marsden's crow, her only companion and a symbol of her bondage and of her position as Marsden's
"kept" woman. The two meet as Allen John, naked, starts to climb
out of the river and onto the shore. He fails at first to see Rosalee, but when he finally does his embarrassment is made clear and
he quickly falls back into the purifying stream, only his eyes remaining above the surface.

Almost immediately Rosalee's "autre monde,"[35] her "otherworldliness," is made clear. Her claim ("I want to be lonesome!
I'm sick of men. ... I never want to see one again!") is visually,
spiritually, and physically substantiated. The water project she lives
near has been deserted, the workers' cabins emptied. Earlier long
low-angle shots of the ladders and cabins filled with men scurrying
along are juxtaposed to later similar shots. This time only wild
dogs run along the wood and rope ladder-bridges, or there is no

The River

activity at all. Rosalee's state of lassitude and ennui, her otherworldliness, is reinforced in her physical surroundings, just as Danny's emotional state is echoed in the landscape twenty years later in
MOONRISE (1949).

The only activity within the shots (even Allen John's swimming
is reduced to being drawn by the current) is the movement of the
train. This is to become Allen John's means of entry into the adult
world of experience: he plans to leave his boat on the river and
move "into town" for the winter. Yet he misses the first train, the
shadows of the machine reflected on his upturned face. This is a
reflection of his twin desires--to stay with Rosalee and to escape
into a new world.

Almost unconsciously, Rosalee sets the table in her cabin for
two, expecting no one but anticipating "something." Again, her
otherworldliness is reinforced as she tells Allen John, "I knew you'd
never make the train," claiming some special foreknowledge. All
the while she is caught in a series of scornful poses, refusing physical or emotional contact with this boy-man and ordering him about.
He does her chores while she stands above him, her superiority and
commanding nature thereby reinforced visually. She refuses to recognize him as a man (Allen John: "If you hate men so much why
invite me to supper?" Rosalee: "You don't count"), relegating him
to the role of servant and viewing him as an innocent child.

In the next shot the two build a house of cards. For the first
time they sit opposite each other at the same visual level. Yet this
equality of position is undercut as Rosalee leans her body over the
table to taunt Allen John again. The card game, reflective of the
cat-and-mouse game she has been playing throughout, takes on an
erotic quality. The erotic nature of the game begins mildly enough,
with Rosalee teasing Allen John about "how many women you've known."
Allen John's answer ("None but you. My mother died when I was a
kid"), reaffirms his innocence and purity, as do his questions ("Are
you Marsden's wife?" "Related to him?"). Rosalee's simple "No"
replies, without explanation, allow her to maintain her enigmatic
quality. Even her final reply ("I've learned that life is better ...
alone") comes without further explanation.

An almost-unconscious attraction grows between the two. Rosalee notices his great height (6'1") and stands against him provoca-
tively (–R –AJ). She turns to him, and just as he touches her and
bends to kiss her the train whistle blows and interrupts the scene.
Allen John, again missing the train, stands at the door, a point-of-
view shot up to the passing train reflecting just how far away both
the train and his dream of a winter in the city are.

The mood broken, the two enter into confrontation. Allen
John, torn between desire and fear asks Rosalee what she meant
when she told him, "You don't count." Her reply ("I meant you
were a boy, and I've known only men like Marsden"), followed by
another enigmatic grin and her stare at the crow, causes him to re-
bel once more. By proclaiming his difference, ("I'm a better man
than Marsden. I'd never treat you like he did"), he reinforces his
separateness from other men and from the outer world itself. Yet
his otherworldliness is not the ennui of Rosalee; it is the otherworldliness of the child existing in adult surroundings. Allen John
leaves the cabin to wait on the train platform and to decide about
his future. Rosalee, painted as the martyr through another shot of
her standing in the doorway, arms stretched out in a position used
most effectively in the war montage in A FAREWELL TO ARMS
(1932), is once again isolated within the cabin and within herself.

Without explanation, the next cut is to Allen John back at the
hearth of the cabin. Rosalee enters the room, pausing at the thres-
hold in the same Christ-like pose. Dressed seductively in a black-
and-flowered negligee, she sits beside Allen John and sucks suggestively upon a stick of candy he gives her. His determination to go
is still strong, and there is one more train to come before rail service is cut off until spring. When he offers to cut wood for her before he goes she taunts him once again ("I don't believe you could
cut enough wood to keep anybody warm"), standing above him as she
did earlier in the film when she ordered him about in the same manner. He attempts to prove himself to her, and once again misses
his train. This time Allen John's response is anger ("You think I'm
a joke, don't you? You think I'll stay here and be laughed at and
made a fool of!") as he stands towering above her, then leaves abruptly.

Time passes, and the film picks up during a winter snowstorm.
Again the juxtaposition of shots comments on the narrative. Borzage
first cuts to the snowstorm without, then to the fire within. There
follows a cut to Rosalee on the bed wearing a white nightgown and
a black kimono, the cold and the fire of the previous shots reflecting
the two parts of her soul that Allen John brought alive and into conflict within her. Her reflections and thoughts of the whirlpool and
of the river, of Allen John and of the barrel in the current, are then
juxtaposed to two shots of the crow in a cage hanging on the wall.
She walks to the birdcage and places the bird above the cage. As
if to tie herself to this image, she then walks to the window, the
bars on the window paralleling the cage, and stands before it. At
this point Allen John returns. She admits to her being "terribly
lonely" without him. To celebrate, they play checkers, but her reaction to his innocence turns to anger and disgust. Viewing the
shadow of the bird and the cage on the wall, she walks over to the
table and lights a lamp, attempting to make the shadow and its symbolic significance to her own life vanish. This fails, however, and
the shadow appears on the opposite wall, this time surrounding Allen
John. In anger, she throws the checkerboard across the room, displaying her first obvious emotion beyond her continual boredom. She
goes to lie on the bed, seductively calling to Allen John ("I'm thinking of you, John Allen ... my heart ... "). He comes to her, and
she puts his hand on her heart, symbolically joining it with her own.
Just as he bends to kiss her, the crow, Marsden's watchdog, flies
off the cage and attacks him. Rosalee, her passions now fully un-
leashed, attacks the crow, desiring thereby to release her soul and
her emotions, and threatening to kill anyone who tries to stop her
("Let me go, or I'll kill you"). She stabs Allen John in her madness, the blade of the knife miraculously bending on impact. He
finally confesses his love for her ("I love you better than anything
in the world") and vows to take her from Marsden, to marry her,
and so to free her.

Rosalee orders Allen John out, once again isolating herself,
so that she need not deal with emotion or action. She locks the door
as if to lock out her feelings. He yells, "I'll take you away from
Marsden," grabs his axe, and marches off. Almost as if castrating
Marsden or, better, Marsden's influence, he begins to chop down
every tree surrounding the cabin, wildly yelling at the same time,
"I'll show you I'm a better man than Marsden." Rosalee's only reaction is to turn from the door, walk to her bed, and to pick up
his gear.

Allen John is found frozen in the snow by none other than
Marsden, who has returned from prison. Rosalee, galvanized out
of her inaction, attempts to revive Allen John. She and Marsden
rub snow all over him and feed him hot liquids. Rosalee begins to
talk to him, to call him back, an image used at the end of DISPUTED
PASSAGE (1939), when Audrey calls Beaven out of his coma and back
to life. She finally confesses her love ("God help me to make you
understand ... I love him. He mustn't die. I love him"), and
Marsden leaves for help. In a white nightgown symbolic of her re-

newed purity, Rosalee, fully awakened by her love and her passion, clutches his hands and kneels by the stricken man. Finally, in what is perhaps Borzage's most sensual and erotic sequence, she climbs into his bed, hugging the naked and comatose man to her, transmitting the warmth of her life force from her body into his, and praying to God throughout ("Let him live ... let him live"). Allen John opens his eyes slightly, and in his delirium, recalls earlier events and images of the cabin, the whirlpool, Marsden, the train, Rosalee's face, and the crow, just as Rosalee did in her earlier daydreaming. He at last returns to the reality of the present, calls her name, and smiles. His first words ("I didn't even go away when you wanted me to") take on an added significance. Her reply ("Oh Allen John! I never want you to leave me! I love you!") becomes their marriage vow, this being reinforced by the slightly high-angled shots of the two and medium close-up that follows. She vows to "go down to the sea" with him in the spring; the two are to begin a new life together. He, no longer the innocent child, and she, no longer the isolated and otherworldly being, have found their souls through each other. As if to reinforce this, the final shot is of Allen John looking up at Rosalee and, by extension, to God, as Rosalee looks up to God. Her complexity and isolation gone, she becomes simply a woman who loves. The two are both reborn in the deadness of winter, the snow becoming an image of rebirth here just as it is used in THREE COMRADES (1938) and THE MORTAL STORM (1940), and the two go off together in the spring. Just as the protagonists in THE GUN WOMAN (1918), SEVENTH HEAVEN (1927), and STREET ANGEL (1928) transcended their environments through experience and love, so too have Rosalee and Allen John moved into a higher spiritual state. They, too, have not so much escaped as outgrown their environment, a motif used even more strongly in MAN'S CASTLE (1933) and LITTLE MAN, WHAT NOW? (1934).

THE RIVER, drawing upon the themes of the earlier films of the 1915-1926 period and upon the religious, spiritual, and romantic base of SEVENTH HEAVEN and STREET ANGEL, becomes a link to the Borzage films of the 1930s as well. What separates it from the other two films discussed within this chapter is its extreme complexity and its extremely sensual elements. Yet with these two films it becomes the clearest statement of Borzagean idealism. Love takes on religious, mystical, and spiritual qualities in SEVENTH HEAVEN and in STREET ANGEL only hinted at in previous films. Love becomes the avenue for spiritual transcendence. Yet THE RIVER, in adding a sensual and erotic quality to this relationship, ties the couple as much to the reality of their selves, their instincts, and their drives as does their desire for transformation. Firmly grounded within themselves, the characters learn to exist in the world and within reality as much as they escape the predicaments of this world. While Chico and Diane are surrounded in a beam of white light and while Gino and Angela walk off into a fog, Allen John and Rosalee plan to go down to the river, into civilization and life, and to rejoin the world. Their transcendence allows an immediate future to be hinted at, whereas no such promise is given the other couples, a fact that links this film to future Borzage works. Similarly, the

endings of the films that follow present the characters on the one
hand transcending reality but on the other hand moving both to another
physical environment and to another stage of existence within the immediate world. Thus, while such problems as war, depression, and
separation as fact are not important, the now-exalted couples continue to exist fully within the realm of immediate reality as well.
Their perceptions are changed. They are changed. No longer do
the two exist as separate or "whole" individuals. They are whole
only as a unit and only as a unit can they exist in their higher spiritual state.

These three films set the context in which almost all of the
later Borzage films work. It is at this point that Borzage begins
to redefine melodrama. In the earlier period the attention shifts
from plot and situation to character; in this period we recognize
most clearly the shift from individual to couple. Individuals begin
by claiming wholeness (e. g. , Chico's statement "I am a remarkable
fellow") yet are gradually shown to have numerous and serious
"lacks"--lacks that are only filled by joining with another individual.
Only then can a catharsis and transcendence take place. In the process the idea of a black-and-white morality is submerged within the
search for knowledge, growth, and regeneration. Borzage de-
emphasizes the Manichean and simpleminded nature of literary and
stage melodrama and devises a melodrama fraught with intimacy and
complexity. While SEVENTH HEAVEN, STREET ANGEL, and THE
RIVER most clearly exemplify this change, it is an idea that resur-
faces continually in the films that follow.

NOTES

[1]John Belton, "Souls Made Great Through Love and Adversity, " Focus! 9 (Spring-Summer 1973), p. 16.
    [2]Ibid. , p. 16.
    [3]Ibid.
    [4]Philip Rosen, "Difference and Displacement in SEVENTH
HEAVEN, " Screen 18, 2 (Summer 1977), p. 95.
    [5]Ibid. , p. 95.
    [6]Ibid.
    [7]Ibid.
    [8]Belton, p. 22.
    [9]Ibid.
    [10]Molly Haskell, From Reverence to Rape: The Treatment of
Women in the Movies (New York: Holt, Rinehart and Winston, 1973),
p. 50.
    [11]Rosen, p. 95.
    [12]Ibid. , p. 96.
    [13]Ibid. , p. 97.
    [14]Ibid.
    [15]Ibid. , p. 98.

[16]Robert Smith, "The Films of Frank Borzage" (part 2), Bright Lights 1, 3 (Summer 1975), p. 17.

[17]Rosen, p. 98.

[18]Ibid., p. 99.

[19]Ibid.

[20]Ibid., p. 101.

[21]Ibid., p. 99.

[22]Ibid., p. 96.

[23]John Belton, The Hollywood Professionals: Howard Hawks, Frank Borzage and Edgar Ulmer vol. 3 (New York: Tantivity, 1974), p. 83.

[24]Ibid., p. 81.

[25]Ibid.

[26]Ibid., pp. 80-81.

[27]Ibid., p. 81.

[28]Haskell, p. 51.

[29]Belton, Hollywood Professionals, p. 83.

[30]Ibid., pp. 83-84.

[31]Ibid., p. 84.

[32]Ibid., p. 85.

[33]Ibid., p. 86.

[34]Ibid.

[35]Henri Agel and Michael Henry, "Frank Borzage," in Anthologie du Cinema vol. 7 (Paris: L'Avent Scène et C.I.B., 1973), p. 260.

3. TRANSITION TO SOUND

Sound had become an integral part of film when DON JUAN, with John Barrymore and Mary Astor, premiered in 1926. Using synchronized music in place of a piano and piano player was not new to Borzage. The three films discussed in the previous chapter each had prerecorded scores and used such sounds as bells and gunfire, in SEVENTH HEAVEN; foghorns, in STREET ANGEL; and train whistles, in THE RIVER. SEVENTH HEAVEN even provided one of the era's hit songs, "Diane." When THE JAZZ SINGER opened in 1927, however, it was the dialogue and the singing, not just the score and the sound effects, that caused a furor. While THE JAZZ SINGER was primarily a silent film, it was the vocal sequences that fascinated and thrilled audiences.

Borzage avoided the use of dialogue until 1928-1929, when he filmed dialogue sequences for THE RIVER, the now-lost LUCKY STAR, and SONG O' MY HEART (1930), starring the famed Irish tenor John McCormack. Although THEY HAD TO SEE PARIS, an "all-talking" picture, opened earlier than SONG O' MY HEART, SONG is thematically and stylistically closer to the films of the 1927-1928 period and was probably produced earlier. The picture is a partial "talky," only McCormack's songs and bits of dialogue being heard at various times. There is a twenty-five-minute concert sequence in which McCormack, as Sean, sings a number of pieces in English, French, German, and Italian. In contrast, the concert scenes in the later I'VE ALWAYS LOVED YOU (1946), here the sequence is extremely static, the camera never moving from its center position and alternating only between medium and long shots of Sean. The camera acts as a member of the audience, taking the same position as the viewer and creating a sense of the viewer being present.

Filmed primarily in Ireland, SONG O' MY HEART has a two-fold narrative, centering upon Sean O'Carolan and his lost love, Mary, as well as upon the love story of Eileen, Mary's daughter, and Fergus O'Donnell. It is, in structure, much like an earlier Borzage film, THE CIRCLE (1924).

Years earlier Sean was forbidden to marry Mary because he wasn't considered "suitable" (rich) enough. Because of this their spirits were broken, and both have been forced to live unfulfilled lives. As a further result, Sean's voice lacks honest emotion, or "ny-aah" as a townsman calls it, and his career as an operatic tenor has never come to fruition. Mary, now deserted by her husband and

forced to live with her Aunt Elizabeth, the "woman who made her
marry for the money was in it, " exists in a completely broken state.
The continued tie between these two is underscored on a basic visual
level through a number of shots intercut between Mary and her family arriving in town and moving in with Aunt Elizabeth, and those of
Sean and his family. Sean even acts as friend and spiritual father
to Mary's son. The boy, Tad, often comes to Sean's home just to
be close to him. Sean, while popular with all the neighborhood children, is seen alone only with Tad. When Sean tells the children a
story, it is a tale of a prince and princess who are separated by
others, and this serves to elevate his love for Mary and their failed
romance to the level of fairy-tale. This idea reverberates throughout the entire film, especially in the magical or fantasy quality provided by the Irish setting.

The problem that Sean and Mary faced years earlier reappears
in the love story of Fergus and Eileen, and the similar stories of the
two sets of lovers act together to reduce the importance of linear
time while illustrating the repetitive nature of events and the idea of
"the circle of generations. " Eileen and Fergus cannot marry because Aunt Elizabeth, the rich head of the family, opposes their
match just as she did the match of Sean and Mary, and for the same
reason. The ties between Fergus and Sean are reinforced when Fergus comes to Sean for comfort and advice. From this early point
in the film shots of Sean and shots of Mary are often followed by
complementing shots of Fergus and Eileen. Furthermore, what happens to one of the older characters is often echoed in the narrative
concerning the younger characters; for instance, when Sean leaves
for America, Fergus leaves for Dublin.

Sean gets a contract to do a number of concerts in America,
and the town gathers at his home to wish him well and to see him
off. Only Mary refuses to join in the celebration ("It's been a long
time since I said ... goodbye ... to Sean"). Yet the two are tied
once again, this time when Sean sings "The Rose of Tralee. " This
song--their song--bridges both the symbolic and actual space separating them, just as the religious medals in SEVENTH HEAVEN and
the portrait in STREET ANGEL served as symbols of union. The
force of the song is so powerful that it draws Mary to Sean. As
Sean sings the words ". . . that made me love Mary, " Mary enters.
The two face each other, and there are intercuts of point-of-view
shots of each, which serve to bridge the chasm created by time and
events while once more visually underscoring their emotional and
spiritual ties. The final shot of this sequence is of Mary alone in
a frame. Sean enters the frame, his presence in her life and his
importance in her world visually re-established.

The tie between Sean and Mary transcends space. In fact, it
is even more strongly depicted once Sean is in America. During
the concert sequence there is a cut to Mary, sitting in a chair by
a window. She "hears" Sean's voice singing "The Rose of Tralee, "
and as the song fades out she dies, and the image fades from the
screen. A few shots later Sean tells his brother, Vincent, that

"during that last song I could have sworn someone was calling my name. " At this point a letter arrives for Sean. Before he can read it, however, he goes out to sing one last song, symbolically titled, "I Hear You Calling Me. " Completing the song, he returns and reads the letter, which is from Mary. Its content stresses the non-physical tie between them:

> Dear Sean,
> You have been in my thoughts always. When things looked darkest--most helpless--I used to close my eyes and call you by name. Instantly you were by my side-- giving me courage to carry on and so I'm calling to you now, for I need you ever.
> I have been ill for a long time, Sean. I may not be here when you come home. So I'm writing to you what is nearest my heart--
> Watch over my children, dear Sean--there is no one else to whom I can turn.
>   Mary

Sean returns to Ireland to intervene on behalf of Fergus and Eileen. Mona, Sean's sister, also intervenes, berating Aunt Elizabeth for her past and present actions ("This house might be full of children's laughter, but you've crushed the joy out of it ... like you crushed the heart out of Mary") and takes Eileen and Tad into her home. The actions that follow--the marriage and Sean's adoption of Tad--offset the lack of any earthly union between Mary and Sean, whose spiritual union, however, has been clearly and completely worked out. Eileen and Fergus, now married, drive off together in a scene recreated as the finale of the later film SMILIN' THROUGH (1942). Furthermore, Sean promises to take Tad with him to America, thereby permanently taking on the role of father to the boy. The final scene, again reminiscent of SMILIN' THROUGH, consists of a series of cuts between Eileen and Fergus hugging in their coach and Sean singing of the "Silver Lining" at the piano.

SONG O' MY HEART is the major transition film between Borzage's silent and sound work. While relying upon his earlier film images and on such themes as the transcendence brought by love and the resulting elevation to a higher plane of understanding, the film integrates music and the meaning of the lyrics in particular in a manner Borzage used later in many weaker films, such as SMILIN' THROUGH and HIS BUTLER'S SISTER (1943). The songs add dimension to the plot and become the expression of the continued closeness and love of Sean and Mary. While visually less striking and less "free" than the films of the 1927-1928 period--the sound camera was far less mobile than the silent camera--SONG O' MY HEART successfully incorporates sound, rather than simply using sound for its own sake. This often makes up for the overly senti-mental nature of the film (especially the "Little Boy Blue" sequence of the concert scene) and the lack of originality of much of the plot. The film is essentially a silent, and it is only after this that Bor-zage works exclusively with sound.

The rest of this period, up until BAD GIRL (1931), is a time of obvious experimentation--but experimentation less with stylistic approach than with the use of sound, with the creation of naturalness in dialogue and in total presentation. The weaknesses of these films are varied and will be noted as they are discussed.

During this period Borzage, one of Fox's leading directors, made two pictures, THEY HAD TO SEE PARIS and YOUNG AS YOU FEEL, with Fox's leading male talking star, Will Rogers, as well as one of Charles Farrell's few talking pictures, LILIOM, an uneven film based on Ferenc Molnár's play.

The first of the Rogers films, THEY HAD TO SEE PARIS (1929), plays upon a number of themes and situations presented in a novel published that year, Sinclair Lewis's Dodsworth. In this film Borzage extends the East-versus-West conflict of a number of his earlier works, such as PITCH O' CHANCE (1915), UNTIL THEY GET ME (1917), THE GUN WOMAN (1918), and SECRETS (1924), into that of the Europe-versus-America, or civilization-versus-wilderness, themes.

The story concerns Pike Peters and his family in the months that follow an oil strike on their Oklahoma property. At Idy Peters's instigation the family, now wealthy, travels to Paris, where almost immediately the disintegration of the unit begins. Idy "outgrows" her husband and, as she sees it, his small-town attitudes. She buys a chateau outside of Paris, pushes her daughter into an engagement with a shallow and foppish Marquis, and attempts to enter upper-class society. The night of Mrs. Peters's ball (which the guests are paid to attend, the amount varying with the title), Pike, symbolically staring down at the party from a place at the top of the stairs, at first refuses to join in, underscoring his resistance to European culture and society. When he finally does join he disrupts the party by entering in a suit of armor. While completely alienating his wife, Peters's openness and lack of pretension impress the guest of honor, a Duke, and the two desert the party, exit upstairs for a "real drink, " and end up asleep in Pike's bed, the suit of armor lying before the bed in a crumpled heap.

Pike and Idy argue over the events of the party and over Pike's desire to return home (she calls him "a small-town hick"). Pike, standing symbolically above her throughout the scene, further refuses to pay the dowry required for daughter Opal's marriage to the bogus Marquis. Realizing that money is ruining the family--an interesting theme for 1929--he decides to return to America and to the reality and the emotional security of home and, by implication, of midwestern values. Before he goes, however, he meets Claudine, and the two devise a scheme to reunit the family by inflaming their underlying sense of Puritan, or non-European, morality. When the family learns of Pike's "affair" they band together to force him to recognize his and, finally, their own foolishness (Pike→ ←Idy/Opal/ Ross). Realizing the truth of their situation and their loss of the prized American value of common sense, the profligate trio repent

They Had to See Paris

and reform. Idy decides that it is time to return home, and Opal
decides to marry the clerk she left behind. The two women hug
Pike, reaffirming the superiority of his attitudes, while Ross looks
on approvingly. In contrast to the isolation of Sam Dodsworth, Pike
and Idy are rejoined once again, their love renewed and their understanding of each other and of their place in the world reaffirmed.

        The second film that Borzage made with Will Rogers, YOUNG
AS YOU FEEL (1931), is based upon a similar conflict of ideas. A
product of the Depression, the film propounds the values of hard work
and thrift yet at the same time stresses a degree of moderation in
both work and play. As Lemuel Morehouse, Rogers is the hard-
working, no-nonsense head of a meat-packing concern. His two sons,
Will and Tom, do little but indulge in the totally hedonistic pursuits
that their money allows them. Will parties every night, returning
home only in time to see his father leave for work. Tom spends
his days exercising his body but never his mind. Their concerns
are completely and pointedly ridiculed, Will's pretentions as an art
critic, in particular. As in THEY HAD TO SEE PARIS pretentions
to culture and the resulting snobbery are criticized severely and
are presented as frivolous and ridiculous. Yet Lemuel, surprisingly,
is criticized just as strongly for his excessively rigid beliefs and
for his absolute and unbending nature. He lives according to a rigid
schedule, never allowing himself a free moment. It is only when he
meets Fleurette that his stodginess and reserve begin to break down.

She is immediately tied to Lemuel when both think that a statue bought by Will is ridiculous and when both end up dressing in the same room by accident. She takes on the role of adviser or instructor, teaching him to drink champagne and to enjoy himself.

Soon Lemuel completely drops his regulated life and starts dancing and drinking and living as hedonistically as his sons. The sons, on the other hand, because of the guilt they now feel for caus-ing their father's "condition, " become hard-working, simpleminded businessmen. After a number of comic and serious incidents, includ-ing a trip to Colorado to investigate a land deal, Lemuel explains that he acted as he did to teach his sons a lesson. They have learned responsibility and have been forced into adulthood. Yet he has learned as well, proclaiming his new creed of fun with moderation ("Anyone is dead who lets life pass by"), just as he is leaving for Paris.

These two films are influenced more by the presence of Will Rogers than that of Frank Borzage. Rogers, a stronger and better-known personality than John McCormack, sets the pace of the films, and it is he, more than the characters he plays, whom the audience came to see. The films, written especially to suit Rogers's image, are tailored to his delivery and style. This is in contrast to some of Borzage's earlier silent films and many of his later sound films in which looks and developed screen personality of an actor or actress are integrated within a role but do not overshadow it--such as with Janet Gaynor in SEVENTH HEAVEN (1927) and STREET ANGEL (1928); with Margaret Sullavan in LITTLE MAN, WHAT NOW? (1934), THREE COMRADES (1938), THE SHINING HOUR (1938), and THE MORTAL STORM (1940); with Loretta Young and Spencer Tracy in MAN'S CASTLE (1933); with Jean Arthur and Charles Boyer in HIS-TORY IS MADE AT NIGHT (1937); and with Joan Crawford in MAN-NEQUIN (1938) and STRANGE CARGO (1940).

Between the two Rogers pictures Borzage directed the screen version of LILIOM (1930). A film visually closest to STREET AN-GEL, LILIOM features dark lighting and large and expressionistic sets, the visual shadows acting as implications of the thematic prob-lems faced by the main characters, Liliom and Julie.

After an uncomfortable, turbulent, and short courtship Julie forsakes her job, family, and the security promised by her marriage to a carpenter and succumbs to the passion that she feels for Liliom. Liliom works as a carousel barker. The image of the carousel, with its bright lights and continuous music, overshadows the two throughout both their courtship and their marriage, acting as a counterpoint to their struggles and unhappiness. The smooth arc that the camera makes when introducing Julie and her friend Marie to the wonders of the park (and, by extension, to Liliom) is in di-rect contrast to what follows. The centrality of the carousel as an image begins here. Between an introductory shot of the two girls in medium close-up and one of Liliom is a long shot of the whole carousel. It becomes from this point on as integral a part of Julie's life as it is a part of Liliom's personality and identity. Yet its

Liliom

continuous and circular motion, and the fact that it never actually
goes anywhere or changes its course, undercut it as a productive
or positive symbol.   The carousel immediately takes on an implication of futility that reflects upon Liliom's life throughout the film.
It is on the carousel that Liliom and Julie meet and touch for the
first time.   Furthermore, the sexual passion of the relationship is
underscored as the pace of the scene and the tempo of the background
music increase steadily as the two ride.   Liliom puts Julie on a tiger, perhaps representative of his view of himself, holds her suggestively around the waist, and even helps her to get the brass ring,
which is symbolic of a wedding ring.   Julie runs away from Liliom
only after he sits on the tiger with her and only after the suggestive
up-and-down motion finally forces her to lose her composure.   The
carousel owner, Musquat, oversees all of this jealously, her anger
rising out of her fear of losing Liliom.

        Julie is consistently depicted as an innocent, and this becomes
even more noticeable in the pet names Liliom gives her--"little
dove, " "pigeon, " "sparrow, " and "little bird. "   All of these reinforce her gentleness and naivete.   This bird imagery is carried
even farther and used to contrast Julie and her feelings for Liliom
with some of the relationships between other characters in the film.
Liliom's downfall comes through the machinations of "Buzzard, " a
criminal type whom Liliom joins in a robbery in reaction to his being "cooped up" in a marriage and after the loss of his beloved job
as carousel barker.

Once Julie and Liliom marry they are forced because of economic necessity to live with Julie's aunt. The two are consistently haunted by the carousel, which is seen outside their window, and the obstacles to their happiness that it represents. In the first scene in which we see Liliom after his marriage he is lying down beneath a large picture window, the carousel and the lights of the amusement park visible in the background. Julie claims that Liliom is trying to make a new life away from the carousel. Yet her words are undercut by the looming image that continually haunts her husband, falsifying her belief and her faith. This iconographic use of an amusement park is presented in much the same way in MANNEQUIN (1938) and in MOONRISE (1949). Liliom's dreams go beyond his present state, taking on an element of fantasy, in the same way that the carousel acts as an almost-magical vehicle of escape. Liliom later looks at railroad tracks and dreams of going to Vienna and of starting a new life in America.

Liliom agrees to join Buzzard in the robbery of a factory payroll after Julie announces that she is pregnant. The strength of the circular image of the carousel is reinforced once more: Liliom's action is destined to bring about tragedy. His life will be "replaced," therefore, by that of his child. Buzzard's offer of "security and the future" becomes, in reality, the eventual peace of death and the unknown future of the afterlife. Just before the robbery Liliom even wonders aloud about the next world and what he could tell God in explanation of his actions. Almost immediately following this the attempt at robbery takes place and fails, and Liliom is mortally wounded. As if to underscore his unimportance in the immediate world once again, the police stand above the prostrate man, while Julie comforts him, and talk of their cigars, their low pay, and the annoying mosquitoes.

What follows is one of the most striking death scenes imaginable. Liliom, brought back to the apartment, is placed upon what becomes his bier. The room is huge and dark, the carousel once again visible through the picture window placed behind Liliom and Julie. The only direct lighting is a candle that stands over Liliom's head, lighting his face. After he finally confesses his love, Julie takes on the role of secular and religious mother as well as that of wife, comforting him ("my boy, sleep") and praying for him. Liliom "hears" the train that will take him to judgment, an idea in opposition to the impotent circular movement of the carousel as well as to his dreams of traveling to Vienna and to America. As he speaks a train emerges from the lights of the carousel, growing larger as it approaches, the background music intensifying as the train draws near. It bursts through the window and into the room, where it stops and where a messenger exits to receive the spirit of Liliom. Once Liliom is aboard the train returns the way it came, this time traveling up through the clouds.

Liliom walks through the train, the lighting throughout brighter than that of the earthly sequences, meeting the suicides and the other dead in their respective compartments. Finally called to the

chief magistrate, Liliom requests and receives permission to return
to earth for one day to "do something" for Julie and for the baby he
fears he will never see and to whom he gave nothing while he lived.
He can do this only after serving ten years in hell as a punishment
for his lack of discipline.

The ten years pass, and Liliom is delivered to earth by the
celestial train. Posing as a beggar before Julie's angular and expressionistic house and gate, he finally meets his daughter, Louise.
She refuses to allow him to touch her or to entertain her with his
card tricks. Her rejection culminates in violence; Liliom slaps her
and then disappears. Louise confesses to Julie that the slap felt like
a kiss, and, as Julie claims to understand, the two women embrace.
It is the memory of Liliom that ties them, not the reality of his life
and death--Louise believes that he died in America, her romantic
conception becoming an extension of Julie's as well as a protective
device. Liliom re-enters the celestial train and exits from right to
left. The women walk off together in a parallel path, once again
being visually tied to Liliom.

This film is much more a fantasy than a melodrama. The
intended and unintended reality of the second half and the general
failure of the heavenly sequences force the film to lose the strength
of the earlier section of the narrative both on the visual level and
on the level of character development. The dark expressionism of
the sets is an important aspect of the narrative, serving to undercut
the romantic and unreal notions of Liliom and Julie. The constant
specter of the carousel and of the amusement-park lights, always
part of the background, likewise undercut Liliom's attempt to escape
his fate, and his dreams of America and of success. The railroad
tracks he sees as an avenue to life become the death train that carries him off. In contrast, the heavenly sequences fail to maintain
this precarious balance. These scenes become reduced to parody,
the images lacking the strength they had earlier. The sets used
throughout this portion of the film, such as the heavenly railroad
and Julie's home, while still expressionistic, are too brightly lit
and fail to create the strong visual level of pessimism that had earlier worked so well. Heaven is too bright; the failure of Liliom's
visit to Julie's house lacks a visual complement. The film ends on
an unsuitably "happy" note, the characters visually tied without any
reason for this coming out of the narrative. The visual and narrative levels of the film do not join here but undercut each other and
make the fantasy and the unreality of the ending seem all the more
contrived and disconnected.

This is a problem noticeable in many of the films of this
period--the ending fails to grow out of the development within the
body of the film and has a "tacked-on" quality that wraps things up
all too neatly. The happy endings of BAD GIRL (1931), AFTER TO-
MORROW (1932), and YOUNG AMERICA (1932), in particular, and
of DOCTORS' WIVES to a lesser degree, do not sufficiently cohere
to the rest of the film, creating an unsettling weakness. Problems
initially of great narrative importance suddenly disappear in each of

these films. In DOCTORS' WIVES Nina's growing awareness of her
place within her husband's world comes about too abruptly to be entirely satisfactory. In AFTER TOMORROW the premarital problems
of Peter and Sidney are dissolved by a deus ex machina--money.
BAD GIRL, while more complex than these other films, suffers from
this same inconsistency.

BAD GIRL, a film thematically close to THE FIRST YEAR
(1926), won Borzage his second directorial Academy Award, the first
being for SEVENTH HEAVEN. Set in the tenement section of New
York, like the later Borzage film MANNEQUIN (1938), the film concerns the relationship and marriage of Dorothy Haley and Eddie Col-
lins, who first introduces himself as "Joe" and only confesses his
true identity after his individuality and difference from other men is
proven. Dorothy is a dress model, and the film opens with her
modeling a wedding dress, a device that underscores her essential
purity. He is a radio repairman who longs to own his own shop.
They meet on a ferry, where, on a bet, she attempts to flirt with
him. Instead of making the natural response, Eddie (still "Joe" at
this point) tells her off, calls her a "show-off," and gives her a
lecture on saving one's money and bettering oneself. He refuses to
have anything to do with women, putting all of his energy into his
work and his dream of owning his own business. Yet he "falls" before Dorothy's innocence and charm, taking her home and opening
himself to her by talking of his past.

A second level in the film is an early comment upon tenement
life. Dorothy lives with her brutish brother, who is sure that without his absolute and stern guidance she will "fall from virtue." Eddie and Dorothy sit on the apartment stairs and observe the people
and the life around them: Paula, a prostitute everyone but Dorothy
snubs; an elderly woman tenant calling a neighbor's relative to in-
form her of the woman's death; and the cries of a newborn baby.
This latter element acts to reinforce the idea of the continuity of
life as well as summarizing a tenement credo stated by another tenant: "born on the second floor to probably die on the fifth." Eddie
alone refuses to accept this fate, his philosophy emphasizing the necessity of money for getting the "things of life." This generally
negative attitude toward life and toward the individual is extended
beyond the immediate environment of this particular building and into
the neighborhood itself. When Eddie is late for a date with Dorothy
the men who pass her as she waits under a drugstore awning believe
her to be a prostitute and react to her as such, snickering and staring.

Dorothy meets Eddie at his room, where he removes her hat
and coat, kisses her, and lifts her off the ground as the rain beats
on the window. This is followed by a fade-out and a fade-in to a
time later that night. After this seduction the two realize that they
will have to marry, since Dorothy's brother will certainly throw her
out of the house. On returning to her home, she is indeed thrown
out by her brother, who refuses even to allow her to take her clothes.
Dorothy is forced to go and live with Edna, her best friend, until

Bad Girl

the time she and Eddie can marry. When Dorothy tries to reach
Eddie the next morning she learns that he has moved out of his apartment and is not at work. She fears desertion, yet soon after she
learns that he went to find a larger apartment and will meet her at
the license bureau.

        Complications disrupt the fantasy of their life together almost
immediately. Dorothy learns that she is pregnant but refuses to tell
Eddie, since she fears that the news will ruin his plans. Eddie learns
the news from Edna. In a scene almost exactly like one used in two
later films, MAN'S CASTLE (1933) and LITTLE MAN, WHAT NOW?
(1934), Eddie stands before a store window and looks in at the furniture that Dorothy wants but that they cannot really afford. The furniture takes on a larger symbolic meaning in this scene, implying a
stability and order that Dorothy, in particular, desires. In the later
films this idea is emphasized even more strongly. In MAN'S CASTLE
Trina stands before a store window longing for a stove that she sees
within. The stove implies stability, and Bill's purchase of it for her
implies his commitment to her and to their continued life together.
In LITTLE MAN, WHAT NOW? a single piece of furniture takes on
this meaning as well as a more mystical importance. Hans buys
Lammchen the three-mirrored vanity table that she longs for even
though it is a tremendous extravagance. There follows a scene in
which she sits at the table, Hans standing behind her and just out of
reflecting distance of the mirrors. Her image, multiplied threefold,
completely surrounds him just as her spirit completely surrounds

his.   The implication here reflects the powerful influence Lammchen
has over Hans and her ability to keep him spiritually alive and buoy-
ant and separate from an encroaching Nazi pessimism.   It is Lammchen who keeps Hans from falling into the despair so prevalent in
the German society of the early 1930s.

The furniture bought by Eddie in BAD GIRL becomes representative of his commitment to Dorothy and their life together.   This
fact undercuts whatever narrative events follow.   Eddie temporarily
gives up his single-minded orientation toward his dream, his selfish
individuality, for Dorothy and for what they have created.   Their
child ties them together even more strongly, reinforcing the reality
of their love just as a child does at the end of both MAN'S CASTLE
and LITTLE MAN, WHAT NOW?

Both Eddie and Dorothy believe that the other does not want
the child and does not want to make the changes in their lifestyle or
in their future plans that a child requires.   Surprised by the new
apartment Eddie leases and by all of the money he spends on the
new furniture, Dorothy reacts with tears and anger to all of this
extravagance, however, after Eddie and his friends talk of the poverty they suffered when they were children.   This again reinforces
her fear of returning to the constricting and killing existence of the
tenement.

To earn enough money for a specialist--since he believes that
confidence in a doctor is what Dorothy needs most--Eddie becomes
a boxer.   Dorothy misunderstands, thinking instead that Eddie has
been drinking and brawling out of anger over the coming child.   She
berates him and leaves him.   Even the arrival of the child fails to
reunite the two.   It is only the news that there is an emergency in
the nursery that finally, and falsely, resolves all of the conflicts.
Dorothy believes it is her baby who is in trouble.   She runs out
only to learn that her son is safe.   Eddie, on the scene by chance,
realizes the truth, and after a perfunctory explanation and resolution, the two exit in a cab holding each other closely, their eyes
and their attention upon their child, the family unit strengthened and
reunited.

The plot of this film, and the continual "twists" that are
mainly due to the extreme failures of communication, fail to sustain
our own fantasy at a sufficiently compelling level.   This is the major problem with the film and with some of the other works of this
period.   Borzage creates a film that touches upon many important
and interesting problems, such as fighting for economic survival in
post-Depression America, romantic illusions as opposed to the realities of the world, and the struggle two people face in order to
learn to understand and love each other.   The atmosphere of the
tenement and the depiction of the life of the working class is well
established and well defined.   Yet the film tends to fall into an extreme pattern of alternating scenes of bathos and "cuteness."

A realistic treatment with a sociological angle is to follow

in 1932, when Borzage deals with juvenile delinquency in YOUNG
AMERICA.   However, this work, like BAD GIRL, loses its force
and power due to its fall into extreme sentimentality and predicta-
bility.   The declining quality of this and some of the other scripts
of this period, combined with the approaching merger of Fox Productions with Darryl F. Zanuck's Twentieth Century Corporation--with
William Fox's subsequent loss of control--probably allowed Borzage
to break from Fox and to take on temporary status as a free agent.

Most of the films of this period lack the overriding feeling
that so effectively infused SEVENTH HEAVEN, STREET ANGEL, and
THE RIVER.   With exception of SONG O' MY HEART these films
fade into topicality and fail to develop any of the spiritual motifs
that enhance the romantic nature of several of Borzage's other films.
In both THEY HAD TO SEE PARIS and in YOUNG AS YOU FEEL the
emphasis is placed upon self-gratification in the immediate world.
In both films Will Rogers becomes a populist extension of an earlier
all-American image created by Douglas Fairbanks, Sr. , representing
the quintessential American male whose common-sense attitudes finally make everyone else look foolish.   In both films the character
Rogers plays is so emphasized that little else really matters.   LILIOM
suffers from this same problem.   Being one of Charles Farrell's
early attempts to master sound, the film concentrates upon his character development often to the exclusion of the others, who become
more types than individuals.   Yet here the visual aspect, while uneven, is far more interesting than any part of the actual narrative.
BAD GIRL fails for many of these same reasons.   The strongest
parts of the film--fear of the tenement, the constrictions of marriage, and the effects of poverty on a love relationship--are de-
emphasized and the more trivial tribulations of the couple are stressed.

Most of these films devolve into obvious moralism, moving
their emphasis away from any real character development or inno-
vative plot and into trite situations and stock responses.   The films
of this period are more interesting as transitional pieces than as
works bearing the mark of an individual director.   Once again Borzage becomes an experimenter seeking to find a place within the
sound milieu.   As in the silent period, the turning point comes with
a film of such great importance that it completely changed the course
of Borzage's work.   When Borzage filmed the adaptation of Hemingway's A FAREWELL TO ARMS in 1932 he not only returned to the
spirituality of SEVENTH HEAVEN, STREET ANGEL, THE RIVER,
and SONG O' MY HEART, but he was able to incorporate the theme
of war and to create a film of feeling, pace, and significance.

4. THE YEARS 1932-1942

Following the great works of his late silent period and the experimental period that accompanied the transition to sound, Borzage entered his most productive and most consistent period of work. No longer tied to a single studio, Borzage moved around, directing films for Paramount (1932), Columbia (1933 and 1934), and Universal (1933) before moving to Warner Brothers/First National (1934-1937) and then Metro-Goldwyn-Mayer (1937-1942). Throughout these years and in the years that followed Borzage continued to refine the thematic and visual style that he developed particularly during his tenure at Fox. His films maintained a consistency of "touch" that made them the recognizable works of a cinematic individualist.

Throughout this period Borzage directed a number of films that can be grouped into large thematic areas. It is within this ten-year period that Borzage directed a cycle of "antiwar" and anti-Fascist films, beginning with A FAREWELL TO ARMS (1932) and culminating with THREE COMRADES (1938) and THE MORTAL STORM (1940). He also studied the effects of economic depression and the ensuing social disorder in such films as MAN'S CASTLE (1933), LITTLE MAN, WHAT NOW? (1934), and MANNEQUIN (1938) and in a number of overtly mystical works, such as SHIPMATES FOREVER (1935), GREEN LIGHT (1937), THE SHINING HOUR (1938), DISPUTED PASSAGE (1939), STRANGE CARGO (1940), and SMILIN' THROUGH (1941), which completely focuses attention on the idea of individual and group transcendence. These groupings are extremely broad and somewhat arbitrary. Some of the films could be as easily placed in one category as another. For the purposes of this chapter the possible influence of one film upon another, or the recognition of direct visual and thematic ties, have decided where a film was placed. In addition to these films there is a group of "lesser" films made during this period that have been forgotten or ignored, such as LIVING ON VELVET (1934) and HISTORY IS MADE AT NIGHT (1937). These prove to be important thematic and stylistic pieces; some, such as DESIRE (1936), have been credited to the creativity of someone else or have a previously unrecognized influence upon other Borzage films.

The categorization of these films serves mainly as a frame of organization and reference. Borzage's basic ideas and beliefs, recognized and discussed in earlier chapters, permeate all of these films. In particular, there are the continued emphases on spirituality, growth, and transcendence, and on the centrality of the male/female relationship. As in the silent periods, Borzage uses some

overwhelming outside force, such as war or depression, as a backdrop against which the transcendent nature of love is clearly mani-
fested. Once again it is not the fact of that outside force so much
as the understanding and growth that arise out of this that become
most important.

It is clear that throughout this period Borzage is still working
out of a melodramatic structure. Yet this structure is changed
even more than in the earlier films. Character traits and character development are still emphasized at the expense of the narrative. Borzage does "accept" one very important structural aspect
of literary and stage melodrama, yet he completely reshapes it,
changing the nature of its importance: it is not so much "evil" that
is set apart and battled against as it is the "real world" and its
problems. The characters in these Borzage melodramas face the
problems that result from conditions existing in and because of the
outside world. The spirituality of the relationships is achieved and
recognized partly through the backgrounds to which they are contrasted. ➤The hostility of these environments becomes both the obstacle to happiness of the couple, the family, or the group as well
as "the very condition of their love. "[1] It must be emphasized, once
again, that the growth, closeness and transcendence into a new moral, intellectual, and emotional sphere that come about, are the "victory" that is achieved. It is not "evil" that is "put asunder" so
much as it is the interdependence of two individuals and their ability
to grow out of their immediate reality and into another more spiritual one, that is emphasized.

> What makes Borzage's melodramas unique is his avoidance
> of extreme conflicts: his characters and their environment
> are not in moral conflict. Rather than externalising his
> plots into moral contest between good and evil in which
> characters defeat or are defeated by the evil that threatens
> to engulf them, Borzage, diffusing the conventional melo-
> dramatic moral polarity, permits the co-existence of sev-
> eral moral and spiritual systems in his films. He merely
> makes a trial of one by contrasting it with another, pro-
> viding the catalyst for his characters' growth out of one
> order and emergence into another, transcendent one. For
> Borzage, it is only through love and adversity that souls
> are made great. [2]

The films made during this period become then the mature testament
of Borzagean ideals and must be studied as such.

Part One: The Antiwar/Anti-Fascist Cycle

A FAREWELL TO ARMS, produced and released in 1932, was
"a handsome and glossy production, with big sets, plenty of extras
and superb camerawork. "[3] Yet Borzage worked against the creation

of any sense of epic scope, [4] concentrating on the love story of Frederick Henry and Catherine Barclay instead of on "war" as the overwhelming fact of the narrative.   What results is an honest tale of
"the human consequences of war ... typified in a story about two
lovers."[5]   The ironic "peace" achieved at the finish of the work
grows out of the realizations made by the two main characters and
out of the contradictions that exist around them.   This new peace
serves to underscore both the uniqueness of their relationship, especially when compared with any others in the film, and of their faith
and belief in each other.

The contrasts and contradictions that exist in the "outside
world" act as forces that attempt to ruin what the lovers eventually
achieve.   The environment out of which their love grows is one of
destruction and insensitivity.   The whole idea of love coexisting with
carnage is at first made to appear ridiculous, if not impossible.   In
this environment alcohol and sex take the place of love and intensity
of feeling and enable the characters to anesthetize pain and to forget
about the death that exists everywhere around them. [6]   Those who exist around the lovers, such as Rinaldi and Fergy, are "bitterly pessimistic characters who try to discourage their friends from an involvement in a serious love relationship."[7]   The Italian surgeon Rinaldi, to whom Frederick is closest, attempts to steer him away from
anything beyond a physical relationship with any woman and with Catherine in particular.   ("Sacred subjects are not good for soldiers,
why don't you be like me--all fire and smoke and nothing inside")
Rinaldi wants Frederick to exist on the periphery of feeling so that
he can function in a chaotic world without losing control of himself
or of his sanity.   Fergy, Catherine's closest friend, warns her
against an emotional entanglement with Frederick, which she feels
will only bring about more pain and suffering.   These two subordinate characters and the reality of the war itself together work to separate the lovers.   Their battle to achieve the peace that they believe
to be within their grasp takes on the epic proportions that the war
as an external reality does not.   Even Catherine's death cannot separate them or destroy what their love achieves.

The narrative and visual fact of Catherine's death sets up a
motif used throughout much of the remainder of Borzage's work.
This motif of two lovers transcending time, space, and even death,
as it appears at the end of this film, is particularly striking in its
use of light and whiteness.   This image, borrowed directly from the
final shot of SEVENTH HEAVEN, as is a great portion of the narrative of this later film, is used even more effectively in both THREE
COMRADES and in THE MORTAL STORM.   In A FAREWELL TO
ARMS Catherine's death allows her to become an integral part of
Frederick's psyche, living within him and allowing the love and transcendence that they shared to take on an aspect of timelessness as
well as of an unfading and unchanging nature.   Their love, in its
strength and in its ability to exist beyond the bounds of the chaotic
external world, negates the actuality of Catherine's death as well
as the destruction of war and the negative attitudes of those who
have given in to the pessimism and emotional destruction of the war.

A Farewell to Arms

     The film opens with a long shot of the beautiful, brightly lit
Italian countryside. The camera pans left to a shot of a man lying
peacefully in the foreground, seemingly asleep but, in reality, dead,
his body mutilated and his left leg gone. [8] In the background is a
caravan of ambulances. There follows a cut to a man bleeding to
death and then one to Lt. Frederick Henry, asleep in one of the ambulances, oblivious to the suffering and, by implication, to the war
around him.

> This opening sequence, contrasting the innocent beauty of
> the landscape with the grim horror and ugliness of war,
> establishes the basic situation of the film: characters,
> surrounded by war's bleakness and horror, surrender them-
> selves to a protective pessimism that prevents them from
> really seeing that war and, at the same time, deadens
> their responses to one another. [9]

     Catherine's introduction belies her pessimism and serves to
foreshadow her later situation. Standing high upon a ladder, symbolically above the other nurses, she is listening to and watching a
scene occurring in the commandant's office. A fellow nurse is being
sent away after a love affair with a soldier, who is now at the front,
and an ensuing pregnancy. Fergy, acting the role of harsh judge,
blames the girl for being weak, echoing the pessimistic and right-
eously unemotional sentiments of the other nurses. Only Catherine
defends the accused nurse's actions ("This is a war, Fergy, and
she loved him") and comforts the girl. Already Catherine is clearly

set apart from the others, her uniqueness underscored in this simple
act of kindness which serves as a clue to her inner spiritual nature.

Most like Fergy in attitude is Frederick's mentor and self-
styled protector, Rinaldi. Rinaldi is the utterly unemotional rationalist scientist and surgeon, a character type especially prominent in
two of Borzage's more mystical works, GREEN LIGHT (1937) and
DISPUTED PASSAGE (1939). His love of surgery is a self-love,
centered upon a love of his own skill and upon the precision and rationality required by it; whereas Frederick calls surgery "dirty, "
Rinaldi sees only its beauty. Rinaldi relates how during an operation he once removed a heart just to observe its beauty and function
as well as to marvel at his own skill. Rinaldi calls Frederick "Baby, "
a term of endearment implying Frederick's innocence and emotional
naivete as well as Rinaldi's belief in himself and in his world view.
Their relationship takes on a more paternal/filial nature than one of
a wartime companionship.

In the scenes that follow the singularity and separateness of
Borzage's lovers is reinforced. Frederick and Rinaldi go to the local saloon and whorehouse, where they can both satisfy their sensual
desires (food, drink, and sex) as well as forget about the war. There
follows a fade-in to Frederick sitting at a table talking to the foot of
a woman who sits up on the table and out of sight, her anonymity
symbolic of her unimportance to the men. Behind him is a shuttered
window out of which we see the lights of the troop carriers and of
the marching men, who move from left to right, an example of "the
war in the background [pervading] the action in the foreground. "[10]
When bombs begin to explode Frederick escapes through the same
window and hides below some stairs, where he meets nurse Barclay,
clothed in her white nightgown. Again the characters are surrounded
by an unclear yet ever-present background of war. The background
becomes strongly symbolic of the chaos of the world outside of the
lovers as well as their present spiritual chaos. The background at
once threatens the lovers and ties them together, placing them in a
world of their own.

A sense of relationship between the couple is picked up and
continued through the cut to the officers' club that follows. The
camera tracks around the room, picking up snatches of conversa-
tions on subjects as varied as war, opera, and religion. Frederick
enters with Rinaldi and is formally introduced to Catherine. The
two soon go out into the moonlight, where the couple's separateness
and their growing relationship are visually underscored. The two
sit at the left of the frame and both face up to Rinaldi. This is
followed by cuts of Frederick looking at Catherine or the two looking
at each other, all other persons out of the frame. The two then
rise and exit left in opposition to the earlier troop movements, where
they sit under a monument and where Frederick talks not of love but
of whiskey. After he attempts to kiss her she slaps him (an image
used later in MANNEQUIN [1938]), claiming to detest the "nurse's-
evening-off aspect of it. " In a soft, moonlit scene she relents, calls
him "sweet, " and lets him kiss her softly first, then much more

passionately. Two bombs go off, a device used to imply sexual union, and there is a cut from Catherine and Frederick to "a shot of
troops and trucks moving from right to left in the foreground, ob-
scuring the lovers in the background."[11] Again war intrudes upon
the scene, tying the lovers in a world of their own and reinforcing
the precarious world in which their love will grow.

The lighting of this scene is continued in the scene that follows. When Frederick returns to the room he shares with Rinaldi
the only light is that of his cigarette. This creates an unearthly
glow, much as the moon did in the previous scene. Here, however,
it is not bombs and lights that end the scene but a swift blackout
caused by Frederick's extinguishing of the cigarette. This serves
to separate his basically unemotional relationship with the rationalist
Rinaldi from the emotional involvement he is entering into with Catherine. His changing nature and his separation from Rinaldi's world
view is underscored in the next scenes.

Frederick, ordered out once again, turns his ambulance around
while on his way to the front and returns to the hospital, where he
stops under an arch, tying this scene to the one in which he met
Catherine; he moves, symbolically, from a shadowed darkness into
the light of the hospital garden. When he finally finds Catherine he
enters into her frame, visually reinforcing the tie between the two
and the fact of their now-joined worlds. After asking if she is all
right he tells her that he has been ordered to leave and hasn't "just
gone away" or deserted her. She, in turn, gives him a St. Anthony
religious medal to "save you from harm." This medal, while lacking the power of the medals in SEVENTH HEAVEN, does serve to
tie the couple in a more than secular bond. This is reinforced in
two ways. The next shot of Frederick is at the battlefield, sitting
among a group of fellow drivers and eating what becomes almost a
"last supper." The men eat bread and drink wine, symbolic of the
flesh and blood of communion. The only lighting comes from the
bombs bursting outside and the light entering through a skylight.
When a bomb does hit their shelter Frederick is wounded badly but
not mortally, as his leg is torn apart and his skull fractured, reinforcing the power of the medal and, by implication, the power of
Catherine's love. It is an ironic twist, however, that Rinaldi's
technical and medical skill facilitates his physical salvation and that
Rinaldi tells him that he will see to it that Frederick receives a
medal for his bravery.

At the end of the film the religious medal is Frederick's only
tangible reminder of Catherine. The two medals become symbolic
of the two parts of Frederick's life, as well as of his internal oppositions. This moment becomes the climax of his struggle. His
survival is due to both Catherine and Rinaldi. Yet, unlike his scenes
with Rinaldi, his scenes with Catherine are moments of peace, in
which the war becomes part of·the background and less of a reality.
The remainder of the film chronicles Frederick's break from Rinaldi's world view and his spiritual journey into a higher sphere.
This is particularly symbolized in his desertion and journey back to
Catherine.

While on the surface a film that condemns the folly of war,
A FAREWELL TO ARMS is, as well, a further development of the
theme of transcendence. This is the second film in which one of the
Borzage lovers actually dies, the first being SONG O' MY HEART.
Here, however, the continued connection of the lovers is one that is
totally "of the spirit." Frederick has no son to adopt and no living
part of Catherine to carry with him. Through her death she becomes
a portion of his soul alone. In many of the subsequent films death
becomes the final step into total union. Just as Frederick and Catherine are finally and fully joined, so too are Pat, Erich, Gottfried,
and Otto in THREE COMRADES and so too are Martin and Freya in
THE MORTAL STORM. Love transcends earthly bounds in these
films and in many of the others that follow and joins the lovers' together beyond the limitations of space, time, and death. While this
idea is played upon in NO GREATER GLORY, the next film to be
discussed, death here serves the singular purpose of providing an immediate lesson for others.

NO GREATER GLORY (1934) is "an allegorical preachment
against war"[16] that sets forth the irony and futility of violence. It
is the story of Nemescek and his struggle for respect and acceptance
by a group, the Paul Street Boys. The ideal of war and of dying
for irrational violence is undercut by the opening scenes, which shift
from the battlefield to the schoolroom. This transition is smoothly
and expertly achieved in a dissolve from a soldier, his arm raised,
declaiming against war as "a foul thing" to a teacher, in the same
physical position, defending war and the taking up of arms for one's
country. Throughout the film the masculine ideal of war is continually negated, in particular, by its reduction to a battle between two
opposing boys' clubs fighting over a vacant lot.

In a thematic parallel with A FAREWELL TO ARMS, outside
reality and the immediate world become background pieces to Nemescek's own struggle to find a place within his world. His purity of
soul makes him both a martyr and a visionary,[17] and his final actions serve as a conversion point for all of the other gang members.
The ending of the film becomes a Christian allegory, with Nemescek
as the Christ figure.

Arising from his sickbed, Nemescek joins the Paul Street
Boys in their fight against the Red Shirts. When he enters the "battleground" all of the other boys stop fighting and stand completely
still. Nemescek then walks up to the Red Shirt leader, attacks him,
grabs the Red Shirt flag, and collapses, the flag draped over his
face like a shroud. His mother arrives, kneels Pietà-like before
her son, and, lifting up the body of her dead child, carries him
away, while Boka, the Paul Street leader and personification of the
"Perfect Friend and Ideal Comrade,"[18] and the other boys follow.

The final scene parallels that of Christ and the stations of
the cross. Nemescek's mother momentarily collapses and is aided
by two of the boys, while a blinding light momentarily shines around
her and her son, creating the effect of a halo. Throughout this scene

In the scene that follows, of Frederick's arrival at the hospital in Milan, there is extensive use of the subjective camera, which
ends only when Catherine bends down to kiss him. At this point only
is there a cut, and Borzage moves from an extreme close-up of her
eye to a medium shot of the two lovers. As when he entered into
her frame at the hospital, this again acts as a point of joining. It
is also the point at which Frederick's self-centered world is entered.
Following this there are extensive scenes of Frederick set against
white backgrounds, such as the sheets of the bed and the walls of
his hospital room, as well as a continued use of large shadows--all
emphasizing the problematical nature of the lovers' union and their
own internal divisions.

When they speak to the priest and confess both their love for
each other and the unorthodox nature of their relationship the shadows
visually underscore their separateness both from the world and from
convention. The priest walks off to the right and out of the triangle
of light that contains the lovers. The marriage he performs is thereby undercut in importance even though the priest is the largest figure
in the frame. The unofficial nature of the marriage--no bans are
posted, the consummation has already occurred--is closely related
to the unorthodox nature of the events that precede it. Yet the spiritual nature of the marriage is visually emphasized not only in the
use of light and shadow and in the presence of the priest, but in
Catherine's continual upward glance: she claims to hear organ music and to smell orange blossoms. Yet the only outward ornament
of the ceremony is the ring Frederick places on Catherine's finger
after the priest leaves, the earthly signs of marriage subordinated
to the spiritual ones. In this ceremony there is no exchange of
signs, such as the medals in SEVENTH HEAVEN, and the priest
only is present to give their relationship a "proper" or socially ac-
ceptable blessing.

The two are soon separated, as Frederick is ordered to return to the front after the head nurse catches him drinking. The
couple spend their last hours at a hotel. A train whistle sounds,
calling Frederick away, as Chico is called away from Diane by the
mobilization whistles and as Bill feels pulled by the train whistle in
MAN'S CASTLE (1933). In a scene parallel to one used at this point
in SEVENTH HEAVEN Frederick lifts Catherine off of the ground,
a physical parallel to her new and exalted state, and cloaks her in
his cape, endowing her concretely but only momentarily with his
protection. It is just before this that she admits her fear of their
deaths--she sees herself or him dead in the rain--and his action
serves as a symbol of the protective nature of their love as well as
of their isolation from the outside world, as emphasized in the rain
outside beating on the window. The train whistle is a reminder of
the inexorable nature of time and echoes Frederick's recitation of
Andrew Marvell's poem "To His Coy Mistress."

Frederick returns to the front while Catherine, now admitting
her pregnancy to Fergy, leaves for Switzerland, a land of neutrality
and peace. Sitting by a candle, she writes Frederick a romantic
letter falsely describing the beauty of her rooms. The camera tracks

around the room as she speaks, pointing out its shabbiness yet reinforcing the idea that in the world of lovers external events and objects have no reality. Catherine exists in a sphere of her own design, in which love allows her to exist in her present state of physical deprivation. A sense of nonphysical communication is created as well. Catherine, speaking to Frederick's picture, tells of her loneliness and fear. In the scene that follows Frederick decides to desert after he has not heard from Catherine--Rinaldi, acting as censor, has had all of her letters sent back. Frederick's priority is no longer the war but the world he has created with Catherine; even the negative actions of Rinaldi aid in rejoining the lovers. He tells the priest that the war and this world, therefore, mean nothing to him. He renounces this world for a more sacred one and receives a blessing and leaves. Throughout his talk with the priest Frederick is in the dark and seemingly alone. Yet once again the outside world intrudes through the sounds of marching boots heard throughout the scene.

That Frederick neither hears nor feels the outside world is brought out even more strongly in the seven-minute "Germanically stylised war montage"[12] that follows. Frederick seems unaware of the horrors around him, and this is emphasized cinematically by the montage being stripped of sound and dialogue, using only blurred effects, such as the beating of the rain and the relentless music. We see shots of soldiers marching, men dying, bombs bursting, fire, people evacuating their homes, and a Christ-like figure who stands in a doorway, his arms outstretched, a Red Cross behind him.

> ... Henry's search for Catherine, set in the midst of all this spiritual bleakness, becomes a metaphorical journey and, because of the strength and explicitness of its image, the sequence emerges as one of the most powerfully direct thematic statements of the film.[13]

The idea is reinforced during the montage sequence by a cut to rushing water and by the escape Frederick makes from the authorities by jumping into the river. When he arrives in Milan it is only to find Catherine gone. Rinaldi finds him, and realizing his errors, he confesses the truth and tells Frederick where Catherine is staying.

The parallel scenes that follow are all achieved through a series of cross-cuts that quicken the pace of the film and spiritually connect the separated lovers. Shots of Catherine having a silhouette made, receiving all of her returned letters, fainting from the shock, and being taken to the hospital are intercut with those of Frederick rowing across the lake and arriving at the hospital. Although Fergy had told him of Catherine's pregnancy, how Frederick knew she was in the hospital is never stated--further evidence of spiritual communication. Although Catherine is told that she will not die, a cut to the rain beating on the window belies this statement, as does the fact that she is completely clothed in white, her head in a nun-like covering, the whole effect being that of a body in a shroud. Frederick

is sent by the doctor to a cafe, where, lost in his thought out "You can't die" just as Catherine gives birth to a still He continues to pray for her almost unconsciously through ments, calling upon the God he feels has forsaken them.

In the final scenes of the film Catherine, knowing th dying, attempts to comfort Frederick. Lying in bed and co in white, except for a dark halo of hair, she alternates bet courage ("I'm brave, I'll not be afraid") and fear ("Don't le die!"). In the background "Liebestraum" ("Dream of Love" while the two confess their undying love and understand that will never be parted, not even in death. Just as she dies bells sound announcing the Armistice. Frederick lifts her completely swathed in white, carries her to the window, an her to the sunlight. Frederick then echoes the words "Peace, reflecting upon both her state and that of the world. The tw last in union, there is a final fade into a bright and clear sl flock of white doves flying across it.

> Peace ironically comes with the lovers' final transc of war. Though Catherine's tragic death finally rel the lovers from war's grip and unites them in an e inseparable way, it also leaves Lieutenant Henry al lost with the new peace.... [The] ending of A FAR TO ARMS presents a paradox that reappears throug director's work: his characters achieve spiritual g through physical loss.[14]

An alternate ending exists in which the chance of Cathe recovery is presented, albeit ambiguously. In this ending, as bells chime announcing the Armistice, it is Frederick who say "Armistice" and Catherine who says "Peace." At this point th hug each other, Frederick kisses her cheek, and there is a fa black. This "American ending" lacks the power, feeling, cont and build-up of the one discussed above. However, Catherine seems to revive.

> Thus the fadeout was on an embrace, with Miss Haye [Catherine] still alive--but it was the kind of gutless ing that allowed the audience to make up its own mind to whether she lived or died.[15]

Borzage made it because the studio feared that the film would b depressing. The ending accepted as necessary to this analysis closer to the one found in Hemingway's novel, and the emphasis placed upon transcendence is closer to Borzage's own thematic s

A FAREWELL TO ARMS is a central piece in any discuss of Borzage's thematic and visual styles. It is especially close i structure to SEVENTH HEAVEN, and in the use of river imagery it is reminiscent of THE RIVER. The film is an important influ upon the works that follow, especially THREE COMRADES (1938) THE MORTAL STORM (1940).

a bugle plays taps, adding to the irony of Nemescek's death. Nemescek, in seeking approval from Boka and the friendship of the other boys, receives only "suffering, illness and death."[19] The irony here is underscored further in a cut from the mother carrying her dead child to that of a dredge that is beginning the construction of an apartment building on the battle site. On a superficial level Nemescek dies for nothing, since the "war" he fought in served no purpose. Yet his death unites the two groups and brings about peace. Nemescek's death, like Catherine's in A FAREWELL TO ARMS, is, then, both ironic and necessary. Yet his death unlike Catherine's, actively brings about peace and does not ironically arrive at the moment that some external peace is declared. Both Catherine and Nemescek do, however, achieve peace and continue to live in the souls of those whom they influenced. Nemescek, unfit for the life of this world, leaves it for the more spiritual sphere of idealism and peace. Death, in this film and in the two that follow in this cycle, is a positive force that completely unites a group of individuals. As a force of separation, death is transcended and serves to allow one individual to become a part of the soul or souls of one or more others. The more striking ending of THREE COMRADES plays upon this idea and grows out of these two films, in particular, as much as it does out of the final scene of SEVENTH HEAVEN. At the end of THREE COMRADES death not only becomes a positive force but an event of absolute spiritual transcendence and of complete spiritual union.

THREE COMRADES is much more than an antiwar or an anti-Fascist work. The film is a study of interdependent relationships and of how four characters, none of whom are independent individuals, seek and find personal peace.

The opening of the film strongly parallels the traveling shot used in STREET ANGEL. The camera tracks through a German military club, cutting to isolated groups of soldiers, who are, however, tied by their cause, and by celebrating the end of the First World War. The next cut introduces and frames Otto, Gottfried, and Erich, separating them from the others in the club. Their first toast ("To us!") best reflects their insularity. Their other toasts--to life, home, and peace--reflect their beliefs and what they seek throughout the film: Erich learns to understand and to share life; Otto, acting as father figure to Erich, seeks to create a home for the three; Gottfried works for democracy and peace by joining an anti-Fascist group.

As if to break completely from the past Otto exits and blows up the plane, "Baby," that he flew throughout the war. The director undercuts this action visually, however, in a tracking shot: Otto throws a grenade into the plane, and the camera tracks back just as the machine explodes. The camera then tracks partially forward, creating an uneven and unsettling effect. This is thematically underscored in the subsequent scenes, which negate the comrades' wishes and their desire for a simple and isolated life.

Following a fade-in to a flaming and smoking globe and a shot

Three Comrades

of "passing years" (1918, 1919, 1920) is a long shot of a bread riot
in the streets. Otto and Gottfried are returning home to celebrate
Erich's birthday. Gottfried, the visionary who strives for peace, is
upset by the political and social situation. Otto, however, thinks
only of the immediate ("We have a home"), refusing to join either
side, the rioters or the visionaries. Otto's words are undercut, as
is his whole self-centered or small-group-centered philosophy, when,
after he makes this statement, the bag he is carrying is ripped open
by bullets and some of the bottles within are broken. Conspicuously
absent from Otto and Gottfried's debate is Erich, the innocent, who
is referred to as "baby" by the other two.

The next cut is to the "Baby" emblem, taken out of the plane
and now placed in the trio's car. The image created by this cut reinforces a recurring Borzagean idea: characters and objects lack
any innate spiritual or material existence of their own, achieving a
meaning beyond physical reality only through relationship to other
characters and objects, through their context. [20] "Baby" thus lives
on even when the plane is destroyed and when the car is eventually
sold. Similarly, characters transcend time, place, and life itself,
as in SONG O' MY HEART and A FAREWELL TO ARMS. It is important to the narrative that "Baby" becomes associated with Erich,
the innocent, and that is is on his birthday that he meets Pat Hollmann.

Symbolically, the comrades' car, constructed from the assort-
ed parts of other cars, races and beats the bulbous but swift touring
car that Breuer, a wealthy industrialist, drives. The three defeat Breuer and "win" Pat for Erich and themselves. Pat enters into their lives,
becoming a part of each of the men, tied to each in a completely different way. She gives to each one, and especially to Otto and Erich, a
"wholeness" that they previously lacked; in return the three allow her to
act out a variety of roles that give her a spiritual wholeness that she
lacked as well. Most importantly, they give her life and a reason to
live. Pat becomes the avenue of expression for their beliefs, thoughts.
and desires.

Pat Hollmann--the name takes on an ironic and later symbolic
significance--is a dying member of the dying German aristocracy.
Her allusions to her declining economic state ("I'm going broke")
reflect her decaying physical and spiritual states as well as the
changing nature of German society. This immediately ties her to
Otto, who claims to be one of the spiritually dead, in as powerful
a manner as her physical beauty attracts Erich to her. Yet her relationship to the three goes far beyond the simplicity of mere emotional or physical attraction, taking on Freudian and Jungian aspects
and complexities as well.

The three men are a "whole" being only if they are considered
as a unit. Gottfried, as superego, is the conscience, the soul, of
the group. Otto, while acting out the role of father figure normally
associated with the superego, takes on the role of ego; the realist,
he is infused with an intuitive understanding of those around him.

Erich, as id, comes to represent the youth or animal of the psyche,
the creature of feeling and emotion. Only Erich is capable of loving
constructively, and only he desires to build a relationship with another being. Pat ties in to each of these aspects. Her actual relationship to Gottfried, while weakest throughout most of the narrative, has
the greatest influence upon her later actions. Her relationship to
Otto takes on many mother-and-father aspects, Erich acting as their
child. Their relationship is anchored in common sense and in a mutual and intuitive understanding. Although her relationship to Erich
goes beyond that of the wife to the husband, and often borders on
the parental, she and Erich share an emotionalism of which the others are not capable. Pat becomes, through all of this, representative of some sort of oversoul or anima. She surrounds the three
and holds them together more strongly than their friendship alone
does.

Because of her relationship with the men the actual marriage
scene takes on a larger degree of importance. After a number of
incidents that point out their essential "earthly" differences (especially an embarrassing Harold Lloyd-like nightclub scene in which Erich's
basted tuxedo falls apart), after Otto convinces Pat that one must
gamble to achieve even a small degree of happiness, and after Gottfried convinces Erich to propose, Pat and Erich decide to marry.
The ceremony is performed at Alphons's cafe, where Erich had
brought Pat on their first date and where the four have often met
in the evenings. "Ave Maria" plays on the gramophone, adding a
religious feeling to this seemingly secular event, at which no priest
is present. Otto acts the part of the bride's father, bringing Pat
down the aisle to Erich. As she and Erich stand together there is
a cut to a group shot of the four, which serves to restate their unity
as well as their isolation as a group. This idea was reinforced
earlier when one of the "regulars" at Alphons's, an ex-soldier who
still lives in the "glory" of the past by celebrating battle anniver-
saries and refusing to accept the reality of the present, is locked
out of the cafe just before the ceremony begins. In a scene much
like one used in a film made later that year, THE SHINING HOUR,
there are cuts between the four that tie them all in a marriage bond.
Furthermore, the special relationship between Otto and Pat is emphasized in the lengthy kiss that they exchange after the ceremony.

Pat and Erich honeymoon at the shore, where there are shots
of the two lying on the beach, talking. He rerecites the wedding
vows and talks of the war, his bitterness revealed for the first time.
She talks of a garden, finally interrupting his anger by telling him
that "we're alive" (even though she still refers to herself as a "fragment"). The two then run off into the ocean, their new life together
and their rebirth emphasized in this symbolic baptism.

Yet they cannot fully escape reality. In the scene that follows, as Erich fantasizes about all of the years that they will have
together, Pat, alone in a medium close-up, counts as a cuckoo
sounds, reminding her of time and the limits it places on their
earthly happiness. It is shortly after this that Pat collapses after

attempting some strenuous exercise. The long high-angle shot of
Erich carrying Pat back to the hotel "seems to epitomize the emotional state of his [Borzage's] characters"[21] and projects the isolation of the two within their world and upon the landscape, visually
bringing out "their inward state and feelings."[22] The same visual
technique was used during an earlier phone conversation between the
two. When Erich first calls Pat to ask her out to dinner a split-
screen effect is used. The two are connected by their placement
within the same frame and by the absence of all other extraneous
material. In this case "the unity of space-time in a love relationship"[23] is reinforced.

     Similarly, in the scene that follows Pat's collapse, in which
Erich calls a doctor, all other objects are removed from the frame.
All of these scenes build up the sense of isolation that Pat and Erich
share and intensify the unity created through their love. The idea
of the nonphysical sense of time and space is further enforced in
Otto's attempt to get Doctor Jaffee to Pat. The quick cuts and the
quick action undercut any sense that the space between the two groupings (Otto/Jaffee and Erich/Pat) has any deterministic force. This
visual technique stems from much of Borzage's earlier work and is
used often in the later works as well. It is recognized especially
in the flat cut to Chico returning in SEVENTH HEAVEN and at the
end of DISPUTED PASSAGE (1939) and HIS BUTLER'S SISTER (1943),
as well as in the moment in I'VE ALWAYS LOVED YOU (1946) at
which Myra and Goronoff, although miles apart, play the same piece
of music at the same moment. When Otto and Jaffee do arrive they
symbolically enter out of a fog and into the clear darkness of the
hotel area.

     Pat's collapse is halted, but she is told that she must go to
a tuberculosis sanitarium no later than mid-October if there is to
be any hope of her survival. Mid-October becomes the climax for
a great deal of the action of the film. Borzage attempts to capture
the intangible nature of passing time in a shot of the wind blowing
through the trees and the city streets. In this way he turns time
into "an almost mystical force that floats his cork-like characters
along, much as the unseen wind does the newspaper in the streets."[24]

     The cut to Gottfried at this point reinforces this idea of a
character being at the mercy of immediate events in an unseen purpose. Gottfried, once a member of an anti-Fascist organization,
left this work to protect the safety and livelihood of the group after
a group of Nazis wrecked his cab. Passing along the street, Gottfried sees his old mentor, Professor Becker, speaking out for peace
on a street corner. A group of stormtroopers enter, and a riot
ensues, the military beat of the background music acting as a counterpoint to Becker and soon overwhelming his words. Gottfried saves
Becker from the mob. A quick cut at this point to Pat ties her
both visually and spiritually to Gottfried. She is being told that she
must go to the mountain sanitarium for her health. Once she is
safely abroad the train, Otto and Erich go to join Gottfried in his
battle. The discrepancy here is obvious, as is the fact of Otto's

untold knowledge of Gottfried's danger. Gottfried, in a high-angle shot, is shot in the back and killed by a sniper and dies, finally fulfilled, in the street ("It took a long time, but I finally made up my mind"). Otto cradles him in his arms in a Pietà-like pose as Erich stands by his side. This religious image is continued in the car sequence that follows. Otto drives, seeking out Gottfried's murderer, as Erich cradles Gottfried while the snow falls around them--an image expanded in THE MORTAL STORM.

The parallel between Gottfried and Pat, begun in these scenes, is now developed more fully. Sandwiched between scenes of Otto seeking revenge are scenes of Pat learning of her need for an operation, her longing for Erich and the other two (she has not been told of Gottfried's death), and a scene in which her gift of a scarf, symbolic of protection and warmth, arrives for Erich, who sits alone at Alphons's. The feeling of sadness is emphasized by the strangers who gather around Erich at the piano and sing to Pat. This sadness is "replaced" by the tenacity of Otto's revenge, which is pictured in the scene that follows. Finally recognizing Gottfried's murderer, Otto follows the man. The cutting between the two increases in pace, building the sense of urgency. Otto is in white driving his car and the assassin in black and on foot. The assassin runs up the steps of a church and attempts to gain sanctuary inside. Symbolically, he is locked out and stands momentarily before the church doors and below the three central mosaic windows, as the "Hallelujah Chorus" rises in the background. He then runs to the left, and attempts to hide in a basement staircase, where he is killed by Otto. Erich is conspicuously absent, thereby kept innocent and pure, untouched by the dangers of Otto's act.

Erich is at home during all of this when he receives a telegram from Pat telling him to "come soon." He calls her, Borzage again employing the split-screen effect to enhance the idea of their spiritual togetherness and of the nonphysical nature of the space between them, and she tells of her operation. He vows to come, and both he and Otto arrive in the mountains soon after, during which time the three attempt to forget the present and its problems and to enjoy these few sacred days of peace.

When told of the operation, Otto sells "Baby." "Baby" lives on, however, by the meaning invested in it by the three and by the fact that the money they receive will save Pat. Pat guesses this and regrets that she is becoming a "dead, dragging weight." It is only after the operation and after realizing that she is saved only for the present, that Otto tells her of what she has given to them--the love, life, home, and happiness that they wishes for in their opening toast. She wishes that she were having a child so that some actual sign of her love for Erich would remain when she is no longer there. She then guesses the truth about Gottfried's death and martyrdom, and it is her understanding of his "brave, proud death for what was right" that cements the spiritual tie between these two. Pat takes Gottfried's words to heart and says goodbye to Otto for what both know to be the last time.

When she sees Erich she tells him to go to South America,
his dream paradise, and even creates the scene for him. He thanks
God for having and loving her, his words symbolic of the spiritual
and religious nature of their union. He then throws his watch away
so as to allow time to stand forever still for them and for their love
to exist beyond mortal time. The scene now set for his final physical and spiritual transcendence, she lifts herself slowly up and rises
from her bed knowing that this final act of will will bring about her
death. Although her action is tantamount to suicide, it is fully justi-
fied in Borzage's belief system. This is visually underscored by the
ascending crane shot that tracks her actions. This "celestial shot"
is far more successful than the medium camera shot used during the
scene of Catherine's death in A FAREWELL TO ARMS. This entire
sequence echoes that of the earlier film. Erich's words, "God bless
you, Pat, " correspond to Frederick's repetition of the sentence "I'll
never stop loving you. " Furthermore, as Catherine repeats Frederick's words of union ("We'll never be apart in life and death") and
then clutches Frederick and dies, so Pat's gesture joins her with
Erich.

The use of the ascending camera gives the viewer the sense
that some supernatural force or presence is overseeing the action.
This idea and the essential purity of Pat's motives is further complemented by the white gown that she wears, which makes her appear
as both a bride of Christ and of a man. She dies so that Erich and
Otto may move on and live. Her action becomes one of absolute and
ultimate transcendence out of the "final physical barrier"[25] of her
body and into Erich. Her suicide, the significance of which was
taught to her by Gottfried, becomes an action that allows her to
achieve a final "state of grace. "[26] Pat walks haltingly to the window and to the sunlight of eternity, and exits on to the balcony and
into the snow. She reaches out, ostensibly to Erich but really to
eternity and freedom. Erich runs up to her prostrate body, hugs
her, and lifts her up, as Frederick did with Catherine in the earlier
film, realizing that she is dead and, therefore, has achieved transcendence. The final shots are of Otto and Erich at the graves of
their two dead comrades. The two friends are going to South America as they had always dreamed. They have spiritually outgrown
their present environment. As they leave the cemetery the ghosts
of their two dead comrades materialize and accompany them, the
four walking off into the horizon and into eternity. Space, time,
and death transcended, the four are forever united.

Made in 1940, two years after THREE COMRADES, THE
MORTAL STORM is Borzage's fullest statement of anti-Fascism and
becomes his most fully rounded emotional and intellectual statement
of humanity's spiritual nature and connection with the universe and
its forces. The elements that assail the earth--snow, thunder,
lightning, rain, and wind--reflect upon both the harsh conflicts of
the world we live in and emphasize our powerlessness, our separation, and our physical weakness.

The film opens with a prologue narration accompanied by

time-lapse shots of a gray sky and "clouds that rapidly gather and move in the wind. "[27] The narrator creates a larger sense of the continuity of time and development, speaking of "primitive man's search for shelter against the wind, rain, thunder, and lightning, "[28] and recognizes the "mortal storm in which man finds himself today. "[29] The "cosmic images"[30] that accompany the words create the feeling that it is not so much the characters or the events of the melodrama that is to follow that are the central subjects of the film so much as it is unseen supernatural forces and their effect upon humanity and life. [31]

An establishing shot of a village surrounded by snowy mountains follows, at once setting the village apart as a separate spiritual sphere as well as creating the sense of it as a microcosm.

> Through the course of the film, we see that Borzage's central characters, Professor Roth and his wife, his daughter Freya, his student Martin and Martin's mother, stand, like these mountains, eternal and fixed in their spiritual purity and strength within a rapidly changing, spiritually corrupt society. [32]

These characters reinforce the sense of philosophical and emotional continuity stressed within the prologue. They share an emotional, spiritual, and intellectual tradition as well as a sense of human goodness. Spiritual and nonspiritual values come into conflict as the film progresses and as "the sides are chosen." Tradition, humanity, and truth stand against Nazism and its destructive philosophy. Nazism not only becomes the destroyer of a specific political or religious set of values but the betrayer of a system of greater spiritual values. [33] It is because of the lack of acceptance of the importance of the past and its lack of spirituality that, while this antihumanitarian philosophy may triumph in the present, it must eventually be destroyed.

THE MORTAL STORM substitutes the family and other emotional and intellectual units for the lovers in earlier Borzage films and even for the group in such a film as THREE COMRADES. [34] Both the family and such larger units as the intellectual community of the university reflect the divisions that arise within the nation, further reflecting the disintegration of society and of the security that was previously passively accepted. Numerous parallel shots mirror this and visually underscore the social changes and the emotional states that they cause.

Two sequences point this out best. Early in the film a fast track follows Professor Roth through the corridors of the university and into the classroom, where students, faculty, family, and friends honor him on the occasion of his birthday. They present him with a statue of a figure holding a torch symbolizing "the knowledge that the professor passes on to his students. "[35] In a slower parallel track that occurs later the camera again follows Roth through the corridors of the university. This time, however, the school has

The Mortal Storm

been placed under the control of the Nazis.   Since he is anti-Fascist
as well as Jewish, faculty members all refuse to acknowledge his
presence or his greetings.   When he enters the classroom, instead
of cheers and applause, there is only an angry silence.   Furthermore, his now-uniformed students challenge his beliefs and facts
that refute the Nazi theory of blood differences between the races,
shout down his scientific rationality and, by extension, his humanism, and leave the room in a body.   Instead of the joyous presentation of a statue, a book burning follows, "which transforms the earlier torch of learning into a bonfire of ignorance, cynicism and
hate."[36] The professor refuses to bow to what he sees as insanity,
symbolically standing above the scene of the burning and watching
it from a balcony, and is eventually sent to a concentration camp,
where his death becomes a sacrifice to truth.

A second set of contrasting scenes not only points up the
changes that take place within the family but present a realignment
of the central group into ties of spirit instead of simply those of
blood.   This scene is mirrored in the final scene of the film, its
power and importance thereby reinforced and the transformation that
has occurred documented visually.   Following the university celebration of Roth's birthday there is a celebration for family and friends
at the Roth home.   The unity of the group is stressed, as are the
individual groupings.   Roth sits at the head of the table, between
his wife and Fritz.   Freya sits between the two men who love her,
Martin Breitner and Fritz Marberg.   Also at the table are Mrs.
Roth's two sons by a previous marriage, Erich and Otto von Rohn,
and Professor and Mrs. Roth's young son, Rudi.

```
           Fritz        Freya        Martin
         ┌─────────────────────────────────────┐
  Roth   │                                     │   Otto
         └─────────────────────────────────────┘
           Mrs. Roth     Rudi         Erich
```

Roth makes a speech about the happiness and pride of his present
life and the joy that his family brings him, hoping that this "happiness continues as long as we live." As if to underscore this, the
only lights are those of the candles on the birthday cake and an
overhead fixture. The outer edges of the frame, symbolic of the
outside world, are dark or shadowed. Freya takes this moment to
announce her engagement to Fritz, while the maid enters and announces that Hitler has been made chancellor. Fritz, Otto, Erich,
and Rudi leave the table to gather around the radio in the parlor.
Martin, Roth, Freya, and Mrs. Roth remain behind, silent and sad-
dened by the news, their actions in contrast to the excitement and
joy of the other group. When the others return to the table the re-
grouping that results reflects the separation-by-belief that has occurred. The spiritual ties that join one group and the political ties
that join the other negate the blood or family ties stressed earlier
when Otto and Erich told Roth that they felt as if they were his natural sons.

> The family seems to crumble around the professor, yet
> the solidity of those who remain gives birth to a new al-
> liance of souls. The two-shots of Martin and Freya, es-
> pecially, create an unbreakable bond between them that,
> like the surrounding mountains, remains invulnerable to
> time and the transitory evils of a Fascist society. [37]

The group now discusses power and political and social matters. There is a debate over freedom of thought and questions concerning what is to become of those "non-Aryans" who think differently. Roth and Martin are closely tied in spiritual conviction by
their answering statements. Roth hopes that "responsibility brings
wisdom" to the Nazi leaders. Martin choruses this by saying "Amen"
and, in an argument with Fritz, by stating his basic credo: "I
think peace is better than war." The look upon Freya's face foretells her growing spiritual and emotional break with Fritz, and their
engagement is indeed broken later. It also serves to strengthen the
evidence of her basic spiritual tie to Martin. This tie later results
in their engagement and "marriage." The final breaking point within
the scene is the sound of the telephone ringing and the departure for
a Nazi party meeting by Fritz, Otto, and Erich.

The table scene becomes the focal point of the film, and it
is referred back to at the end of the narrative, when the shots act
to "emphasize the eternal and timeless nature of the professor's,
Martin's, and Freya's beliefs." [38] Otto and Erich return to the
family house after Freya, attempting to escape with Martin into
Austria, is killed by a Nazi patrol led by Fritz. The brothers
stand in the living room of the now-empty house, next to the window

through which the falling snow is seen.   This image links this scene
to the prologue and to Freya's death.   Erich speaks angrily of Martin's escape, remarking upon the political and social freedom he has
achieved through his escape into Austria.   Otto repeats Erich's words
("He's free") but qualifies them so that they take on a greater meaning ("Free to think as he chooses").   Erich cannot accept this, realizing that Martin's freedom and his beliefs themselves will bring
an end to Erich's Fascist philosophy ("Free to fight against everything we believe in").   Once again, Otto qualifies this, his words
reflecting his growing separation from Fascism ("Thank God for that").
Erich then slaps Otto and exits just as Fritz did earlier.

Otto, disillusioned with the "rigid Nazi dogma that has destroyed
his family,"[39] is converted to the humanitarian philosophy of the
Martin/Roth/Freya group.   Yet his acceptance of this has come only
after the loss of everything that once was meaningful to him, and
his triumph is qualified by his sadness and loss.[40]   He then walks
slowly through the empty house.

> Borzage's tracking camera shows us what he sees and sug-
> gests what he remembers: it tracks from Otto's face
> through an empty room to the dining room table.   It looks
> where Freya used to sit and we hear her voice on the
> soundtrack, repeating what she said at the professor's
> party.   The camera angle changes to reveal the professor's
> empty chair, then goes past the chair to the shadow it
> casts on the floor as the professor also speaks.   Borzage
> pans up to Martin's seat, accompanied by a reprise of
> Martin's refusal to convert to Fascism.   Dollying-out into
> the hallway, the camera fixes on the shadow of the pro-
> fessor's torch-of-knowledge statue and the soundtrack re-
> calls his speech when the statue was given to him.[41]

This final scene, playing upon the philosophical and spiritual
divisions set forth in the earlier table scenes, becomes one of final
transcendence for the spiritual or humanist group and completely
separates those three--Roth, Martin, and Freya--as well as Otto,
from the illogical and base Fascist philosophy.

Throughout much of the rest of the film these divisions and
ties have been strengthened.   The two groups presented in opposition
at the table develop and grow in opposing directions.   Roth is sent
away to a concentration camp.   The last time he is seen his hair
and beard are completely white, his hands shake, and his face is
lined and tired.   Yet he refuses to lose hope or to believe that the
values that he believes in are lost forever.   In one scene he sits
at a table, his voice strong, a single lamp above him lighting his
features and those of his wife, all else, including his Nazi guard,
in darkness.   This scene, in contrast to the earlier dining table
scene, is much like the final transcendence scene of SEVENTH HEAV-
EN.   Roth and his wife, much like Chico and Diane, are bathed in
a beam of light.   All others in the frame--the priest in the earlier
film and the guard here--exist in darkness: they are present yet

they do not really intrude upon the spirituality and understanding of
those in the light.

Martin and Freya "grow together" as well, their similar spirituality and humanism tying them in a love relationship far stronger
and deeper than that which existed between Freya and Fritz.   They
are tied visually as well as idealistically at the confrontation scene
at the dinner table.   Freya later asks Martin, who soon after isolates himself from the increasingly Fascist university and from
Fritz, Otto, and Erich, to join them at a local inn, imploring him
not to break up their lifetime friendship ("Don't desert us now.
You're so sane").   The two then join the others at the inn, Freya
once again seated between Martin and Fritz.   Martin is seated in
a position similar to that which Freya occupied at the Roth dinner
table, his tie to the professor and, by extension, to the professor's
beliefs, subtly reinforced.

Borzage tracks through the inn from right to left, as the local villagers who are at the inn sing drinking songs, laugh, and talk.
A group of Nazi officers enter and soon after lead the crowd in a
patriotic military song glorifying their Nazi leadership.   Borzage
again uses a parallel shot to comment upon an earlier scene.   This
time the camera tracks back from left to right.   The crowd is now
a unified body, everyone standing, arms raised in Nazi salute, and
singing in unison.   Only Martin and Freya face each other, in visual
and spiritual isolation, their position in opposition to that of the
crowd.   A few moments later, after again arguing with Fritz over
pacifism, Martin exits to help an elderly professor who is being
beaten by a group of Nazis after refusing to join in either their song
or their salute.   Freya exits and joins him.   She later defends Martin's action to Fritz, echoing Martin's pacifistic leanings and finally
breaking off her engagement ("I can't live in your world!").

Martin and Freya continue to meet at the idyllic farmhouse
where Martin lives with his mother.   The house and Mrs. Breitner
both reflect a tradition and a set of beliefs that range back over
time and family and that are in opposition to the Fascism in the
outside world.   Professor Werner comes to Mrs. Breitner for sanctuary, and Freya comes there to find peace.   When Martin and Freya
later attempt to escape to Austria and freedom (Freya had been de-
tained in an earlier escape with her mother and Rudi for having a
manuscript of her father's with her) the two finally confess their
love.   Martin's mother, an aged matriarch, "marries" them in an
unorthodox ceremony sealed with "apple wine from the fruit of Martin's tree"--the tree of life--which they drink out of a traditional
"bride cup. "   Instead of a marriage at a church, they celebrate
their marriage before the universe and before God at the foot of
"our mountains, " Mrs. Breitner blessing them and asking God to
do the same ("Bless my son and his wife").   The two then drink
out of the cup, say "Amen, " and leave their isolation for asylum
and peace in Austria.

The contrasting shot that follows, of a Nazi meeting, visually acts to increase the separation of Martin and Freya from the Nazis, and from Fritz in particular. The meeting takes place in a dark back room. The men are seated around a large, ugly wooden table, in contrast to the Roth table scene. And in contrast to the final scene of Roth in prison, the room is evenly lit by a metal fixture with a swastika carved into it. Fritz is sent to lead a patrol to capture Martin and Freya ("Allegiance to the Reich comes before human relationships"). This separation is further continued in the ensuing chase scene, as Freya and Martin attempt to cross the border and escape the Nazis.

As the two attempt to ski to safety Freya begins to lag behind ("Everytime I look back you seem to be smaller.... You're so very tired.... Your face is so small and white"); she even asks Martin, symbolically, "We're not lost are we?" At this moment there is a cut to Fritz and his Nazi patrol. This is immediately paired with a long shot of the couple that contains a crucifix-like shadow in the lower right portion of the frame. This image again reinforces the religious nature of their union and of their escape. As the sun rises over the mountains Martin calls Freya "my strength" and promises never to fail her. In the chase scene that follows high-angle long shots of Martin and Freya are set against medium close-ups of Fritz and his troop. Placed against the backdrop of the mountains and sunshine, Martin and Freya seem to become a part of nature. The high angle of the shots reinforces their isolation and their entrance into and existence within their own spiritual sphere. When Freya is finally shot it is just after a low-angle shot of the Nazis and a close-up of Fritz, which increase the sense of their immediate power. There is a shot of Freya's blood upon the snow, which reflects upon her union with the elements of nature and which echoes the prologue. In a scene much like the ending of A FAREWELL TO ARMS Martin lifts the dying Freya into his arms and carries her across the actual and symbolic border and into freedom ("We made it, we're free!"), as village church bells sound echoing the true peace that Freya finds in death and in union with Martin.

At this point the final confrontation scene between Fritz, who killed Freya, Erich, and Otto occurs, as does the track around the deserted table. At the end of Otto's "walk" he leaves, spiritually reborn. The snow falling outside echoes Freya's death, her joining with the elements, and her continued spiritual presence. As if to extend the image, there is a cut to the outside of the house and to a close-up of Otto's footprints being filled in by the freshly falling snow. This last shot "represents in its purity and whiteness, not only Otto's regeneration but also the larger triumph of eternal spirit over the transitory and ephemeral actions of individual men."[42] Otto, like Freya and the others, becomes integrated with "the invisible, cosmic forces that dominate the mortal storm in which man repeatedly finds himself."[43] The fact that his footprints are "erased" again reinforces the fact that his earlier actions, and by extension, the actions of all men, have only transitory meaning or importance.

The film's cloud-filled prologue and snow-filled conclusion

look away from the lesser reality of specific characters
and events and towards a greater, more abstract reality
of the divine presence that animates the natural world and
gives meaning to its inhabitants. [44]

The ending of THE MORTAL STORM, like the other films
discussed in this section, reinforces the Borzagean idea of transcendence out of one spiritual sphere and into another. The increasing
complexity of this notion is reflected in the increasing complexity
of the images Borzage uses to identify it. These films, and SEV-
ENTH HEAVEN as well, create a "line" of complexity that joins
them both thematically and visually. Chico and Diane transcend their
immediate sphere at the end of SEVENTH HEAVEN, as Frederick
and Catherine do through Catherine's death in A FAREWELL TO
ARMS, as the comrades do as a unit at the end of both NO GREAT-
ER GLORY and THREE COMRADES, and as Freya, Martin, Roth,
and Otto do at the end of THE MORTAL STORM.

What sets these films apart from the others, however, are
the visual images Borzage uses to create a sense of direct relationship. SEVENTH HEAVEN ends with Chico and Diane bathed in a
holy white light that signifies their transformation. This image is
developed and strengthened in A FAREWELL TO ARMS, when Frederick lifts the dead Catherine up to the sunlight and, by implication,
offers her to heaven and to God. Catherine, like Pat in THREE
COMRADES, is shrouded in white, her purity and transcendence as
a bride of Christ visually underscoring the narrative. Pat's death
is even more spiritually significant due to its sacrificial nature and
due to the group transcendence it brings about. She makes the comrades "whole men, " as her name (Hollmann) implies. Nemescek's
death in NO GREATER GLORY has the same result. THE MORTAL
STORM ties all of these ideas together. The film not only ends with
the symbolic marriage of the couple and their transcendence, an idea
visually reinforced in the high-angle shots of Martin and Freya against
the mountains. Their marriage thematically ties them to the other
couples within these films and reflects upon the spiritual and religious nature of their love. This love allows for their eventual transcendence. Yet the final images of this film--the deserted table
and the footsteps in the snow--create an even stronger sense of some
"divine presence" that oversees the world and of the transitoriness
of human actions. Borzage reaffirms the spiritual nature of the
world itself, especially through the images of the surrounding prologue-
epilogue shell.

Visual and thematic ties exist among all of these films as a
group, but also link them with the rest of the Borzage corpus. While
such films as MAN'S CASTLE (1933) and LITTLE MAN, WHAT NOW?
(1934) are ostensibly "Depression" films with an economic base, their
final scenes grow out of the works that precede them and reflect
previously stated Borzagean values and ideals. Their transcendence
themes and their endings, in particular, join them to the films discussed in this section as well as to many of the others that follow.

Part Two: The Meek Shall Inherit the Earth

In the films to be discussed in this section war and violent
upheaval are replaced by economic deprivation as the background
against which the primary and central love relationship develops.
As in the other films, social chaos is prominent, yet, once again,
the reality of the physical setting is not all-consuming or important
as a fact in itself. The characters are detached from this immediate reality, and it is their relationship as well as their movement
into a state of "grace" that becomes central to the melodramas.

> Unlike the physical oppressiveness of the anonymous en-
> vironment surrounding King Vidor's characters in THE
> CROWD (1928) or OUR DAILY BREAD (1934), Borzage's
> depression setting is less a physical than a spiritual threat
> to his characters. What endangers Borzage's characters
> is not the depression's poverty or unemployment, but, as
> in LITTLE MAN, WHAT NOW?, the spirit of decadence
> and aimlessness with which it pervades them. [45]

The separation between these films, the antiwar and anti-
Fascist films, and some of the earlier works, such as SEVENTH
HEAVEN and LILIOM, is not complete: all these films have visual
ties, as well as share a number of themes. In particular, the theme
of "individual pride and ego, its inherent limitations, and the necessity for the individual to go beyond it"[46] ties the films of this sub-
section to the others discussed previously. MAN'S CASTLE (1933),
LITTLE MAN, WHAT NOW? (1934), and MANNEQUIN (1938), grouped
here because of their ostensible economic "theme," thus have ties
to the earlier BAD GIRL, which is set against this same background.
Yet these films, the first two in particular, are far more involved
and complex and are thematically and visually closest to SEVENTH
HEAVEN and THE RIVER. Their influence upon later films must
be noted as well. MAN'S CASTLE, for example, is an obvious pro-
totype for THE BIG CITY (1937) and HIS BUTLER'S SISTER (1943). [47]
What separates these films from the antiwar cycle is the increasing
importance of the mystical element. This comes to fruition in such
later films as GREEN LIGHT (1937), THE SHINING HOUR (1938),
DISPUTED PASSAGE (1939), and STRANGE CARGO (1940). MAN'S
CASTLE (in particular) and LITTLE MAN, WHAT NOW? are seminal
pieces in this movement, as they take on increasingly mystical overtones. These elements are far less visually "jarring," however:
no "beam of heavenly light" or overwhelming burst of sunshine and
snow appears in the last frame. These films are visually more subdued, often substituting a gauzy and soft effect for an overtly visual
"sign" without losing any of the effect or the thematic power.

MAN'S CASTLE differs from other Borzage works in that the
plot is concerned less with the narrative movement to transcendence
that we see in most of Borzage's other works than with presentation
of a complex set of visual shifts that underscore the plot progression

throughout. [48] The film is structured mostly in individual scenes,
each an entity in itself, which gives the film an episodic quality. [49]
Out of the visual and thematic interrelationship of these scenes a
flow results.

> An overall progression occurs in the style from the begin-
> ning to the end of the film--one from the pictorially lush
> compositions reminiscent of some of Borzage's silent films,
> especially STREET ANGEL--to a kind of compositional
> simplicity, even to the point where obvious kinds of com-
> positional design are completely absent; something which
> occurs in his films as early as THE RIVER but did not
> become fully developed until the late 30s. [50]

The progression is not simply a linear one but much more a constantly moving process in which each scene criticizes or develops
conceptions presented in an earlier one more by inference than by
obvious design. [51]

MAN'S CASTLE resembles SEVENTH HEAVEN both in its
narrative and its visual structure. Bill, like Chico, while harsh
and skeptical of institutions--here, marriage and steady work--is
essentially generous and warm. He refuses any commitment to
another, and his "self-sufficiency and independence seem, at first,
to be great strengths." [52] In truth, he is more directionless than
free, and his liberation from convention and constriction is an illusion. Even the "promotional costumes Bill wears--the 'Gilsey House
Coffee' neon sign or the Gotham Eatery sandwich board--betray the
falseness of his liberation from ordinary concerns, and ... reflects
the absurdity of the freedom which his eccentricity and egoism have
given him." [53]

The film opens with a scene of Central Park at dawn, shot
in soft focus, not even the characters sharply or clearly defined.
Bill, dressed in a tuxedo, is feeding the pigeons. The camera moves
slowly right to reveal Trina, watching Bill's actions and crying si-
lently. When she confesses that she hasn't eaten in two days he
takes her hand and leads her into a restaurant. Moving out of their
separate worlds and their concerns with their own actions and problems, the two are joined within a shared world of their own in the
restaurant scene. They are in the frame together, the rest of the
crowd being blurred, indistinct, and unimportant. Bill is concerned
with Trina only insofar as he desires to impress her. Trina is
concerned with the food before her. Only when the two must face
the consequences of their action--Bill cannot pay for the meal and
must explain his plight--that the crowd comes into focus and the
couple's world is recognized as being part of the larger world.

This idea of their connection and their separation from the
outside world continues once they leave the restaurant. As they
walk along the street they pass many people, who are visually separated from them by a distortion of scale (the result of back-projection).

Man's Castle

The strange separation between Bill and Trina and the surrounding crowd suggests both their isolation from the rest
of the world and, perhaps, the notion that their isolation
comes from a falsely bizarre envisioning of that world on
their part.   The presentation of that envisioning is dis-
torted and unnatural in that the strange back-projection used
suggests even within the scene that it is a state which
contains internal contradictions and cannot endure
permanently--and, consequently, that the specific kind of
isolation in which Bill and Trina act (an isolation made
possible by the envisioning described) cannot endure either. [54]

Bill takes Trina to his home, a Hooverville by the harbor, after learning that she has no home and nowhere to sleep. Against a soft-focus view of the city that emphasizes the illusionary quality of his words, Bill confesses bits of his philosophy. He tells Trina of how easy it is to live, of what the train whistle that they hear means to him ("Here I come ... like a long-distance call"), and of his belief in the ultimate goodness of humanity. This latter point once again undercuts his outward gruffness and isolation, tying him closer to Trina.

The shantytown is a visual extension of the romantic and subjective quality created by the soft-focus long shot of the city. The details of the shantytown are indistinct, a reflection of Bill's romantic statements about life and living. The fact that Bill sleeps on an unroofed barge is a reflection of both his fear of being tied to something firm and his desire for some form of security. Like the sandwich board that he wears later, the image becomes representative of Bill's tie to a world in which he does not or cannot participate: he can exist only on the fringes of that world. In true Borzagean fashion, both the barge and the sandwich board, as well as the shack into which Bill and Trina move, are images of varied nuance and implication.

This shack replaces the barge and becomes the couple's "safety zone," representative of both the peaceful nature and emotional strength as well as the uncertainties of their relationship. Created out of bits and pieces of material and salvage, it becomes "their defense against the outside world."[55]

> Structurally, it [the shack] contains both of their personalities. Trina's stabilising and ordering nature is seen in the stove, the curtains, the washboard and the basin; Bill's quest for freedom appears in the sliding window in the ceiling that looks out on the blue sky and flying birds.[56]

The objects in the shack are relatively indistinct from one another and from Trina. They are tonally less separated from Trina and, by extension, her desires, than from Bill. These same objects become identified with both Bill and Trina, however, becoming representative of "materializations of part of hers and Bill's egos, or sense of themselves."[57] The shack belongs to them and is symbolic of their relationship.

> But, as in earlier scenes, the style here begins to criticize its own notions. The difficulty of discerning separate objects suggests a kind of anonymity or non-specificity to that part of their identity which the objects give them. To attach the characters to a specific set of objects stylistically would be no more appropriate than assigning them a specific kind of style was in the opening scene or a specific kind of isolated space was in the restaurant scene. Borzage, as always, is struggling to liberate his characters from any specifics which might ensnare them in a false

materialism--either via an overly limited romanticism centered on surface beauty (the opening) or via too great an
attachment to specific spaces or objects. [58]

A conflict arises, however, between Trina's immediate and
long-range wants. She tells Flossie, another shantytown inhabitant,
that she has "everything anyone could want, " yet in the next scene
she stands before a store window gazing longingly at a stove. The
stove represents more than Trina's attachment to objects; actually
it is reflective of her desire for security and commitment. Bill's
abrupt refusal reflects his wanderlust, and his refusal to be anchored
to anyone or anything. To give in to her desire would be almost to
announce his emotional commitment to her. Yet as soon as she goes
home he gets the money needed for a down payment by becoming a
process server and buys the stove on an installment plan.

When Bill brings the new stove into the shack after bullying
Trina and asserting his power this object stands out among their non-
descript possessions. The new stove is seen in the foreground in
close-up, the implication being that it is an extension of Bill's ego[59]
and of his domination. Trina gets on her knees before the stove,
bowing to it as if before an altar and, by extension, to Bill's domination. The stove represents both Bill's tenderness for Trina as well as
his importance to her and his superiority.

At the same time, the strange disparity between the stove
and the background of the frame again begins to suggest internal contradictions. Materialized ego stands out so obviously ... in Borzage's usually balanced visual field, that
it seems almost anomalous. [60]

Furthermore, this becomes a reflection of Bill's inner discontinuity,
being placed in contrast to his attraction to the train whistle and its
implications as well as his unwillingness to take off the masks he
wears before both Trina and the larger world. The disparity between
Bill's actions and his words is reflected further in the cut that follows Trina's kneeling before the stove.

Bill is next seen standing on stilts, an advertising ploy, and
this takes on a number of symbolic implications. Beside the direct
contrast with Trina's kneeling before the stove, Bill's being on stilts
reflects his self-image and self-importance. Children group around
his "legs, " and, as if to reinforce his importance in their eyes and
in his own, he gives one an "autographed" baseball. The direction
that his life is taking, however, is stressed as well, since in advertising "Ye Gotham Eatery" he is earning enough money to pay the
first installment on Trina's stove. Even though he has not fully recognized or accepted his commitment to her and their life together,
we see his unconscious movement toward that commitment. This
scene is a striking parallel to the one in STREET ANGEL when Angela falls off of her circus stilts after seeing two policemen. In her
case, as in Bill's, the precarious position of her life is reflected by
her precarious balance on these false legs. That Bill and Trina go

through an orthodox wedding ceremony performed by Ira, a one-time
minister who acts as the conscience of the shantytown, is of less importance than one expects. (That Trina wears a forty-year-old dress
is significant, however, as representative of Borzage's Victorian view
of women and of Trina's central and almost Victorian role in the drama itself.) It is only later that an actual commitment is realized.
What occurs for Bill much later is an acceptance of his responsibili-
ties to Trina and then the couple's mutual transcendence of their immediate "real" and spiritual worlds. The ceremony, unlike those of
the couples who consent to marriage in previous Borzage relationships, does not symbolize any outwardly understood or recognized
bond. Bill continually fights against being tied down, and it is this
refusal that eventually leads to his later aborted escape.

The "special" quality of Bill and Trina's relationship is further
expressed in the Bill/Fay and Bragg/Trina contrasts. Bill meets
Fay, a showgirl, when he delivers a subpoena to her. They meet
again later while he is on stilts as he passes by and looks into her
apartment window. Obviously attracted to him, she propositions him
and later offers him a job as her bodyguard. This, and the image
of glamour that she offers, are undercut by Bragg, Bill's friend, who
propositions Trina at the shack in a scene bracketed by two of Bill
and Fay. Bragg's attempt to seduce Trina is crude and his attraction only physical. This is a further opposition to Bill, who constantly refers to Trina in comically disparaging nature as "skinny"
and "gawky."

Trina's sureness about Bill's fidelity is brought out in the next
scene, as is Bill's struggle between egocentricity and dependence.
When he returns to the shack Trina is not angry; kneeling to him as
she did before the stove, she refuses to listen to any of his excuses,
telling him that they are unnecessary. Lying on his bed, Bill listens
to this without understanding her attitude and her sureness of his love
at all. This is reinforced visually in the shots that follow. Bill lies
down on the bed, staring up at the sky through his "skylight" and
then at Trina, moving around the shack. This same shot pattern
occurs after the dinner sequence, when Bill presents Trina with a
flower. Once again his dual "allegiance" is stressed, his desire
for freedom (the sky) and for domesticity and emotional attachments.

> One begins to sense a kind of separation between the images
> of Bill and the close-ups of the things he sees, almost as
> if they were in separate spaces. The camera, by assum-
> ing Bill's position, represents the nature of his seeing, of
> his relationship with the things around him. By expressing
> this relationship in point-of-view shots, Borzage crystal-
> lizes Bill's whole view as an egocentric one: rather than
> attempting to enter other objects, to free himself from his
> own ego and understand other things, he remains fixed in
> one position, and his view of life is entirely as he sees it
> from that position. It is almost as if he sees everything
> as revolving around him ... and thus seeing them as sep-
> arate from himself. [61]

Bill cannot resolve his inner tension and contradictions and
cannot fully commit himself to love as Trina can. This is stressed
even more in their separate reactions to the news of Trina's pregnancy. The two lie on the bed, and through the series of two-shots
that follow Borzage visually underscores their dependence and interconnection while undercutting Bill's earlier words ("how much I like
a girl ain't nothin' to bet money on.... I'm liable to be all steamed
up today and washed up tomorrow") as well as his statement of how
Trina only suits him now. Trina's words reinforce this image. Even
if Bill goes away, she will always have him, since she will have his
child. It is at this point that Bill rises and exits from the frame.

> This ... expresses formally ... what Trina has just said:
> that Bill and Trina are inextricably united forever--in ef-
> fect, that neither exists as an individual apart from the
> other, thus apparently ending all justification for Bill's as-
> sertions of freedom and independence. [62]

Bill's subsequent attempt to "escape" and "hop a freight" for
freedom is undercut by this and by the power that Trina and her love
have over him. Bill jumps aboard the freight, his face looking back,
troubled. In the series of cuts that follows a sort of telecom-
munication occurs, as there are cuts from Bill to Trina at home,
on the bed, back to Bill, and then again to Trina. Space becomes
unimportant as love transcends any spatial fixity. The interdependence of the two and their essential unity is reinforced. Even the
sounds in the background--the train and the music--are shared by
the two. The tie is cemented when Bill jumps the freight and returns to Trina. When they later meet at the market her words
("You're a free man, free as a bird") are undercut, as is his belief
that he can still be free. This is visually stressed in their separation from the background of the market and in their obvious unity.
Still claiming that he desires freedom, Bill decides to rob a ware-
house so as to provide Trina with money for the baby, a narrative
parallel to LILIOM. Still feeling that he can "buys off" responsibility,
he plans to take a freighter to China, thus leaving Trina behind.

The robbery Bill and Bragg plan fails, and Bill is wounded.
Returning to Trina, he announces his presence by a toy soldier--
symbolically small against the environment in contrast to his earlier
inflated idea of himself on stilts. When he confesses the motive for
his actions she tells him, once again, that her only need is him and
that she doesn't want to "pull him down." She attempts to free him
by telling him he can go if he desires, but, she knows that, like the
birds, he can't "fly all the time." Both finally break down and cry,
their responses in concert for the first time, and Bill refuses to
leave without Trina. Their obstacle, Bragg, is removed when Flossie shoots him ("We're useless, no-good people, you and me"), thus
freeing the two.

Bill and Trina flee together, leaving their shack and all of
its objects, including the stove, that previously held them down. The
two "hop a freight" for a new start, having outgrown their environment

and their separation as well as the chaos that existed around them.
The two are seen lying in a boxcar, their transcendence echoed not
only in this religious setting (the boxcar is covered in straw like a
manger, and their child is due at Christmas), but by the ascending
camera that accompanies this. Their spiritual liberation is reflected
in this shot. The idea that they are detached from their restricting
environment reverberates, and "they seem to float freely in space,
triumphant and eternal in their love. "[63] No longer fragmented, the
two are now spiritually whole through their interdependence and through
their chosen unity.

Again characters are subordinate to the overriding unity. As
in other films of this period, transcendence of the immediate or "real
world" reflects the spiritual rise of the characters. Not so much escaping evil or conquering it, the characters rise above their own limitations and in union grow out of their present. MAN'S CASTLE, like
the previously discussed films, stresses this as well as Borzage's
idea that the actualities of space and time have no meaning. MAN'S
CASTLE, like the film that follows it, LITTLE MAN, WHAT NOW?,
reaffirms life in a manner closely tied to the films discussed earlier
in this chapter. These two films, in particular, celebrate life and
its physical continuation in pregnancy or birth, as well as create a
sense of spiritual transcendence. While the films work through different means, they all reaffirm the interdependence of the group.
The earlier films view death as a means of finding spiritual union;
MAN'S CASTLE and LITTLE MAN, WHAT NOW? reaffirm the spiritual nature of life. In all of the films the "real" environment is
not so much escaped as transcended. While in the other films death
allows for this, the idea of the nonspatial fixity of love and commitment stressed in all of these films overwhelms any sense of loss
that results. Characters, whether they be living or dead, are permanently joined spiritually. It is the resulting state of "grace" that
becomes most important.

LITTLE MAN, WHAT NOW? again reaffirms this spiritual
sense while, like MAN'S CASTLE, presenting us with two characters
who grow out of their environment and into a greater spiritual union.
Lammchen and Hans escape the cynicism of the decadent and depression-
ridden German society of the 1920s by achieving a spiritual transcendence that gives them greater strength than that possessed by the
others around them. Unlike Trina's and Bill's, their love is easily
confessed, their interdependence an easily accepted fact. Lammchen,
like Trina, becomes a "redemptive presence, "[64] saving Hans from
spiritual depression and from a fall into Fascism by giving him hope
for the future. Lammchen's power is more easily recognized than
Trina's, however, and Hans's innocence "counteracts the cynicism that
surrounds her and her husband. "[65] Hans outwardly has little of the
tough skepticism and gruffness of Bill, his need for Lammchen recognized by him as much as by others. The two couples differ in
how they achieve transcendence, yet both films end by taking similar
thematic directions.

LITTLE MAN, WHAT NOW? plays upon the basic theme of

MAN'S CASTLE, and in much the same manner. The depression environment, like the villain in a melodrama, threatens the spirit of
the characters. [66] The world-at-large, and the force of depression
in particular, act to "beat down" Hans, Borzage's "Everyman. " As
the prologue implies, only love acts as a force for salvation.

> The story of LITTLE MAN is the story of EVERYMAN and
> the question of WHAT NOW? is the WORLD'S DAILY PROB-
> LEM, a problem that men can only hope to overcome by a
> courage born of great faith in the hearts of women.
> Against the tide of time and chance, all men are little--but
> in the eyes of a woman in love, a man can become bigger
> than the whole world.

The film opens on a rainy day in postwar Germany. The
camera slowly tracks in to a street speaker who expounds upon equality and the injustice of German society, the need for a "new day. "
As the camera moves in for a closer shot of the crowd there is a
dissolve and a parallel shot of Hans standing on a street corner and
waiting for Lammchen. Set apart from the crowd and the "outer
world, " the lovers exist, both visually and thematically, in a world
of their own. Lammchen's entrance jolts Hans out of his despair,
and her presence moves him from his intense listening to concentration upon her ("I'm too rich in having you, you're too poor in having
me").

Hans believes in accepting life peacefully and in keeping one's
place contentedly. Yet his words ("nothing very wrong happens to
the peaceful") and the general atmosphere of the gray skies and the
rain undermine his optimism. The rain, in particular, is a comment
upon the spiritual depression that exists throughout the society in
which the film takes place. This image is used often in Borzage's
films, from STREET ANGEL (1928) to HISTORY IS MADE AT NIGHT
(1937). As if to compound the immediacy of their problems, Lammchen learns that she is pregnant.

Lammchen, introduced originally by a series of sudden close-
ups on the street corner, becomes "an amazing source of positive
energy, counterbalancing the negative forces around the couple. "[67]
She constantly brings Hans out of his state of despair, in the doctor's
office and later in Berlin, for instance, allowing him to function in
a disruptive society. Their ensuing marriage becomes not only representative of their emotional bond but also of stability in a world of
increasing confusion. Their marriage is kept secret from Kleinholz,
Hans's employer, who desires him as a husband for his plain and
dumb daughter. When Kleinholz catches Lammchen and Hans at the
park and fires Hans, it is only Lammchen's love that stops him from
falling into total despair. This is reinforced in the scene in which
Hans and Lammchen ride the merry-go-round. Lammchen, having
eaten all the dinner salmon, runs away and hides. When Hans finds
her and calms her fears, the two ride the merry-go-round, the outside world blurred and seemingly unimportant. Once again visually
isolated from the outer world and tied to each other, the two are

Little Man, What Now?

assured of survival. The following dissolve from the ride to the
train wheels acts to carry over this scene.

        Because of the economic depression Hans cannot find another
job, and the two go to Berlin to live with Hans's step-mother, Mia
Pinneberg.   Mia reflects most clearly the corruption of the society
around the couple.   She is perversely attached to her dog, is interested only in money, throws wild parties, and, it is intimated, runs
a house of prostitution.   Her relationship with Jachman, the man
she lives with, and her scornful attitude toward Hans and Lammchen
and their relationship, reflect the "all-consuming depravity that she
and her world represent for the young couple. "68 Mia and her blurred
sense of values become as much a part of the blurred outer world as
did Kleinholz.   Each serves as a cynical contrast to the innocence
of the young couple and the valiancy of their fight for survival. Furthermore, any help that the couple receives they are forced to pay
for.   They must pay Mia an exorbitant rent of 100 marks, and
Lammchen is forced to serve as a maid during Mia's parties. Jachman only offers to help Hans if Lammchen will become his mistress.
Only when he learns of their coming child does his attitude change.

        Lammchen continues to act as Hans's strength, and her grow-
ing importance is visually reflected in the dressing table that he buys
her.   The two stand before a store window, once again separated

from all others and framed by the plate glass. As in MAN'S CASTLE
and BAD GIRL, the camera looks at them from within the store, the
dressing table in the center foreground. In a later cut to their apartment Lammchen sits before the three-mirrored dressing table, with
which Hans has surprised her. As she sits before it her image is
multiplied, reflecting upon her spiritual importance as well as upon
the power of her influence over Hans. "The reflections, shown as
bright images that emanate from her, transform her, as she sits in
front of the mirrors, into a source of light and strength. "[69] This
image is even more startling than Borzage's cut to her arrival at the
start of the picture. Each, however, reflects upon Lammchen's importance and the importance of the couple's relationship.

When Hans finally learns the nature of Mia's income he takes
Lammchen away from the corruption. The two are now to live alone,
the narrative now reinforcing the visual images recognized earlier.
The apartment that they do find is rented to them by a wagon driver,
who comments upon Lammchen's courage at having children in these
days. The apartment itself, like that in SEVENTH HEAVEN, is a
garret above a furniture store consisting of one large room with ac-
cess to the roof ("a gateway to heaven"). Hans at first fails to see
its charm or its significance, being angered only by what he sees as
its shoddiness and inconvenience, such as the fact that one can only
reach it by climbing up a ladder. His anger turns into a tirade concerning the unfairness of life itself, thus reflecting back upon the
street speakers he heard earlier and Lammchen's positive power over
him.

Yet Lammchen once again pulls him out of despair, and Hans
kneels before her, crying, "Take care of me, please. " In their garret the two are able to find refuge from the "outside" world and
from the encroachments upon their happiness. This encroachment
continues to grow, however, since soon after Hans loses the department-store sales job he recently found.

The fact of Hans's unemployment, while important, is undercut by Lammchen's tripled image when he comes to her. Again she
becomes the "romantic deity-figure through whom Hans finds redemption from the decadence ... in his world"[70] and from the tribulations
he faces. This image is even more strongly presented by Lammchen's wearing an ornate white silk dress covered with iridescent
sequins. Lammchen stands out of the bleak environment, her power
again stressed. In contrast to the pessimism of the early scenes,
Hans does not fall into the despair that surrounds him. This we
know to be due to Lammchen, for only when Hans is separated from
her does he begin to falter. When he cannot raise the money for
her confinement he meets a Nazi sympathizer who convinces him to
go to a meeting. Hans drifts over to the meeting, where, knocked
down by the police, he picks up a stone in anger. Realizing what
has come over him, he returns home ashamed.

Juxtaposed to this and to his return is the birth of their child.
When Hans returns to the garret he kneels before Lammchen and the

child, both in white and both shot in soft close-ups. As if confessing his sins and his fears ("Poor little fellow, what now?"), he vows to "begin again and take care of our son." Reacting to both his momentary identification with the mob and to the love unit in which he now exists, he realizes that the three will survive. Lammchen echoes this most clearly ("Isn't he small and helpless--but life can't be any bigger than he is because he is life, isn't he?, and we've created him. We've created life so why should we be afraid of it?"). As if to "cap" their growth, Heilbut, Hans's department-store friend, enters, offering Hans a job in his store in Amsterdam. Lammchen and Hans, having outgrown their immediate surroundings and having defeated the decadence and corruption of their society, leave Germany for the new life that is symbolically represented in their child. The two have triumphed "over life's negativity through their creation of a new, pure, positive being whose redemptive power lies in the fact that it is nothing but life itself."[71] Like Chico and Diane, Gino and Angela, Rosalee and Allen, Eddie and Dorothy, Frederick and Catherine, and Bill and Trina, Lammchen and Hans have moved out of the immediate realities of their world and into a sphere of greater understanding and spirituality. Through Lammchen's faith and power the two begin anew. Their creation and acceptance of their love reflect their ability to create as well as their ability to transcend and to begin again. In one of Borzage's more powerful ideological statements life begets both life and a renewal of hope.

MANNEQUIN, more closely tied to BAD GIRL than to the two films just discussed, juxtaposes the ideas of economic success and emotional fulfillment. The first section of the film "is a stark portrait of a lower-class girl who makes a bad marriage and is stuck, dependent on a lazy and unreliable man."[72] More than this, it is a comment upon tenement life and a working girl's dreams of escape. It is thus an amalgamation of later-1930s "women's films" and general 1930s escapist fantasy. The middle section of the film is devoted to Jessie's rejection of her husband and of her attempt to become an individual. In true Borzagean style, the final section is both the "dream escape" and, more importantly, the "coming together" of Jessie and Hennessey through a bond of shared love and equality.[73]

MANNEQUIN opens upon a factory at five o'clock and moves to Jessie's walk through the streets of New York's lower East Side to her Hester Street home. Entering her apartment, she immediately joins her mother in the kitchen while her out-of-work father lounges in the parlor. She kiddingly fantasizes about her higher aspirations-- green fields and a pheasant dinner--revealing the two opposing sides of her personality. On an immediate level she exists within the real world of poverty and emotional despair. Opposed to this is her romantic nature. It is this latter part of her personality that, through true love, eventually triumphs. Jessie's sense of entrapment is further revealed visually in a number of shots in which she and her mother are seen through the bars of the kitchen pipes. Her superior position within the family and her usurpation of the position as "breadwinner" is further brought out in the dinner scene that follows: while her father nominally sits at the head of the table, it is Jessie who stands above him and oversees the situation.

Jessie's dual nature is reflected by the flickering bulb that lights the tenement stairway. This, like the train whistle in MAN'S CASTLE, becomes a metaphor for the spiritual atmosphere in which Jessie and the others exist. It is an intangible force that cannot be corrected, reflective of something much deeper. [74] Jessie continually attempts to fix the flickering bulb and is later trapped in the darkness when the light goes out, just as she is trapped in her present environment.

Jessie sees her love for Eddie as a way out of her problems. Yet their relationship and their opposing dreams undercut the romanticism of Jessie's feelings. Eddie takes her to an amusement park and beach, where she draws a circle representing the world that they exist in alone. Yet as she talks of the moon he talks only of work, and while she looks at the surrounding lights, all shot in soft focus, he talks of money and of fights. When Jessie returns home that night and is trapped in the dark hall she runs down to Eddie and begs him to marry her and provide her with a "way out" of her environment.

The wedding-reception scene that follows gives the greatest insight into the realities that Jessie's romanticism has blocked from her view. Immediately a contrast is created by the deep focus that replaces the earlier soft focus of the beach and that serves to undermind Jessie's romantic dreams. Jessie, dressed in a black wedding dress not much different from the black dresses she wears throughout these scenes, sits in the background of the frame, seen between Hennessey and his associate Briggs in the foreground. Hennessey is a Horatio Alger-type of hero, the self-made man who has risen from the slums. Very much a romantic, he sends champagne to their table. He, like Jessie, has a dual nature, and his seeming business realism is undercut later, as is Jessie's emotional romanticism. When Eddie, who recognizes Hennessey, and Jessie come over to thank him, Eddie, taking on the role of pimp, offers Jessie for a dance. Hennessey is overwhelmed by Jessie's own romanticism, which is symbolized by the "beautiful and helpless" violets that she holds. Still the innocent and still believing in fairy tales, she dances with Hennessey only until the song "Always and Always" plays. When she hears this she stops dancing with him and returns to Eddie, this being "their" song. Eddie, seeing only what he can get from this situation, offers to forget this fact. It is Hennessey who makes him dance with Jessie, who sings the song to him as well. The song later serves to tie Jessie and Hennessey: when Hennessey proposes the song is playing in the background.

Visual images that first appear at this point bind Jessie to Hennessey and separate her from Eddie and her blind romanticism toward him. When Jessie and Eddie arrive at their new apartment Jessie stands framed before the window and talks of the beauty of the river and the lights outside. Eddie is conspicuously left out of this interior frame. This becomes a visual correlative to Hennessey, because later he is framed before an office window, the harbor seen outside. Jessie is still the romantic, however; she dreams aloud at this point just as she did earlier at the amusement park. She, in

contrast to Hennessey, has no realistic conception of what is really
"outside" and of the realities of the world itself.

Eddie's true personality is revealed in the scenes that follow.
Not only does Jessie go off to work the next morning while Eddie remains in bed, but he takes her last five dollars. It is at this point
as well that he tells her that she ought to work in the chorus as there
is more money in it. She does so, and this becomes the manner in
which she is reintroduced to Hennessey.

When Jessie goes to one of Hennessey's parties, she stands
before an unflickering lamp and talks to Hennessey. He admits to
having thrown these parties only in the hope that she would attend so
that he could be with her again. Exiting onto the patio, she speaks
rhapsodically of the city and of the lights, unconsciously incorporating Hennessey into her dream world. When she claims that all she
needs in life is three rooms Hennessey is entranced and kisses her.
She slaps him and leaves, but he stops her by having the elevator
brought back up before she reaches the ground floor, an act stress-
ing his financial and emotional power. He apologizes and takes her
home in a cab, a parallel to the scene when Jessie and Eddie returned home from the wedding reception. He fails to understand that
she is not attracted by his wealth and wants to see her three rooms,
to understand their specialness. What he witnesses instead is a scene
in which the couple who actually own the apartment argue with Eddie
over its return and over the condition of the furniture. Jessie is
forced to leave her romantic dream house and return to the tenement
life she wanted to escape so badly. The original "reason" for her
marriage is thus negated.

Jessie begins to realize more of Eddie's true nature, yet she
still loves him enough to forgive his lies. This fact is visually con-
veyed when she walks into the hall bathroom and stands by a window
looking out on the river. Not only does this contrast with her earlier happiness, and not only is she again framed alone in an interior
frame, but a flickering exterior light surrounds her as it did earlier.

Through a number of ensuing scenes Jessie and Hennessey are
visually connected. When Eddie is arrested Jessie gets the bail money
from Hennessey. Not only does he give it to her without question,
but goes with her to see to Eddie's release. Eddie misconstrues
what is really happening and refuses to hear Jessie's defense. Visually, however, his accusations are supported: Jessie stands beside
Hennessey, and the two face Eddie (Eddie→ ←Jessie/Hennessey).
Furthermore, the strain between the two is recognized when they
wait for the subway. Eddie stands alone in the foreground as Jessie
waits in the background. When they get on the train they sit opposite
another couple who hug and touch throughout. Eddie refuses to touch
Jessie, arguing with her instead, and Jessie's dream and her reality
are placed in sharp contrast.

The climax of this first section of the film comes in a scene
that follows soon after. As Eddie and Jessie's father lounge smok-

ing in the parlor, they discuss the unfair state of things. Jessie's
father suggests that Eddie go on relief as "the country owes it to
you." The two demand their dinner, and there is a cut to the two
women, once again framed by the bars of the hot-water pipes and
surrounded by steam. Jessie admits for the first time how important money is, and her attitude reflects her increasing discontent and
disillusionment. In a striking monologue her previously silent mother
breaks down the last vestiges of Jessie's faltering idealism:

> "There are some things I've been wantin' to tell you....
> About what you've got and what you want. What a woman
> gets. A woman's supposed to lead the man's life. Her
> man's life. And women are made that way, occasionally.
> Woman's weakness is supposed to fit in a man's strength.
> Her respect pays for the security the man gives her. But
> now you, Jessica, you've got strength of your own. You
> can do things. Not just dream about them ... like most
> women."
> "What are you trying to tell me, ma?"
> "Make a life for yourself. Always remember what it is
> you want. Get it. Any way you can. If you have to, get
> it alone."

Soon after this Eddie broaches the idea of Jessie divorcing him, mar-
rying Hennessey for money, divorcing Hennessey and remarrying Eddie, their financial problems thereby being overcome. It is only at
this point that Jessie sees through Eddie's veneer and walks out, declaring scornfully, "Women are weak and men are strong. My mother wasted her life trying to prove that."

In the second section of the film Jessie gets a job as a model
and repays Hennessey the 100 dollars that she borrowed for Eddie's
bail. This not only frees her from Eddie and from that part of her
past but makes her somewhat more equal to Hennessey. She refuses
his request for a date ("for now and always"), declaring that she
wants to stay alone. This statement implies that she now believes
herself to be "whole"; however, this is visually and symbolically sub-
verted when Hennessey attends a fashion show in which Jessie is modeling. He wears a cutaway, and she, for the first time, wears a
white gown much like a wedding dress, symbolic of the purity of
their eventual relationship. She finally consents to have dinner with
him, at which time he offers to buy her clothes and a car. Rejecting his materialism, as she had rejected her earlier romanticism,
she refuses his offers and holds on to her freedom and independence.
It is only when he confesses his love for her, claiming he fell in
love when she slapped him, and that he has enough love for both of
them, that she consents to the union, believing that she has found
happiness since she is no longer vulnerable. Indeed, Hennessey
treats her more like an equal and no longer like an object. She enters this marriage in a far more realistic state of mind and refuses
to lose her identity or what she sees as her "wholeness" by refash-
ioning herself in his image.

The last section of the film tends to become much more of a romantic idyll and lacks the raw power and realism of the earlier tenement sequences. The split between the tenement milieu and Jessie's aspirations for a better life becomes more a split between realism and fantasy. Jessie and Hennessey marry in Paris and settle into three rooms of an Irish cottage for their honeymoon. The reality that they attempt to leave behind soon intrudes again, however, with a cable from Briggs that announces that Hennessey's business--the reality underlying their illusions--is in danger due to a threatened strike. Jessie mistakenly believes that his business is more important than they are, yet realizes that while all she wants is "here," there are obligations "over there." Having tasted her dream, she must return to Hennessey's world and to his combined dream and reality.

When they do return Hennessey is ruined. He stands before his office window overlooking the harbor, signing away his business assets to pay off his debts. Hennessey isn't unhappy, since he still believes that he has what is really important to him in Jessie. Once again the daylight outside of the window echoes both his understanding and his actual "wholeness"; he understands that "wholeness" is achieved only by interdependence. Yet he may lose Jessie, who, refusing to bow to Eddie's blackmail, decides to leave Hennessey rather than hurt him. She too now understands that there is something greater than her own well-being. Hennessey confronts Jessie just as she is about to leave. Eddie enters as well, and Jessie and Hennessey stand united in opposition to him (Eddie— —Jessie/Hennessey). Jessie then confesses Eddie's schemes and her fears. It is only when Hennessey laughingly confesses his bankruptcy that she refuses to leave, offering him her jewels and her help in getting "three rooms and a start." She now gives herself freely in a relationship of emotional equals. Together they will create their own world and "build a circle" around themselves. Earlier false illusions destroyed, the two find their dreams in the reality of mutual dependence.

Jessie and Hennessey, like both Trina and Bill and Hans and Lammchen, begin from a point of inequality and grow together into interdependence. Jessie, however, becomes a much stronger, less ethereal heroine than either of these other women. Unlike Trina and Lammchen she is disillusioned by love and by economic realities. Yet like these two she finds herself in a separate sphere at the end of the film. Having outgrown and readjusted her former ideas, she can give herself to Hennessey and can share with him. Their economic reconstruction becomes symbolic of her emotional reconstruction and of the unification of the two previously opposing sides of her personality. Having escaped the fetters of her past and of her illusions, she is capable of growing and changing.

Hennessey, like Bill and previous Borzage "heroes," loses his illusion of melodramatic "completeness" and in his understanding of his incompleteness is finally able to grow. No longer desiring to buy things for Jessie and to place her upon a pedestal, he is finally able to treat her like an equal partner. Their relationship, like those of

Trina and Bill and Lammchen and Hans, becomes one of spiritual
equals. Through their growth all have been able to transcend their
immediate surroundings and to move into some more spiritual sphere.

All three of these films--MAN'S CASTLE; LITTLE MAN, WHAT
NOW?; and MANNEQUIN--work out of a basis of economic hardship
or deprivation. What threatens the couples, however, is not so much
lack of money as their own personal selfishness. This is especially
true of Bill and Trina and of Jessie and Hennessey. Only Hans and
Lammchen are different. Hans has much less of the bravado of the
other two male characters, his dependence on Lammchen being recognized by the two from an early point in the film.

As in the antiwar and anti-Fascist films, the fact of the problems of the "outside world" is not as important as the feeling of spiritual loss that results. The mood of these films is somber in that
the sense of emotional depression and fragmentation in each is extensive. Yet the spiritual and emotional leaps that are finally made
create a feeling of almost religious joy at the end of the films. Later
in this period this idea of a pseudoreligious and spiritual awakening
and transcendence takes on a far more mystical tone, and the characters go through a more obvious "religious" conversion that allows
for their transcendence.

Part Three: Suffer the Rich

In STRANDED (1935), one of Borzage's most overtly allegorical films, Lynn Palmer, who works for the Traveler's Aid, guides
lost and confused souls to their destinations. [75] She not only makes
sure that a young woman, jilted and pregnant, is taken to a hospital
to receive proper care, but listens to an old woman talk of her past
glories and delivers four immigrant brides to their prospective husbands. She touches every phase of life from birth and youth to old
age and death, providing consolation and direction. Her relationship
with Mack Hale, a cynical, tough and unbending engineer much like
Bill in MAN'S CASTLE and Hennessey in MANNEQUIN is cast in the
traditional Borzage mold: her love "helps him outgrow the cynical
egotism and blind, hardheaded independence"[76] that not only blind
him to the suffering of others but that interfere with their relationship. The bridge whose construction he is supervising becomes a
symbol for the bridge to understanding that he crosses. Love here,
as in most other Borzage films, redeems those who find it. Lynn
learns not only to give "en masse" but to give intensively as well.
She finds a greater fulfillment through her relationship with Mack
and a greater "wholeness" in her life. Mack loses his cynicism and
exchanges his inflexibility for understanding. In one particularly symbolic scene, much like the "calling back" scenes of MAN'S CASTLE
(1933), DISPUTED PASSAGE (1939), and HIS BUTLER'S SISTER (1943),
Lynn sits over a wounded and unconscious Mack telling of her love.
Shortly after he revives, and while at first he refuses to accept the

importance of her job, since he sees those in need of help as misfits
while she sees life "in terms of human beings," he does admit his
love for her.   When they finally do unite it is because his perceptions
have changed, and he recognizes that her function of building with
people is as important as his function of building with steel.

At one point in the film Lynn upbraids Velma, a "society girl"
who is volunteering at the Traveler's Aid only to please her mother
and to be able to meet her "unacceptable" boyfriend without being
seen, for her lack of commitment and for her overall selfishness.
Unlike Lynn, whose own wealth is secondary to her work, Velma's
wealth allows her to live a useless and idle life.   Velma's self-
centeredness separates her from Lynn and acts in opposition to Lynn's
ideals.   This dual attitude toward the rich--Velma is as negative as
Lynn is positive--is a striking feature of a number of films of this
period and in some ways reflects an ambivalence that probably grew
out of Borzage's own poverty and his later rise.   Yet despite this
ambivalence Borzage experiments with the rich in these films much
as he did with the poor in other films.   While money is an important
narrative aspect of such films throughout his career as THE GUN
WOMAN (1918), THE Nth COMMANDMENT (1923), THE FIRST YEAR
(1926), STREET ANGEL (1928), SONG O' MY HEART (1930), LILIOM
(1930), BAD GIRL (1931), AFTER TOMORROW (1932), MAN'S CAS-
TLE (1933), LITTLE MAN, WHAT NOW? (1934), THE BIG CITY
(1937), THREE COMRADES (1938), and MANNEQUIN (1938), and
while the rich are found in such other films as SEVENTH HEAVEN
(1927), THEY HAD TO SEE PARIS (1929), and YOUNG AS YOU FEEL
(1931), neither is stressed as much as it is in the films to be discussed in this section.   And while these films are not as striking or
as powerful as some of the earlier efforts, they are important as
reflections of Borzagean ideals and beliefs.   LIVING ON VELVET
(1935), DESIRE (1936), and HISTORY IS MADE AT NIGHT (1937) may
lack the powerful visual and thematic qualities of some of the earlier
works, but they are important not only as "Borzage films" but as
seeming oddities made by Borzage during his most prolific period.

LIVING ON VELVET (1935) centers upon what essentially becomes the "rebirth" of Terry Parker after several years of drifting.
Having lost his parents and his sister in an air crash in which he
was the pilot, Terry believes that his survival was due to some divine error and that since then he has been living on borrowed time.
His continued fascination with airplanes reflects his aimless floating[77]
as well as his preoccupation with danger and death.   In contrast to
the view expressed in most other Borzage films, Terry's love for
Amy Prentiss alone cannot rejuvenate his soul.

Terry's relationship to both Amy Prentiss and Gibraltar Prit-
cham takes on some of the complexity of the relationships of the four
friends in THREE COMRADES.   Gibraltar, as his name implies, is
the rock on which Terry relies whenever he needs help.   He and
Amy, whom Gibraltar loves as well, act as Terry's symbolic parents
and work against his honest belief that "I had no right to live ... no
right to take advantage of a miracle."   These two struggle to revita-

lize his soul and to get him to stop giving "someone up there" another
chance to get him.

Terry meets Amy at a party that she is giving, and the two
immediately fall in love. The fluid movement of the camera reflects
this primary emotional smoothness, as do the words that the two exchange. When Terry and Gibraltar enter the camera pans slowly from
right to left. When Terry meets Amy the reverse occurs and reflects the changed direction that both of their lives are soon to take.
Terry and Amy walk, dance, exit right, onto the balcony and out of
the party ("The ideal time to leave any party is at the beginning").
Visually replacing Gibraltar by this parallel yet opposite action, Amy
soon after takes his place as emotional support as well. The lovers'
dialogue underscores Amy's intuitive understanding of Terry as well
as their unspoken love.

> Terry: "I'd like to say something ... something ... "
> Amy: "I know. It isn't necessary. "

Later, as they are isolated in a softly hazy medium close-up, the
darkness of the night surrounding them and isolating them, she clears
away the only obstacle in the way of their joining:

> Terry: "You're Gibraltar's Amy. "
> Amy: "Just Amy. "
> Terry: "He loves you. "
> Amy: "Not too much. "
> Terry: "You love him. "
> Amy: "Not enough. "

Gibraltar, later realizing what has happened, unselfishly and without
recrimination gives Amy up to Terry ("You're happy, that's all that
matters") as a father gives away a bride, accepting what he recognizes to be inevitable. Amy even takes his place in Terry's bathroom, holding Terry's robe as Gibraltar did. He later gives the
bride away at the wedding, again reinforcing his role as father. Only
Terry has second thoughts.

> Amy: "I love this Parker fellow. "
> Terry: "Gibraltar can give you everything. "
> Amy: "But I don't want anything. "
> Terry: "With Gibraltar you're sure of happiness. "
> Amy: "That depends on what you call happiness. "
> Terry: "I'm miserable. My life stopped two years ago.
>   You'll never know a minute's rest or a day's con-
>   tentment. "
> Amy: "Oh, it all sounds so wonderful. "
> Terry: "All right. Get your hat. "

Once married, Amy immediately takes on the role of mother
as well as that of wife. The two move into a Long Island cottage
owned by Gibraltar, this image being an extension of the separation-
of-the-lovers idea in general, as well as of the garret homes of the

lovers in both SEVENTH HEAVEN and LITTLE MAN, WHAT NOW?
and the shanty of the lovers in MAN'S CASTLE in particular. As
Amy fixes things up she directs Terry away from the useless task
of polishing pantry knobs and tells him to get the electricity turned
on and to get a telephone. She also asks him to shop for bread and
salt, symbols of domestic happiness and love. Instead of these es-
sentials he brings only romantic luxuries like shrimp, pâté, caviar,
and anchovies and completely forgets the rest of his errands. Terry
is as dependent as a child, a creature of whim and fancy with an extremely short attention span. Amy, the realist, directs his actions
and continually attempts to move him forward and into responsible
adulthood.

When, at Amy's prodding, Terry goes to the train station the
next morning so that he can go to the city to look for a job, he and
Amy watch and copy the actions of the other husbands and wives.
Attempting to fit into the societal mainstream, they adopt the outward forms of their immediate social sphere. Yet this is immediately undercut by Terry's basic inability to join in this world until
he exorcizes his demons: he joins the other men on the train in a
bridge game even though he does not know how to play, and when he
returns home that evening he still has no job and has squandered
whatever money he did have on a dachshund. Two visual images
that immediately follow point up the increasing failure of Amy and
Terry's adult relationship. When Terry returns home he sits on the
floor between the chairs of Amy and of Gibraltar, who has come for a
visit. Again his place as child is emphasized. Also, it is at this
moment that he hears the sound of a plane outside and rushes out to
see it. The plane, as a tie to his haunting past and his notion of
his own doom, continues to have a hold on him that is much stronger
than that of Amy's love. This undercuts the hope that Amy can reform him ("for himself more than me") and it is at this point that
she decides that she will give Terry up if she fails. The scene that
follows reinforces this. Again arriving home late and without a job
or an explanation, Terry berates himself for being outside of the
mainstream and for being "on the wrong side of the road ... on the
outside looking in. " He sits dejectedly and alone on the stairs as
Amy exits to her room.

Their growing emotional rift is halted temporarily when Terry
receives a return on an earlier worthless investment that is really
a gift from Gibraltar. Yet their continued differences are apparent:
Amy wishes to use the money to redo the house while Terry wants
to buy "rugs from Damascus ... spices from India ... and there's
something I must get for myself. " That something is an airplane.
This becomes, for Amy, the final sign or recognition of her failure,
and, berating his general attitude and his selfishness for the first
time, she leaves him.

> "This attitude of yours toward life, this contempt you have
> for people in the world, all this dashing around of yours,
> all the flying about, the unhappiness, the unrest mean just
> one thing--there's a void in your life, a distinct and ter-

rible void. I thought that when I married you I could fill
that void. I thought I could take what was wrong with you
and right it, but I haven't. I've failed. I haven't cured
you of your trouble; I haven't righted what was wrong with
you. Why I haven't even made you happy ... really....
Please, Terry, don't talk. Don't even touch me. "

Love alone is not enough to "cure" Terry nor is it enough for
Amy. After the two confront each other once again and Terry tells
Amy that her desire to get inside his brain and heart is unreason-
able, Amy returns to the city. Her dream defeated, she returns to
her former reality. Yet Amy is still unhappy and decides to live
Terry's way, to "live on velvet" and not lose "one precious moment. "
Surrounded by adoring men, she attempts to forget the past and the
future. Her reverie is interrupted, however, by a phone call. In-
tuiting that something has happened to Terry, she learns that he has
been in an auto accident. Once again he miraculously escapes death.
This deus ex machina serves to resolve the drama quickly. Amy
confesses her love and her willingness to change for him if only he
will live. In the final scene Terry, now recuperated, offers to set
her free:

Terry: "Amy, there's something I've been saving to tell
           you at this moment. You've been a grand nurse
           and certainly a grand companion, but the job's
           over. You're free, Amy. "
Amy: "But I don't want to be free. Freedom's over-
           rated. "
Terry: "You mean that darling? Do you?"
Amy: "Yes, Terry. "
Terry: "As I lay on the ground that night looking up at
           you, I realized that I wanted you more than any-
           thing else. "
Amy: "As you lay on the ground that night, Terry, I
           told you that I loved you more than anything else.
           I said it then and I say it now. Do whatever you
           like, be whatever you want to be. I want you. I
           love you. "
Terry: "If you love me you'll stop talking about a Terry
           Parker that doesn't exist anymore. "

The two then look up at heaven and at the statue of General Sherman
they walked to when they first met. Amy echoes an earlier line of
Terry's ("Love, General, something I learned from an old Indian
chief whom I befriended as he lay dying in the Black Hills of South
Dakota") as the camera pulls back and up in an ascending crane.
Terry and Amy have become a single spiritual unit. Their repetition of each other's words reinforces this as do the religious implications of the dialogue just quoted ("As I lay ... "). This last shot,
like those of MAN'S CASTLE and THREE COMRADES, adds a spiritual level to their regeneration and echoes their transcendence into
a sphere of greater spirituality, understanding, and love.

LIVING ON VELVET reflects a change in Borzage's work.
While in many ways a throwback to earlier films, both thematically
in its portrayal of women as multifaceted in importance and visually
in its final shot, it also foretells a stylistic change that will be especially important in later films. Terry, unlike other Borzage "heroes, " never conceives of himself as "whole, " recognizing his internal fragmentation throughout. Furthermore, Amy and Terry are continually attempting to fit in and join society and not to move into a
sphere solely inhabited by themselves. Only when Terry finally and
unsatisfactorily settles his past does he move into adulthood and,
therefore, out of the past and into the present. Until the last scenes
of the film Amy and Terry's relationship fails because Terry cannot
face the present or the future and cannot give anything of himself to
someone else. The love of these two is not a mutual love of equals
but more a mother-son love, a fact recognized especially in Terry's
inability to act on his own initiative. Even at the end, when Amy
nurses him back to both an emotional and physical health, their problems remain unsettled.

There is a complexity to this film that does not appear at first
viewing. And while the ending "cleans things up" satisfactorily, Terry's
cure is too quick and Amy's denial of herself too out of character.
The ending's simplicity belies the complexity of what has occurred
throughout. Despite Amy's words, love is not enough in this case.
Terry, predating many of Borzage's later and more neurotic characters, must redeem himself. [78] This is unsatisfying here because the
car accident succeeds without reason where numerous air crashes
failed.

While LIVING ON VELVET structurally resembles MAN'S CAS-
TLE, unlike this earlier film events in the narrative do not grow out
of each other. The strength of Amy's leaving, unlike Bill's in the
earlier film, is undercut by her externally motivated return. She is
not "called back" like Bill, nor does she return freely. Amy's return is a negation of individuality and serves to make her not so much
interdependent with, as dependent upon Terry. At the finish of the
film the two are not really interdependent at all and do not, together,
create a new whole. They are each dependent on each other in an
unhealthy way. Their words cannot negate this, nor can Amy's pro-
testation against freedom. The film fails in its ending much as some
of Borzage's earlier 1929-1931 sound films did and as DESIRE does
later.

Similar to LIVING ON VELVET in emphasis, yet far more a
sophisticated comedy than a spiritual drama, is DESIRE. Filmed under the aegis of Ernst Lubitsch, the head of production at Paramount,
the film is less in the Borzage mold than in the Lubitsch tradition of
sexual innuendo and verbal and visual wit. While it is marked by a
noticeable degree of Borzagean sentimentality, the film is closer to
a Lubitsch film like TROUBLE IN PARADISE (1932). What makes
this something of a Borzage film is the use of romantic close-ups to
"personalize" the action, in contrast to the depersonalization of the
long shots and the soft focus often applied at important moments. [79]

The Lubitsch touches are recognizable not only in the general atmosphere and in the sexual undertones of the film but in the antagonism/
joining nature of the plot. Early in the action Madeleine's car, an
all-white limousine that matches her all-white outfit, is tapped by
Tom's. Later the two race their cars along French and Spanish
highways. Both events "suggest the characters' sexual antagonism
and attraction. "[80]

Madeleine is continually hiding her "true self" from Tom,
thereby fighting off not only what she feels for him but her eventual
reformation and redemption as well. This "charade" motif begins
early in the film and continues throughout. Madeleine is first viewed
in soft close-up, her face hidden behind a white veil. Later, when
she is trying on a rope of pearls, we see her face through a mirror
only. Her scheme for stealing the pearls demands that she first pose
as the wife of the psychiatrist Pauquet and later as the wife of the
jeweler Duval. In much the same manner, throughout the latter portion of the film she refuses to admit her love for Tom, hiding her
emotions behind a cool exterior, while earlier she pretended to love
him while she didn't. [81] Shots of Madeleine and Tom together are
often broken by interrupting lines, such as a car window or the bar
of a piano, and it is only during the latter portion of the film that
the two are framed together without obstruction. Unlike that of Carlos, the master thief, Madeleine's avarice is only skin deep. It is
the reality that Tom offers and not the illusion of reality that Carlos
provides to which Madeleine finally succumbs. At the end of the film
she leaves her castle in Spain and joins middle-class society, which
is Tom's reality, as the wife of an automotive engineer in Detroit.

The denouement and resolution amount to not only a post-
Production Code confession-apology-redemption scheme, but, as in
THEY HAD TO SEE PARIS, European sophistication and mores are
overwhelmed by American pragmatism and moralism. Madeleine is
"beaten" by Tom, chastened and made repentant. She returns the
necklace to Duval, and Duval and Pauquet stand as witnesses while
Madeleine and Tom are married. Marriage becomes Madeleine's
"sentence, " and she is paroled in Tom's care.

Madeleine's change is not due to a transcendence but a chas-
tisement and a realization of the "error of her ways. " Tom's hard-
nosed persistence defeats her as much as her own weakness of failing to be as cold and unfeeling as Carlos. Importantly and symbolically, these two come off of the mountain and join the "real" world
of working people at the end of the film. While Madeleine does grow
out of her immediate world, Tom is simply returning to his. The
game is over and Tom is the winner. Morality does not defeat Madeleine's immorality nor does good defeat evil. Although Madeleine
is reformed, there is no sense of any great moral awakening. Romantic love, in contrast to the transcendent kind, simply breaks down
her defenses.

Few moments in the film make it a recognizable example of
Borzage's work, and while the film overflows with sophisticated charm

it often lacks feeling.   The dinner scene in which Tom and Madeleine
are framed between two candles is perhaps the best example of Borzagean visuals, and the belief that Tom will forgive--something Aunt
Olga, another member of Carlos's jewel ring, didn't accept in a similar situation forty years before--and that love will soothe and unite
does reflect a degree of Borzagean idealism.   There is a lack of
"humanism" in this film that makes it more a romantic and comic
work than a work of melodrama.   Yet the film is important not so
much in itself as in its influence upon a Borzage film of the following
year, HISTORY IS MADE AT NIGHT.   This latter film plays upon
both thematic and narrative conventions found within DESIRE: Irene
Vail, like Tom, is a Midwesterner, and both fall in love with Euro-
peans whom they bring to America.   This later film is tied visually
and thematically to more recognizable works as well.   Influenced by
DESIRE, HISTORY IS MADE AT NIGHT synthesizes sophistication and
feeling in a way that DESIRE does not.

        HISTORY IS MADE AT NIGHT is Borzage's most sophiscated
romantic film.   Filled with softly lit close-ups, it evokes a sense of
romanticism unparalleled in any other Borzage work.   While Michael
Mahern sees it as "a shameless pastiche of thirties romantic and melodramatic clichés,"[82] the romantic atmosphere created by Borzage
works so well that the viewer often forgets the number of narrative
discontinuities.   Unlike most of his earlier works, this film lacks
the sense of social adversity that is suffered by the truly "lower
class" characters found in SEVENTH HEAVEN, STREET ANGEL,
MAN'S CASTLE, and MANNEQUIN. [83] Yet Irene and Paul still inhabit a world that is hostile to their emotions.   And even though they
exist in the social sphere inhabited by the rich, they exist in an emotional sphere much like that of other Borzage couples.   Just as in
earlier films poverty becomes an obstacle to happiness, in this film
money, as personified in Bruce Vail, becomes perverted into a negative power that separates the lovers.   The "pairing" structure of the
plot, in which scenes of Irene are bracketed first by scenes of Paul
and then by contrasting scenes of Bruce, emphasizes the strength of
this perversion in the same manner that the camera acts to undercut
Bill's bravado in MAN'S CASTLE.   Furthermore, true to the structural form of many romantic comedies of the 1930s, such as IT HAP-
PENNED ONE NIGHT (1934), HOLIDAY (1938), and NINOTCHKA (1939),
the eliciting of the truth during the final scenes of the film allows the
final and unobstructed union of the lovers to occur.   True to the thematic and structural form of other Borzage films, however, the main
characters not only "come together" at the end but they transcend
their immediate world, their union becoming one of spirit more than
one of body.

        Married to a wealthy expatriate American, Irene Vail--the
name takes on a great deal of significance in the course of the film--
is an American girl from Kansas who leaves her husband because of
his insane jealousy.   Her husband, Bruce, decides to discredit the
divorce she seeks by staging an incident in which a "lover" is found
in her room the night before the decree becomes final--thus not only
nullifying the divorce but making sure that she is never able to ob-

tain another one.   When her husband's chauffeur forces his way into
her apartment at the Hotel Triumph--only at first is the name ironic--
and stages the scene, Paul overhears the commotion and enters to
save Irene.   Visually, Paul is placed in the shadows with a hat pulled
down over his eyes, thereby covering his face and, symbolically, his
motivations.   To protect Irene he pretends to be a jewel thief and
"kidnaps" her.

Once in a cab Paul explains why he did what he did and returns her jewels just as he symbolically gives her back her identity
as well.   The two then go out for some champagne at the Chateau
Bleu.   They are the only guests present in this fantasy world, and
Paul draws a puppet ("Coco") on his hand who "asks" all of the questions that Paul cannot ("Why are you married?"; "What made your
husband do that to you tonight?").   Refusing to reveal herself, Irene
directs "Coco" to tell Paul to "ask me to dance."   What follows is,
perhaps, the most overtly romantic scene of any Borzage film.   Seen
from a high-angle level that acts to isolate the two within the frame,
Paul and Irene tango.   Like Cinderella, Irene's slippers continually
slip off, and Paul, her prince, replaces them.   Finally she tosses
both of them off and dances barefoot.   In the next shot the camera
tracks past Irene's discarded shoes and the fallen mink cape that she
clutched protectively around her neck earlier and follows Irene's naked feet, "around which her lace nightgown swirls."[84]   While her
identity is still a mystery to Paul, she unspeakingly reveals more of
herself to him than she ever had to Bruce.   This one scene fashions
their love affair into a fairy-tale mode, an idea used again in MOON-
RISE (1949) when Danny takes Gilly to the deserted plantation.   Their
happiness is undercut by Bruce's decision to kill the chauffeur whom
Paul knocked out.   In blaming Paul, whom he believes to be Irene's
lover, he hopes to be able to keep her for himself.   The tie between
the scenes is strengthened by the song "Tango of Love" ("I Get Ideas"),
which both Paul and Irene dance to and which is an indirect reference
to Bruce's jealousy and his plan.   This scene does not, however,
lessen the truth or the importance of Irene's next statement, "Tonight
is what I've waited for."   Exiting from the darkness that foreshadows
the danger that follows, she leaves her romantic haze at dawn and
returns to the reality of her apartment only to find both Bruce and
the police there.   Shocked into an immediate reality, she agrees to
go away with Bruce so as to save Paul from arrest, the rope of
pearls Paul returned giving Bruce his clue to the "truth" and becoming symbolic of a noose.

The film begins to fall into a melodramatic rather than simply
romantic form and pattern.   Yet the ethereal aspect remains.   Asked
by his friend Césare if he has known Irene for long, Paul replies,
"Forever," thereby expressing the timelessness of their love.   Learning of her departure through a newspaper story, he calls her ship-to-
shore.   While during their first meeting she was in white, she is now
in silver.   Throughout the film she wears white or some derivative
of it whenever she is with Paul in contrast to the black outfits she
wears during her scenes with Bruce.   During this scene she moves
out of the shadows and into the light as she speaks with Paul, telling

History Is Made at Night

him that she left Paris because of her love for him, and that she can
never see him again.   This scene is closely followed by a confrontation with Bruce, who enters and attempts to seduce Irene, offering
her a second honeymoon and a new start.   When she refuses his caress turns into a stranglehold.   Her emotions released by the phone
call and by this act, she confesses to Bruce that she would "give my
soul" to be with Paul and informs him that it was his jealousy that
allowed her to find Paul.   This scene is paired with one that follows,
in which Paul, "feeling" that Irene is in trouble without being told,

decides to follow her to New York. Their communication becomes a
thing of intuition, unbounded and unhampered by distance. Paul and
Césare, the chef at the Chateau Bleu, together go off to find Irene.

Irene, like Jessie in MANNEQUIN, uses her looks to escape
from her present situation. She, too, leaves her husband and gets a
job modeling clothes. Paul, now in New York, gets a job at (the
significantly named) Victor's, the swankiest restaurant in the city.
The two are separated only physically by Bruce and the power he represents. Although she has walked out on Bruce, Irene cannot break
from him completely. Circumstances intervene and force her to be
reconciled with him once more. Calling her into his office, he shows
her a portrait of her that he commissioned. The portrait, much like
the painting of Angela in STREET ANGEL, represents what is within
Irene and what only Paul can understand. In it she is dressed in a
white flowing gown much like the nightgown of the earlier scenes, with
the artistic equivalent of soft focus around her face. This is the only
way that Bruce can possess Irene, yet this is the possession of an
image alone. Bruce owns the portrait and nothing more. Within the
film frame Irene is placed on the right, dressed in a black suit and
completely separated both emotionally and spiritually from the man
she now hates. She returns to him only because she desires to protect Paul. A man has been arrested by the French police for the
chauffeur's murder, and Irene believes him to be Paul. To save Paul
she will sacrifice herself and her own happiness by staying with Bruce.

To "celebrate" the two go to Victor's for dinner; Irene, again
dressed in black, finds Paul there and laughs. She returns alone to
the restaurant later that night to explain to Paul that she wasn't laughing because he was a headwaiter but out of relief at finding him safe.
Irene stands at the top right of the frame, a curved wall acting as a
bridge to Paul, seated in the lower left corner. This distance, the
greatest possible within the frame, is symbolic of both their physical
separation and of their superficial spiritual separation. The wall becomes representative of their deep spiritual connection and love. Irene
crosses through the darkness and over the distance to Paul, implying
their eventual reunification even before it is actually realized. [85]

In the scene that follows the two play at being married. She
is now wearing a white apron and cooking him dinner. Later, during
the walk through the park, she wears his pale topcoat. This scene
acts as if to negate the physical time that has passed and the separation since they first met. Its importance is underscored by the fact
that the two were to have met at a Parisian park the day that Irene
was forced to leave for America with Bruce. The two cannot, however, escape reality, and "their romance can't exist apart from the
world." [86] Before they can run away to Tahiti (which has the same
dream and Edenic implications that South America does in THREE
COMRADES) they must, Paul decides, return to France and clear the
innocent man arrested for Paul's "crime." Echoing something implied
in Angela's "last supper" actions in STREET ANGEL, Irene pleads
with Paul not to "let them take tomorrow from us," not realizing that
what they share can never be taken from them.

On the ship returning to France we learn from Bruce that Paul
has confessed to the newspapers but that he will probably never be
convicted of the crime since, in effect, he was defending a woman's
honor. Realizing that he can never win Irene back now, Bruce orders the captain of the ship, which he himself had built and named,
ironically, the Princess Irene, to break the over-the-North-Pole record, knowing that the waters are full of icebergs. The ship becomes
a microcosm of the chaotic world in which these two exist. [87] Moving through a heavy fog much like that which engulfs Gino and Angela
during the final sequence of STREET ANGEL and out of which Otto
arrives with Jaffe in THREE COMRADES, a continually moaning foghorn, like the cuckoo in THREE COMRADES, forebodes both the inexorable passage of time and the increasing danger. As the ship
moves deeper and deeper into the fog, and as the foghorn sounds become more and more ominous, Irene and Paul draw closer and closer together. At one point Irene stands alone in the fog crying. Paul
enters her frame and comforts her, telling her once again to "think
only of today" and to make the fullest of every moment that they can
share. Even though neither knows that Paul will probably never be
convicted of his "crime," it is Paul who has an ultimate faith in their
love and, though he does not admit it, in the future. Even a re-
enacting of their first meeting, complete with the same meal and the
same music, fails to draw Irene out of her despondency. Once again
she leans on his shoulder and cries.

Disaster finally arrives when the ship strikes an iceberg. A
panic ensues, representative of the chaotic outside world, as passen-
gers scatter to lifeboats, bells and whistles sound, and the ship is
abandoned. Paul saves Irene, bringing her out of her cabin and placing her in a lifeboat. She refuses his aid and escapes. While all
of this occurs there is a cut to Bruce listening to the news of the
disaster and the report that few, if any, will survive. He exits into
his office, writes out a confession to the Paris police, and shoots
himself before an "altar" of Irene's portrait. This portrait, depicting Irene in black, corresponds to the clothing/color motif used throughout the film and, further, corresponds to the pairing structure discussed earlier. The first portrait (the dream image of Irene in white)
is hanging on the Princess Irene liner, now, significantly, the lovers'
domain. This scene has much the same effect as one of the final
scenes in STREET ANGEL. In the film as moral drama, Bruce, the
representative of evil, is destroyed. In turn, good prevails, at least
for the present.

At this point there is a cut back to the ship (thus preserving
the pairing structure), where Paul and Irene, in their own separated
world, sit on a stairway above the noise and movement of the deck
area. They capture all possible emotion and knowledge in these few
moments and create an eternity. "At a loss to express their love,
they simply gaze into each others' eyes and babble about their respective youths. "[88] The "conversion" that occurs, while "disjointed
and nonsensical, "[89] is expressed in their looks and, especially, in
their eyes. Their souls now fully opened to one another, they are
finally and fully joined. The spirituality of the moment is further

echoed by the hymn ("Nearer My God to Thee") that rises around
them. It is at this point that a disembodied voice announces that the
ship will not sink.

> The miracle that follows when the ship suddenly stops sink-
> ing is generated not by the intensity of the lovers, nor even
> by the collective good will of the ship. The ending simply
> asserts that the forces of evil lack total power. They can
> disrupt the world, but can never destroy it. There will al-
> ways be some force to divert man from a direct collision
> with destruction. The Devil may be at hand, but with God
> lies destiny. [90]

Separated by the fog and by their position physically above the others,
Paul and Irene move into a world of their own. While their love defeats the immediate evil that surrounds it, it does not destroy evil
entirely. In the film's melodramatic structure evil is destroyed only
temporarily and is destined to rise again. The question is not one
of final defeat or victory but of momentary advantage.

Irene struggles to find her identity in this film much as Terry
does in LIVING ON VELVET and as Madeleine is forced to do in
DESIRE. Within this film, however, Irene consciously desires and
acts to free herself from money, and by extension, the evil it em-
powers in her attempt to free herself from Bruce and from his power. When she "loses" her mink cape and slippers in the opening
dance scene at the Chateau Bleu with Paul she "loses" the immediate
emotional hold that Bruce and his money have over her. She finds
both romantic and spiritual love with a poor headwaiter. Her growing lack of interest in wealth reflects the growth taking place within
herself. Love gives her the means to realize her own strength and,
in doing so, to give up her present and to seek the future. This occurs in the two other films discussed in this section as well. Although the final car accident in LIVING ON VELVET is in essence a
deus ex machina, it does allow both Terry and Amy to realize the
strength and the importance of their love. In DESIRE love overrules
Madeleine's desire for "things" and allows her soul to open up to
Tom and to what he offers.

In their overwhelming reactions against money and all that it
represents, however, these films lack much of the power that is evident in many of the films whose stories grow out of poverty or out
of some greater emotional deprivation or despair. Without these aspects the films, particularly in their endings, while interesting, lack
the emotional power of the other works. Borzage only gets close to
the feeling of his earlier films in HISTORY IS MADE AT NIGHT. In
this film spatially fixed bonds are broken down and the characters
develop a strongly intuitive and spiritual relationship and communication. The final moments of the other two films suffer from a basic
problem found in Borzage's early sound films, in that the endings do
not sufficiently grow out of the events of the narratives and so lack
conviction. The cohesiveness of HISTORY IS MADE AT NIGHT is in
one respect due to an increasingly overt movement into mysticism

that overrides many of the melodramatic plot elements. This mysticism will be discussed in greater detail in the section that follows.
The mysticism we find in this film grows out of the mystical elements
of such earlier works as SEVENTH HEAVEN, STREET ANGEL, and
SHIPMATES FOREVER, and is more fully developed in the films that
Borzage directed between 1937 and 1940 in particular, and that influenced some of his later work, such as HIS BUTLER'S SISTER (1943)
and I'VE ALWAYS LOVED YOU (1946) as well.

Part Four: Mysticism and Conversion

> The positive optimism of Borzage's work as a whole rests
> on a deeply felt belief in love as a redemptive force. In
> film after film, he presents a couple, reveals that one or
> both have fallen (in the Miltonic sense of the word) into
> seemingly incurable melancholia, bitterness or despair,
> then oversees his characters' restoration to an edenic state
> of innocence through the purity of their love.... The ther-
> apeutic and redemptive nature of Borzage's love relation-
> ships gives his films a quasi-religious quality. As a re-
> sult, though his early films are primarily romantic in out-
> look many of them contain religious elements. 91

The religious and spiritual elements of Borzage's narrative
are reinforced by lighting and visual techniques, most often in close-
up. In the latter half of the thirties, however, this religious bent
becomes increasingly central, and the films themselves become spiritual in a more overtly religious sense. What is stressed is less some
central love relationship than "a more general concern for the spiritual well-being of not only his [Borzage's] lovers but other characters
around them."92 The salvation of the characters is not so much
through love, but through their conversion to a spiritual system. 93
Love becomes important less for itself than for the greater insight
and sense of divinity that it provides. Love becomes the result or
representative of spiritual transcendence more than the actual object
of achievement.

This overtly mystical pattern is seen most clearly in four
films directed by Borzage between 1937 and 1940: GREEN LIGHT
(1937), THE SHINING HOUR (1938), DISPUTED PASSAGE (1939), and
STRANGE CARGO (1940). It is also an important aspect of THREE
COMRADES (1938), especially in the ending, in which the relationship
of the four, two living and two dead, moves beyond time and space
and into eternity.

Throughout Borzage's earlier films the transcendence of the
individual or of the couple out of the immediate world and into a
quasireligious one of spiritual understanding is an important thematic
and visual element. In a film as early as SECRETS (1924) an aging
woman "calls" her husband back to life. In SEVENTH HEAVEN (1927)

a religious miracle brings Chico back to Diane as if from the dead.
In MAN'S CASTLE (1933) the birth of a child due at Christmas takes
on immense Christian symbolism. NO GREATER GLORY (1934) "uses"
an individual as the means of conversion for a group. Nemescek's
death becomes a redemptive action for the group, uniting the opposing
street gangs behind the body of the fallen boy and his grieving mother.
This film in its emphasis on group conversion foreshadows these later
films, as does the conversion that occurs in SHIPMATES FOREVER
(1935). This latter film reverses the conversion idea: Richard Melville III is converted from his apathy and atheism, becoming a "be-
liever" after the sacrifice of seaman Lawrence.

 Entering the naval academy at Annapolis on a dare, crooner
Melville constantly finds himself in opposition to the rest of the ca-
dets. Refusing to give his heart as well as his mind to the service,
he continually finds himself separated from the cadet group of which
he is at least nominally a part. He lives alone and studies alone,
refusing to accept or give help. His only emotional tie is to June
Blackburn, the woman he loves. Their relationship (visually similar
to that of Terry and Amy in LIVING ON VELVET in their meeting,
in particular, which follows the same pattern as that of the earlier
couple in its immediacy and its right-to-left and reverse movement)
is the only one that Melville upholds; he is cut off from his father,
Admiral Melville, head of the academy, by his obstinately anti-Navy
bias and by his lack of commitment. Playing upon an earlier "service" film, FLIRTATION WALK (1934), which is more a male love
story than a strict male-female romance, the love of the couple is
placed secondary to the idea of the group. Melville's conversion is
not due to his love for June nor to any lesson his father teaches him.

 Melville sings the once-rousing song "Shipmates Forever" that
he has written almost as a hymn, surrounded by his comrades and
tied to them spiritually and emotionally for the first time while prac-
ticing aboard ship. This is the first clue to his changing attitude.
His conversion comes only through the boiler-room fire that purges
Melville of his doubts and imbues him with belief and commitment.
Cadet Lawrence runs into the boiler room to shut off the oil
flow and so save the ship from exploding. While attempting to do
so he collapses. Melville realizes that Lawrence is in there and goes
into the inferno to help him. Shutting off the oil, he drags Lawrence
and himself out. Both are so badly burned that their identities cannot be distinguished ("the scalding and fire made them alike"). The
two have become one, Melville identified only by his naval academy
ring. Lawrence's death allows for Melville's emotional and spiritual
rebirth. Lawrence, like Christ, dies so that another may be reborn
and may join the group. Completely bandaged, like Judy at the end
of THE SHINING HOUR, Melville realizes this, and a reconciliation
with his classmates and with his father ensues. He is welcomed into
the group ("we want you back"), and, when he finally leaves the hospital, is hugged by the men and visually integrated within the group,
his central position no longer one of opposition but of emotional centrality. Later, standing before Lawrence's grave with tears in his
eyes (another parallel, since Lawrence cried when he heard the hymn-

Shipmates Forever

like singing of "Shipmates Forever" earlier), he pays silent tribute
to his "brother," the grave before him reinforcing the idea of Lawrence's sacrifice, and the sea beyond him, Melville's rebirth.

Like Otto's conversion at the end of THE MORTAL STORM,
the actions and sacrifice of Lawrence, representative of the group
spirit, act to convert the individual in a religious or spiritual sense
to the ideals of the group. The love relationship of June and Melville is subordinate to Melville's relationship with the group. In the
films of the later thirties this situation is somewhat reversed, and it is
an individual who, after going through some great ordeal, is not only
converted but converts the group as well. This pattern, played upon
in the group conversion of THREE COMRADES, holds true for all of
the films that will be dealt with in this section.

In a discussion of GREEN LIGHT (1937) mention should be
made of the earlier DOCTORS' WIVES (1931) and the later DISPUTED
PASSAGE (1939), films that deal with the "gradual conversions of
agnostic doctors to a belief in something outside of themselves, to
a discovery that, through sacrifice, they can become part of a redemptive spiritual system."[94] The men of science, Judson Penning,
Newell Paige, and John Beaven, come to understand that scientific
rationality is secondary to a universal faith[95] and that a life lived
only according to rational principle negates the possibility for both
understanding and human contact. It is not so much science that is

"wrong" but the absolute devotion to empiricism that is dangerous. Furthermore, in both of these films, the conversion of the central character leads to the bedside regeneration and purification of all of those who exist around them and within their physical and spiritual sphere.

One of Borzage's "transitional" films, DOCTORS' WIVES (1931), is centered on somewhat the same conflict as both GREEN LIGHT and DISPUTED PASSAGE: the devotion to science rather than humanism and love. DOCTORS' WIVES is the story of Dr. Judson Penning and his wife, Nina Wyndram. In traditional Borzage fashion, and much like the opening of STREET ANGEL in particular, the two meet at a scene of tragedy. Nina's father, shot against the white bedsheets to give him a spiritual look, is dying. Going for help and entering what appears to be an empty cab, she meets Penning, explains her situation and takes him to her home. Penning, with her when her father dies, eventually takes her father's place as the center of her life, even calling her "Lamb," an allusion to her innocence, as her father did.

Nina gets a job in Penning's lab, where she feminizes the surroundings with flowers and pines away at Penning's failure to notice her. Berating a lab monkey for this same offense, she is overheard by Penning and is asked out to dinner. As in LIVING ON VELVET and SHIPMATES FOREVER, it is during this first date that the two fall in love. Penning proposes to Nina, who is dressed in white and carrying white flowers. Yet her commitment is undercut both by her childish-look and by her answer to his proposal ("You'll make a divine playmate"). Since she fails to realize what she must give up, Nina's offer to help him to become a great doctor after he confesses that he feels himself to be only a "society doctor," catering to rich patients' silly ills, becomes more a child's dream and a game. On their honeymoon their passion is interrupted by a call from a sick patient. Penning's commitment to his work is continually placed in conflict with Nina's romantic desires. Her life, as she says, eventually settles into a routine of "killing time waiting for Jude."

Nina's position as child as well as her attractiveness are reinforced when we meet Penning's colleague and friend, Karl Ruyter. Ruyter, who calls Nina "little girl" at their first meeting, is a career researcher who exists totally alone, sharing his life and emotions with no one. Yet Ruyter is fascinated by Nina, allowing her into his "sanctum sanctorum," his lab, and she is fascinated and impressed by his selflessness. Ruyter confesses that he would give up everything for one thing only--the "sincere love of a beautiful woman"-- implying that empiricism and humanism cannot exist together in his universe.

As the narrative progresses Nina loses patience with Jude's devotion to work and duty, seeing Ruyter as "a blessing ... comfort, solace and refuge." Ruyter finally admits his love for her, warning her that there is "death and destruction in it." She finally leaves Penning during a party, dressed in black for the first and only time, and drives off alone.

The Ruyter-Penning conflict arises when Penning finally recognizes Ruyter's love for Nina after Ruyter allows Nina to visit his
lab.   After the two later confront each other Ruyter sacrifices himself and his happiness by attempting to commit suicide.   Penning
reads about it while at Good Samaritan Hospital, the place where Nina
becomes a nurse, her nun-like devotion making her now feel "useful
[and] happy." Penning operates on Ruyter, giving him the few weeks
more of life Ruyter requested to help others.

Nina and Penning reunite after this, Nina entering into actual
adulthood.   When the two return home they are again interrupted by
a phone call.   Understanding her new role and secondary status, Nina
announces herself as "the doctor's wife," becoming a part of Jude,
inseparable and without an individual identity.   With her transformation complete, her rite of passage achieved, Penning once again messes
her hair and calls her "wonderful."

For all of its chauvinism, DOCTORS' WIVES sets up the para-
digm for the conflicts developed in both of the later "doctor" films.
Although here the emphasis is on Nina's "conversion," which is reflected in her nun-like nurse's garb, the other films center on the
changes that occur within the doctors themselves.   Nina learns the
importance of her husband's work and learns to accept her secondary
place within his universe.   Penning, at first a mere society doctor,
learns to give himself to greater things as well.   His contrast to
Ruyter is obvious: Ruyter represents true scientific research and
commitment to an empiricism that becomes humanitarianism.   His
sacrifice takes on Christ-like aspects.   He gives himself to death
for the sins of Penning and so that Penning can change and win back
Nina.   Penning's operation on Ruyter is an act of tremendous significance because it follows their confrontation.   Penning goes beyond
petty feeling and acts to save something greater.   In doing so he
takes on the aspects of Ruyter that he lacked and becomes whole,
since he now embodies not only humanism, in his ability to love,
but empiricism, in his devotion to science.   He becomes in essence
the "whole man," as Nina becomes the "whole woman."   Their love
and joint devotion to scientific duty make them interdependent and,
therefore, one.   They cannot exist as wholes if they are apart, and
at the end of the film, this is recognized and accepted subconscious-
ly by both.   Penning wins Nina back as a wife and companion and
less as a daughter, since she has lost her naive innocence.   Not
only have they changed, therefore, but their relationship has changed
as well.   Although not one of the equals, neither is it any longer
one of father and daughter.

The conflict in this film between science and love is settled
not so much by a "spiritualization" that occurs within Penning alone
as by this fact coupled with a conversion within Nina.   In the later
films a singular and important shift occurs: the conversion is strongly centered within the doctor himself due to his own conflicts and is
much more strongly developed.   Both Newell Paige and John Beaven,
changed by circumstances, move toward an understanding of devotion
and duty.   Love is only one element of their conversion.   The doc-

tors in these later films are converted from their entire way of being, their belief system being changed in the process.

This is a subtle shift in Borzagean attitudes, since all of the
previous elements of transcendence are present. Yet in these later
films, beginning with SHIPMATES FOREVER, it is more a conversion than a simple transcendence. Transcendence and conversion,
like Borzage's images, are both multifaceted terms. Whereas transcendence arises out of a natural growth pattern, conversion arises
out of some individual crisis of belief. DOCTORS' WIVES predates
the conversion films. Although Judson Penning does indeed undergo
a conversion, becoming a doctor devoted to working for others, his
conversion is overshadowed by the change that occurs in his wife.
Nina, while understanding Penning's devotion to duty by the end of
the film, subordinates herself completely as Penning's wife and loses
the individuality that conversion figures again. Furthermore, conversion implies a more overt acceptance of a part within a new belief
system, whereas no such decision occurs in the transcendence films.
A complete change occurs in Melville, Paige, Beaven, and the full
groups of characters in both THE SHINING HOUR and STRANGE CAR-
GO. This change is due to more than the recognition and acceptance
of love as a romantic and spiritual bond and goes beyond the newly
found interdependence of the couple or the group. The change is subtle, and the "conversion" films do not completely replace those that
center upon transcendence. The two themes work together: conversion necessitates transcendence in that it requires an internal awakening and change just as transcendence necessitates conversion to
some other belief or belief system. Yet the different emphases do
exist, and the two strains have a tremendous effect upon the later,
post-1942 films, especially MOONRISE (1949).

GREEN LIGHT (1937) plays upon much of the science and humanism conflict central to DOCTORS' WIVES. The story centers on
Newell Paige and the rite of passage that he undergoes. The film
opens with a high-angle long shot of a busy street and moves to a
close-up of Paige's car and to Paige himself. There is then a return to a view of the larger area and of the traffic jam created by
Paige's conversation with a policeman. This opening parallels the
structure of the film itself in its movement from the group situation
of the hospital to one concerning the individual experience and the
individual's regeneration before returning to a larger group regeneration and conversion.

Paige is an excellent surgeon, yet his attitude toward his responsibility is somewhat cavalier. He is briefly contrasted with his
colleague and friend, Stafford, a serious researcher seeking a cure
for spotted fever. The mystical element of the film is provided by
Dean Harcourt, a religious figure of an unnamed denomination whose
religious ideals, true to the Borzagean pattern, are more humanistic
than dogmatic. Paige is "introduced" to Harcourt by Mrs. Dexter,
a seriously ill patient. Dexter is a religious stoic[96] who is inspired
by Harcourt and who in turn inspires Paige to his redemption. The
physical and temporal reality of space is transcended in this initiation

Green Light

when, as Mrs. Dexter listens to a Harcourt sermon over the radio,
the camera moves from a close-up of her to that of the radio and
then fades into Harcourt's church auditorium itself. In a parallel
movement the camera tracks in closer to Harcourt and finally to a
close-up of the Dean as he preaches on our unsteady progress through
life.   This parallel camera movement ties Harcourt to Mrs. Dexter,
and Paige to both of these spiritual figures.   Harcourt's speech is
an exhortation that is, thematically, addressed directly to Paige.   In
it he talks of humanity being stopped by many things that we can
neither understand nor control.   These are the "red lights" that we
must accept and learn from through suffering before we can continue
in our progress.   When we learn the green light returns, and we,
and civilization, continue our "inexorable march into eternity."

Mrs. Dexter is given courage and confidence by this speech
and by her greater faith.   She relies upon it when told that her much-
needed operation must be delayed because her doctor is in Milwaukee.
Reminiscing instead about her girlhood and again expressing her belief
in the power of her faith, she then picks up a picture of her daughter.
As in the radio scene, there is a fade-in to her daughter and a friend
coming out of a church in England.   This ties not only Paige and
Mrs. Dexter but creates a nonspatial tie between Phyllis Dexter and
Paige, which becomes an essential element of the narrative.   Their
connection is further reiterated by Phyllis's talk of her mother and
of her mother's love for Paige's dog, Sylvia.   At this moment, once
again tying Phyllis and Paige in a larger, albeit unrecognized, sphere,
Borzage fades-in to Sylvia running along the seashore with Paige,
who, deep in thought, asks himself aloud, "What's it all about?"--the
"it" referring not only to life but to religion, faith, and commitment
to a belief.   There is a cut to Harcourt, who, having overheard all
of this, engages Paige in conversation.

Paige can only talk of the present, refusing to see more than
"today's pains" and, by implication, an immediate existence.   Har-

court, calling himself a teacher more than a preacher, sees himself
as being in the same business: he, too, cures the sick, only his
emphasis being different, since his concern is with human souls and
with eternity. Creating a visual and thematic link between the two,
the rest of the film concerns Paige's restless change and his eventual
unification with Harcourt's ideals, which result in his regeneration
and conversion. Later, after he leaves his position at the hospital,
Paige seeks to cure a disease that has afflicted not only the generations of the past and present but will afflict the future if not stopped.
His work shifts from its orientation completely to the present to one
that spans all time and all people, just as Harcourt's work does.

Refusing to delay Dexter's operation any longer, Paige decides
to operate on her himself. She accepts her fate, declaring herself
"ready" as she lies on a white bed dressed in her white gown. Like
Catherine in A FAREWELL TO ARMS and Pat in THREE COMRADES,
her spiritual purity is emphasized by her angelic or nun-like garb.
Endicott, Mrs. Dexter's assigned doctor, enters during the operation,
his mind more on his stock-exchange losses than on his duty to the
patient. Pushing Paige aside, he operates and makes an error in
procedure that causes Mrs. Dexter to hemorrhage and die. Endicott
will not accept the blame, however, and Paige is tried by the hospital board instead. Refusing to go against his mentor and believing
himself at fault, Paige sacrifices his own career by refusing to tell
the true story or to let his faithful nurse, Ogilvie, do so either.

In her moral confusion, Ogilvie goes to see Dean Harcourt for
counseling, rejecting Paige's sacrifice and his belief in "eventual justice" and claiming that "one gets what one fights for [since] only the
fittest survive." Her ideology, more secular and Darwinian, separates her from Paige and from understanding the journey he must
undertake. Although she loves him, it is more a romantic love for
what he can do and for what he appears to be. Her later conversion
is all the more striking because of her spiritual state at this time.
Harcourt, after looking into her eyes and into her soul, recognizes
her love for Paige and forces her to turn from her present-oriented
and secular philosophy, as he will later force Paige. Telling her of
civilization's "greater destiny," he compels her to admit that it is
not individuals who count so much as "what effect our actions have
on others." He convinces her that she must respect Paige's reasons
for his actions, paving the way for the eventual group conversion that
follows later. Harcourt's belief is in the individual's ability to progress without outside help and by working through his or her own
problems with the help of faith only.

Ogilvie secretly loves Paige, and her desire to protect him
is much like a mother's desire to protect her child. She is paired
with Phyllis Dexter, daughter of the dead patient, who comes to Harcourt for comfort just as Ogilvie is leaving. The two become two
parts of a whole, often wearing outfits of opposite shades or similar
pattern, until Ogilvie's love for Paige becomes a part of Phyllis.
Ogilvie, like Harcourt, is a spiritual being, often dressed in a white
nurse's outfit. Her friendship teaches Phyllis to love unselfishly.

In fact, Paige meets Phyllis at Ogilvie's apartment. Introduced as "Walker," a name with implications of Paige's search and journey, he and Phyllis, much like Terry and Amy and Melville and June, fall in love immediately. Yet their love takes on an almost occult quality. Paige, recognizing his love, echoes the words heard from Harcourt earlier, "Without warning, an entire future may be created." As if to reiterate the fact of his growing spiritual restlessness, he goes to Harcourt, recognizing him for the first time. Paige wants to argue about "everlasting life" and, as a pragmatist, desires to break down Harcourt's faith with empirical arguments. Harcourt, "turning the other cheek," praises Paige and Paige's religion of loyalty and honor instead. Harcourt, a physical cripple, as opposed to Paige, who is an emotional one, tells Paige to go forward and upward. Paige, at first echoing a Marxist dialectic--"Religion is a kind of opiate to be used by people with hurt sensibilities to be lulled into drowsiness"--is convinced he must leave Endicott and the present behind and, so that he can survive, must go and find "something to live and to die for."

When Paige meets Phyllis once again as he is leaving Harcourt's study, Phyllis finally discovers who Paige is after he uses a medical term unknowingly and talks of his dog, Sylvia, whom her mother wrote her about. Leaving Paige, she confronts Ogilvie to find out the truth. Ogilvie, refusing to admit her love for Paige, defends him as "born good." When the two go to find Paige he is gone. Paige, we learn, has gone to join his friend Stafford and to work for humanity without the fame and glory found in the city hospital.

Refusing to rest, Paige works incessantly. He writes to Ogilvie, who relays his messages to Harcourt and Phyllis. Phyllis, now more in love with Paige than hating him, desires to join him and to help him. Her desire to sacrifice all for him becomes tied to the idea of sacrifice on the whole in the scene that immediately follows this one, in which Paige injects himself with spotted fever to test a vaccine he has devised. The vaccine is apparently successful, and the two are united, however, as Phyllis arrives soon after. Seeing their love as fated, the two forgive each other and join together.

> Phyllis: "It had to happen. It couldn't be any other way."
> Paige: "Your mother?"
> Phyllis: "A split second. The knife slips. You didn't do it deliberately. She would have been the first to forgive you."
> Paige: "Do you forgive me?"
> Phyllis: "No. I hope you'll forgive me. I had to learn not to hate."

Phyllis, influenced by her mother and by Harcourt as much as Paige was, goes through her first conversion. She learns to believe in Paige and in her love for him, just as he has learned to believe in something greater in his work and in his sacrifice for humanity. Love takes second place to their joint devotion to something outside of themselves. As if to reinforce this, Paige collapses with the fever and is nursed by Phyllis.

Phyllis and Stafford are joined by Ogilvie and Endicott, who, out of guilt and out of love for Paige, promises to save him. Ogilvie gives Phyllis courage, their personalities merging, a fact reinforced when they wear almost identical outfits. Phyllis gains strength from Ogilvie's spiritual love of Paige. Ogilvie breaks down soon after, and it is Phyllis who takes responsibility and who forces Ogilvie to regain control. The four gather around Paige's bed, their group faith acting to recall Paige to life. As the sun rises Paige reawakens and learns that he's won. The group action not only regenerates Paige but regenerates the group. All are converted to another way of being. Due to the influence of Harcourt and Mrs. Dexter, their lives completely change. Paige and Phyllis, now spiritualized and understanding not only love but belief in each other and in the "inexorable parade into eternity, " are last seen sitting in Harcourt's church. The camera, paralleling the original tracking shot, moves forward to a medium close-up of the two as Harcourt asks, "Who can understand the ways of God?" The two have been converted to Harcourt's belief system, and the echoes of "Amen" rise around them. Yet the enclosed sphere that these two join stretches beyond the church itself. Ogilvie, her romanticism and love for Paige "given" to Phyllis, becomes a creature of religious spirit, sacrificing herself for a greater good, and joins Stafford, another creature of spirit more than of body, in his research. These characters, and Endicott as well, not only transcend their immediate world but find something to give themselves to that is beyond themselves. Not content simply to find interdependence within a couple or small-group unit, they are all converted to the self-sacrifice, understanding, and unending progress of Harcourt's vision.

DISPUTED PASSAGE (1939) works out of the same framework as GREEN LIGHT. Much like Newell Paige is John Beaven, a medical student who seeks, unconsciously, to use science to shield himself from emotion and from life itself. Beaven, however, is even more a tabula rasa than Paige. In his almost innocent state he becomes the battleground for the ideas of others--the science of Forster, the scientific humanism of Cunningham, and the love Audrey gives him--out of which he must develop a "wholeness, " which is achieved by the joint conversion that ends the film.

There is, throughout the film, a constant sense of struggle between Beaven's unity with others and his separation. His separation is due to his overwhelming concern with scientific empiricism and his desire to pattern himself after Forster, an embittered doctor who, after losing his fiancée, closed himself off to all emotion. It is Forster's idea of "pure science" that attracts Beaven first. Only after much thought will Beaven turn to Cunningham's idea of humanistic and not strictly empirical science.

Beaven, who unpacks a Bible and a picture of his mother from his bag first, went to a small theological school, which causes Forster to refer to him as "Brother Beaven." Instead of uniting his spirit and mind, Beaven separates them and forces his spirituality virtually to disappear. He turns to Forster's philosophy that there is no place for theology in medicine and, thereby, to pure empirical research and treatment.

At graduation Cunningham is guest speaker. When he speaks
of powers "greater than our own" and of the necessity of a doctor's
love for his fellow human beings he acts as a direct contrast to Forster and to Forster's ideology. When Cunningham speaks Forster is
seen in the background, as much a part of the frame as he is a part
of Cunningham's idea of the unity of humankind. When Forster speaks
no such unity is present. Furthermore, when Cunningham speaks
there are long shots that connect him to the students, once again tying the entire group into a single spatial and spiritual entity reflective of Cunningham's greater vision.

A subjective pan used to show Forster's point of view during
an early lecture becomes a visual device that emphasizes Forster's
separation from others. This pan reinforces the sense of "spatial
separation between perceiver and perceived"[97] and also links them.
Through this subjective pan the space between professor and students
becomes an integral part of their relationship. This idea of spiritual
and physical integration of all things is most obvious when Cunningham talks to the students, just as Forster's separation-in-integration
becomes most clearly presented by the use of this camera device.

Beaven respects Forster for his ability and desires to "use"
Forster as a source of knowledge, yet he hates Forster's personality
and world view. This ambivalence continues when Beaven becomes
his assistant. Though visually placed together on the classroom stage,
they are not a unified spiritual group. Their conflict develops further
when Beaven meets Audrey Hilton, Cunningham's ward, who reflects
Cunningham's ideology as well as being representative of an Eastern or
Asian sense of life. Audrey, born in America but raised in China
by foster parents, perceives Beaven's hidden humanity, seeing through
the rationalist exterior and into his soul.

Soon after Beaven joins Audrey and Cunningham at their lake-
side home, leaving his duties behind as well as his stern persona.
Forster seeks to thwart their relationship, yet he cannot interrupt
the natural course of emotions. Even when he later succeeds in convincing Audrey that she is ruining Beaven's career, his actions lead
to his own eventual conversion, much like Rinaldi's in A FAREWELL
TO ARMS.

The first step in Beaven's conversion to humanism and to a
oneness with a cohesive spiritual ideology is his trip to Cunningham's
lake. Cunningham, like Harcourt, becomes his spiritual adviser,
opening Beaven's soul to humanistic ideas. The lake scenes take on
a baptismal quality much like that of Pat at the seashore in THREE
COMRADES. Beaven sits beside Cunningham, learning of the beauty
of medicine and the error in building a wall around oneself. Forster's attempted interference--he calls Cunningham's home to order
Beaven back--goes unheeded, as Beaven begins to turn his back on
Forster's strictly rationalist and empiricist philosophy. Beaven admits to the wall he has built around himself; he is tied to Audrey,
since, as Cunningham reveals, she has built a wall around herself,
the result of her Chinese/American cultural conflict. Both admit

later that they are seeking to enter into life and no longer to avoid it.

Beaven's attitudinal change becomes apparent from this point. Whereas earlier, after operating on a boy and then merely leaving, now he gets him a hospital job and takes a personal interest in his well-being. Forster, realizing the implications of this, berates him and his lean toward Cunningham's "spoon feeding" ideology. Beaven admits his change later to Audrey, confessing his love for her as something he fought against but now recognizes as his salvation. While at first refusing to break down her own wall, since she believes that they are of two different cultures, she soon after accepts his love and her own Americanism.

The final conversion is set into motion unwittingly by Forster. Forster convinces Audrey to leave Beaven, making her see that Beaven cannot carry out both his commitment to her and to his work. When he confesses this to Beaven, who has received a telegram signed in Audrey's Chinese name, Beaven quits his position and decides to go to China to find her. His decision, made while he stands in the light and while Forster stands in the shadows, physically frees him from Forster's hold over him. Once in China he stops at a make-shift French hospital. Breaking away from his earlier position, that he loved only Audrey without any commitment to humanity itself, he remains at the hospital when he realizes that he is needed, this commitment acting as the sign of his spiritual salvation. [98]

> The shooting grows dark, the objects in the background become less clear; finally Borzage tilts the camera and distorts the space in the frame. Beaven's presence there is like a final descent, a commitment to surrender his iron ego--and that part of his love for Audrey based on pride and personal gratification--to larger ideals. Borzage sees Beaven's true commitment to love, any true commitment to anything, as inevitably leading to this surrender. [99]

When Beaven is hurt in a bombing raid after attempting to save an old woman and a child (emphasizing his closeness to the cycle of life) it is Forster who comes to save him. The French doctor, La Ferriere, provides transfusions from his own arm, this shared "life blood" tying the two both spiritually and physically, and emphasizing Beaven's new commitment to things more spiritual, something that La Ferriere already understands. Beaven does not rally after the successful operation, however, and even Forster admits that there is nothing more that science can do. Yet Forster does not understand that to help himself, as La Ferriere states, Beaven must will himself to live from within his soul. Forster refuses to accept this, rejecting the idea of any mystical power being more effective than science. It is only Audrey's arrival and her words ("I am here to stay ... come back to me") that begin to give Beaven a will to survive. He utters the word "Audrey" and lapses back into a coma.

Forster, Audrey and Dr. La Ferriere are grouped around
Beaven's bedside, hoping he will awaken from his coma.
This is the scene of final transcendence: after committing
himself to love, to helping others over himself, Beaven will
be saved from death by--in Forster's words-- a "miracle,"
and thus incorporating himself, Forster, Audrey, La
Ferriere--all things--into the general spirituality of the
film. [100]

Following a pan from Audrey to a hole in the ceiling and the
night sky is a dissolve to the same hole in the daylight and a return
pan to Audrey. Beaven then awakens, again calling for Audrey and
telling her "don't go." The Frenchman says a prayer as Audrey
reaches out her hand to touch Beaven. Her action, representative
of some greater agent of regeneration, brings him back to life just
as her words did earlier. At the same time Forster touches his
shoulder, ostensibly trying to apologize to both and negating his total
belief in science. Calling Beaven's recovery a "miracle," he too is
converted into a new and transcendent spiritual system. He is joined
physically, in the touch he shares with Audrey and Beaven, as well
as spiritually to the others.

The shot in which the people are rigidly arranged in positions we have already perceived from a different angle,
gives an almost electric feeling, as if saving energy is being transmitted between people. [101]

The force that the three share and that permeates their world is made
more visible by this action[102] as is the joint conversion that occurs.
Beaven, like Lazarus, returns from the dead. Audrey restates her
commitment to Beaven and to their love. And Forster, most jar-
ringly, is brought away from his total empiricism and his belief in
pure science and turns to a more spiritual outlook. The miracle he
speaks of refers as much to his transformation as it does to Beaven.

DISPUTED PASSAGE, like the other films of this section, rel-
egates the central relationship to a place of secondary importance.
Beaven and Forster are not saved by love itself but by the acceptance
of "a more general faith, of which Audrey's love is only a part." [103]
Each character attains a new spirituality in the course of the film,
as well as a new understanding and wisdom. While Beaven's conversion is most "steady," occurring gradually throughout the film,
it is Forster's that is most striking, his realization coming suddenly
and more overwhelming than the conversions of the others. The relationships between these characters take on less important and "emotional weight"[104] than the final relationship that they share when their
spiritual separations dissolve. No one of them has any real independent effect, and the three, as with all things in Borzage's universe, only take on power and importance in their interconnection.

Love, in both GREEN LIGHT and DISPUTED PASSAGE, becomes only one aspect of the spiritual universe. Only when a more
general faith is accepted do the characters go through some conver-

sion experience. Furthermore, only then are they joined in some spiritual subuniverse that exists within the larger spiritual realm. Men and women, like objects, have no meaning outside of this, and, there-fore, the characters take on a two-dimensional aspect, a fact reflected in the lack of high-contrast lighting or spatial depth. Even Forster, when he lectures to the class, is reduced in importance not only by the high-angle shots, which reduce his presence within the frame, but by his lack of physical presence or density created by the lighting. [105] Lacking any real "place" in the world, the characters' belief in their own importance is undercut and their conversion and transcendence made inevitable. [106] The conversions in these two films are different from Nina's in DOCTORS' WIVES. Not only are these two rational-ists, as well as Endicott in the former and Forster in the latter, brought into and made a part of a larger spiritual reality (in contrast to Nina's new subservience) but they are chastened out of their indiv-idualism as well (in contrast to Judson Penning's victory). This idea is essential to the mass conversion that occurs in THE SHINING HOUR, as is the defeat of isolationist individualism and general selfishness.

In THE SHINING HOUR spirit and body become two separated forces that, when unified, bring a sense of wholeness in interdepen-dence to two lovers. The film, like LIVING ON VELVET, opens with an airplane shot that reflects all of the characters' aimless float-ing. [107] On the plane is David Linden, who has come to break up his brother Henry's engagement to showgirl Olivia Riley.

Olivia, a dancer, lives in an emotionally isolated world of sensual desire. Like David, she has the love of someone (Henry Linden) yet is unable to love in return. Her dance, shown in medi-um and long shots, becomes representative of her self-enclosed world. Dressed in a shiny silk dress that not only points up her sensuality by reflecting light but that calls attention to her, she dances enclosed in a spotlight that is symbolic of her emotional isolation and her own belief in her wholeness. Instead of being able to dissuade Henry, David, too, falls in love with Olivia.

Olivia and David, both sensual characters only, share a sexu-al attraction that they later recognize to be destructive. Further-more, there is a class condescension in David's attitude, which we later see in Hannah, Henry and David's sister, as well. David, a member of the Wisconsin "gentry," scorns Olivia's Tenth Avenue up-bringing, a theme played upon later in HIS BUTLER'S SISTER. David's attraction to Olivia is underscored in the scene of Henry and Olivia's marriage that follows. As in THREE COMRADES, Henry, Olivia, and David are all bound through the camera cutting during the cere-mony scene. David, who earlier spoke for Hannah, echoing her words, is now bound to Olivia as closely as is Henry.

Henry and Judy, David's wife, share a sense of romantic idealism that their respective mates lack. They are representative of one end of the spiritual and emotional spectrum, relegating their own individuality to a place of secondary importance. [108] Judy, in particular, is "hopelessly in love with David," as she confesses to

Olivia, lacking any regard for herself as an individual and willing to sacrifice her own happiness for his.

Hannah Linden is more a mother to her two brothers than a sister, often placed in the rear of the frame and overseeing the situation before her. She constantly interferes with Henry's life, in particular, her relationship to him bordering upon the incestuous. She takes an immediate dislike to Olivia for both sexual and social reasons, consciously acting as a Cassandra and prophesying doom.

These five characters are interconnected not only by their shared name and home but by their shared emotions. They range from the spiritual (Judy and Henry) to the purely sensual (Olivia and David); each is in some way incomplete. Olivia and David are almost all gratification-oriented, their selfish individualism blocking their integration into the spiritual world around them. Henry and Judy, in particular, are more sacrificing and spiritual. Judy is willing to sacrifice herself and her happiness for David. She takes an immediate liking to Olivia because of a "feeling," as she terms it, welcoming her into the Linden home and accepting her as an equal.

David's change, due to his attraction to Olivia, is recognized in his return to piano playing, something he has not done in a long while. This sign causes a small furor, Judy staring and Hannah clutching her hands tightly, seemingly recognizing what this means. David, realizing what is happening to him, pursues Olivia without looking at the consequences of his actions. Olivia, attempting to keep him at a distance, talks only of Judy and of the home she (Olivia) and Henry will soon build. David's horse ride with Olivia becomes symbolic of his pursuit as well as of her attempted rejections not only of him but of her own sensual desires.

Olivia does not really feel that she belongs in this world that the Lindens have inhabited for so long and are so much a part of. Unlike Judy, who was born and raised nearby, her cultural conflict is evident, as is her unsettled emotional state. She and Henry kneel before a model of their new home, with Judy standing above them, visually and thematically taking on the guardian angel role that she maintains throughout, while Hannah and David oversee from behind. The incomplete home itself becomes symbolic of the emotional gaps in the union that exist around them and of the lack of the characters' integration within themselves and within their unions. Olivia's changed social existence does not satisfy her. Soon after, when Judy plays a record ("Mood Indigo"), Olivia unconsciously begins to sway and to dance around the room. As in her opening dance, she exists alone, forgetting those around her. Following this Olivia confesses to Judy that she married Henry not out of love but because she liked him, because she was alone, because she no longer liked the people around her, and because she simply wanted to be married and Henry was the nicest man she knew. Judy confesses the same situation, admitting David's lack of love for her.

At a party given by the Lindens that night the tie between Judy

The Shining Hour

and Henry and that between Olivia and David are cemented. Wearing dresses of similar design, the two women are recognized as similar; yet in their growing awareness of the situation their difference
is shown in how they react.   Judy, recognizing her blandness in
David's eyes, desires to be more like Olivia.   She confesses to Henry that she wants David to think of her when he hears a certain song
or, walking into a room, to "know I was there. " This is followed
by a scene in which Olivia and Hannah are again placed in confrontation, Hannah calling Olivia a "disturbing influence, " and one in which
David calms Olivia and dances with her, the first time she has shared
her "spotlight" or her isolation with anyone else.   Olivia walks off
to the lake, where she and David, who follows later, finally kiss.
Although Olivia realizes the importance of their actions, David does
not:

> Olivia: "What happens next, David?"
> David: "I hadn't thought. "
> Olivia: "You should have. "

Not only is she wiser and more worldly than David, but she sees the
consequences of their actions, whereas his "type"--those who have
always gotten what they wished without trouble--does not.

          Shot against what is obviously a studio set much like the Ha-
waiian set where Dick Dorcy and Kit Fitts fall in love in FLIRTA-
TION WALK (1934), the romanticism of the scene is undercut by
Olivia's "premonition, " as well as by the scene that preceded this

one, in which a town boy attempts to seduce Olivia and to kiss her.
While David can stop the boy's actions in this scene, he fails to see
it as a comment upon his own intentions and does not reverse his decision. Olivia, on the other hand, does see it as such, laughing at
the scene as well as at herself and her reputation.

When David returns to Judy, he admits that he's been "wrestling," a double entendre implying his emotional state as well as his
physical actions. As the two talk Judy faces left and David looks
straight ahead. The cut that follows, to Henry and Olivia, visually
extends the narrative ties found here and earlier. As they talk,
Henry faces right and Olivia forward. Thus through the two scenes
Henry is once again tied to Judy (H→ ←J) and Olivia is once again
tied to David (O↑↑D). Spirit is thereby tied to spirit, and sensuality to sensuality. Olivia makes a last effort to convince Henry to
leave the farm; he agrees, but it proves to be too late.

When the party ends the new groupings take on importance.
Henry is seen with Hannah, Olivia with David, and Judy with Olivia
and David. When Henry and Hannah finally confront each other over
Olivia, Hannah's unconscious incestuous desires become clearer, as
does Henry's recognition that he and Olivia must leave if they are
to save their union. Olivia tries to do the same with David, significantly ordering him to stop playing the piano. Both realize just how
alike they are and, as Judy enters, the two are placed in opposition
to her (D/O→ ←J). When David leaves, after Judy symbolically fixes
his tie and tells him "now you can go ... you never could take care
of yourself," Judy tells Olivia that all that has occured has been
"right" and that she will give up David so that at least two of the
four of them will be happy. On learning of Olivia's plan to go away,
Judy tells her that "leaving changes nothing," thereby implying that
a climax of some sort is near and necessary for a resolution.

A fire that destroys Olivia and Henry's new home, set by a
temporarily deranged Hannah, acts as this climax. While it is undercut in importance by its formalistic composition and its lack of
mystical force,[109] it does bring about the final transformation. The
fire does not become a separate event as much as a resolution of
the important scenes that preceded it. Olivia, standing with Judy
and watching her home burn, stares vacantly and proclaims, "I've
lost it before it was ever mine"; the "it" implying not only the home
but her dreams as well. Judy, watching Olivia cry, runs into the
fire to sacrifice herself for Olivia and David. Olivia, like Melville
in SHIPMATES FOREVER, however, follows her in and, clutching
her in a Pietà-like pose, carries her out of the flames.

The resolution conversion that follows occurs at dawn. Olivia
confesses to David that Judy acted to free them and admits that while
they are free now it is not in the way Judy anticipated. Both realizing that they have changed, that they now know themselves, and that
neither is as good as Judy is since her love is of the greatest kind.
They do realize how much they have and how little they really are in
the larger scheme of things. Olivia tells David that he will be for-

given and leads him to Judy's door, where, as she stands outside of
the couple's interdependent wholeness, David kneels beside the bed
of the bandaged Judy, whose eyes look from Olivia to David. Judy
nods and Olivia closes the door on the two and on their world. Standing at the top of the stairs, she looks down to Henry and Hannah and
admits that Hannah was right all along and that she, Olivia, does not
belong here at all. Henry tells her that they've hurt her as much
as she has hurt them, implying that now they can start afresh. Shot
at a high angle, symbolic of her renewed state and of her power, the
scene is reminiscent of Irene's return to Paul at the restaurant in
HISTORY IS MADE AT NIGHT, the staircase, like the wall in that
scene, tying them and bridging the seemingly overwhelming physical
and emotional space between them. Olivia, confessing her love for
Henry after she descends the stairs from her higher spiritual as
well as physical position, exits to leave the farm, her marriage, and
this newly created spiritual sphere itself. It is a chastened and converted Hannah who sends Henry after her, asking both of them for
forgiveness and whispering a silent prayer as Henry jumps onto Olivia's car and as the two, united for the first time, exit into the ro-
manticized background of the landscape.

What has occurred is a group conversion, the isolated physical
area of the five becoming symbolic of their new spiritual sphere as
well. While David and Olivia are most obviously converted into this
new general faith, Hannah, Henry, and Judy undergo a change as
well. Hannah is chastened after her temporary madness, and her
return to sanity becomes an entrance into a greater spiritual understanding and an alignment with the family as a whole. Henry learns
to accept and understand Olivia, losing his earlier blindness toward
her conflicts. Judy, while the most spiritual character throughout,
joins with the others as spiritually interdependent equals. She and
David, like Olivia and Henry, are rejoined as body and spirit, become
interdependent and their relationships make them "whole. " Not only
does the group go through a conversion, therefore, but the couples
are firmly joined to give the group its foundation and stability. The
spiritual elements (Judy and Henry) being joined with the physical
ones (Olivia and David), the "wholeness" of each of the couples ties
them as their marriage vows never did. Each of the couples in
their unification by conversion moves out of the individual sphere and
into a larger one. The individuals and couples transcend their surroundings and themselves by their love and by their new understanding and faith; and by their larger conversion they join together as a
whole or total spiritual and emotional unit of interdependent parts.
While some of the dialogue of the last scenes is too explicit ("I'll
never forget last night"; "A love like that ... "), the sacrifices made
surpass any banality. The spiritual purity and the "quasi-religious
awareness"[110] attained allow the five to be spiritually awakened and
to develop a sensitivity outside of their individual concerns. What
occurs after the fire is not only a baptism but a rebirth. This rebirth encompasses all five of the characters, their actions being
interconnected and interdependent. Both the close-up cutting, especially noticeable in the latter sections of the film, and the shifting
pairings of characters ally and join the characters, and particularly
Olivia and Judy, in a "sympathetic alliance. "[111]

Borzage's ideas of group conversion and mystical faith are most clearly depicted in STRANGE CARGO. While such later films as SMILIN' THROUGH (1942) continue to rely upon the conversion theme, no other film is so thoroughly mystical or quasireligious.

STRANGE CARGO, condemned by the Catholic Legion of Decency for its supposed immorality, is Borzage's testament to conversion. In a three-part structure similar to that of MANNEQUIN, one third of the film is set in the jungle and swamp of a penal colony in French Guiana. Here a colony of prisoners lives apart from the "free" world, marching lifelessly through an ironically bright, sunlit prison compound yard. The film's opening, an overhead long shot, separates the prisoners into an isolated world, not so much a spiritual sphere as an intellectual or physical one. The second third of the film is a long sea voyage that takes on the same symbolic function as Newell Paige's journey West and John Beaven's journey to China; in each the physical journey is representative of an emotional and spiritual one that leads not only to transcendence but to conversion. Humanity is here, as in the later film THE MORTAL STORM, in combat with the elements, yet here people are more obviously in combat with their base nature and with evil itself. The journey here acts as a baptism, like Pat and Erich's in THREE COMRADES and like the baptisms of fire undergone in both SHIPMATES FOREVER and THE SHINING HOUR. It is while on this journey that the characters' spirits are changed and that they either begin or complete their conversion under the guidance of the Christ-like Cambreau. The final third of the film, the return to land, emphasizes the movement out of an earlier perverted Eden and the reintegration with the immediate world. In this world, inhabited by both good (Cambreau) and evil (Hessler), humanity (Verne and Julie), through reason and faith, is allowed to redeem itself.

The first shot of Verne is during his emergence from the dark into the light after a thirty-day solitary confinement, a movement that foreshadows his later journey into the spiritual "light" and reveals the internal wrestling, as recognized in his hand gestures, that Cambreau will help him to understand and resolve. [112] Verne is a character of physical energy and strength, full of life amidst an incredible physical and sensual deadness. [113] His refusal to stop fighting continually forces him to attempt to escape, and what he terms his lack of honor and respect toward traditional mores makes him try again when given a chance to work on the honor system outside the walls of the prison compound.

Verne's physicality and strength contrast directly and markedly with the physical and emotional weakness of the other prisoners. His response to Julie, the cabaret girl he sees on the wharf, is overwhelmingly sexual. The two eventually respond to each other on an emotional level that transcends the purely sexual. At first, however, Julie refuses to respond at all. Verne's sexual attraction is seen in the manner in which he picks up her discarded cigarette, sniffing and tasting it suggestively before he smokes it. Physically forcing her to agree to meet him, (an echo of his claim that there is "nothing a man can't get through to be free"), Verne promises to come to her that evening.

While the men regroup in line and begin to return to the prison Verne slips out and runs off into the jungle. Mysteriously, Cambreau appears and takes his place. The mystery of Cambreau, his attempt to let Verne run free, and the reason for his being on the island are never explained. He is on the opposite end of the spiritual and emotional spectrum from Verne, being purely spiritual and selfless and eventually acting as the catalyst during the spiritual journey and conversion that follow.

Verne arrives at the club where Julie works, using the symbolic cover of darkness to hide his actions, just as he continues to hide his inner self. Even though she turns him over to the authorities, Julie is forced to leave the island and, thereby, to go on a spiritual journey of her own. Verne is returned to the compound, once again locked behind bars and placed in a cage. His return to physical confinement echoes his unconverted nature and his spiritual incompleteness and isolation.

There are other members of the convict group who plan an escape and who join in what becomes a conversion journey. Telez is a prisoner who is constantly reading the Bible, claiming that while all of the others have forgotten God, he alone will be forgiven for his sins and will escape torment in Hell. Telez's protestations of belief are false and his belief only a self-serving one. Yet he is a creature of insight. He refers to Hessler as the Devil, a role that Hessler chooses for himself at the end of the film. Cambreau knows Hessler's name and who Hessler is without ever being told. This once again gives Cambreau a mystical and unearthly aspect. Hessler debates with Cambreau, and their opposition is not unlike that of Christ and Satan. Hessler declares that all of the prisoners are spiritually dead, only "waiting for their bodies to die." Cambreau works against this. Their conversation is shot in separate frames, representative of the unstated ideologies that separate them from one another yet that coexist within the text of the film and within the larger moral universe.

Cambreau debates with Verne as well after Verne refers to Hessler as "superman." Also shot in separate frames is Verne's argument with Cambreau, in which he berates Cambreau's reading of the Bible, calling it a "waste of time." The force and the truth of his statement are undercut, however, as Verne knows the entire book by heart, having read and memorized it during a six-month solitary confinement. The two debate the idea of humanity being created in God's image, Cambreau quietly claiming that there are qualities of God in all of us, while Verne, the pragmatist, asks him why, if he believes so strongly, he doesn't part the sea and ease their escape. This is what metaphorically occurs when Cambreau quietly becomes the spiritual leader of their escape journey while Verne and Mall, another prisoner, fight it out for physical leadership.

Attempting to supplant Verne's leadership and to rid the group of his presence, Mall attacks Verne, forcing him to be confined to a hospital ward and making him unable to join their escape party. When Verne awakens he finds a Bible beside him, which Cambreau has, unseen, left for him. Within the book is an escape-route map that will lead Verne to the shore. The map takes on religious implications as well, and the journey becomes a spiritual as well as a physical one. While this image is only seen once, its importance, which is felt throughout the film, is underscored by Verne's overtly satirical yet true statement that the book has allowed for his "day of salvation."

The jungle phase of the film begins here, with Verne's escape from the hospital and with the following shots of the other two separated bands of escapees. This is preceded by a high-angle shot of the jungle that reinforces the idea of the isolation of these groups within a physical and, later, an emotional sphere.

The parallel journey of these divergent groups (Mall/Cambreau/ Hessler/Dufond; Flaubert/Telez; Verne; and Julie) ends at the shore, where a boat has been hidden. Before they arrive, however, there are scenes in which Cambreau's higher spiritual status is made even more evident. Hessler, dumbfounded by Cambreau's intuitive knowledge, such as his ability to find hidden trails, asks Mall, but really himself, just who Cambreau really is. When Mall answers "just another prisoner" Hessler's only response is one that points up his uncertainty and his growing realization ("He's got to be"). This once again equates the two as spiritual and intellectual equals in their opposition. While Telez unquestioningly accepts Cambreau as Christ, Hessler cannot do so.

Cambreau is further recognized as a spiritual leader when he wanders away from the group and intuitively finds his way to Julie. He stops her from killing the lumberman, Malfeux, whom she has run off with. The source never revealed, a voice like Cambreau's tells her that her freedom will not be won that way. By revealing "the word" to her, he forces her to drop her knife and to save her soul. Verne mysteriously arrives at the shack as well and stops Malfeux from hurting Julie, protecting her physically, as Cambreau had offered spiritual protection. She feeds him, and the two exit holding hands, unified as physical beings, sharing their isolation in the jungle. Verne leads her through the jungle much as Cambreau leads his group, the importance of the two being equal just as spirit and body exist together and in equal parts within each human being. When Verne and Julie stop for the night he recites a "quasi-erotic passage from 'The Song of Solomon'--'Behold thou art fair, my love ...'--his earlier, crude, physical attraction to her [seeming] to deepen into an emotional engagement."[114] This is the beginning point out of which their new relationship grows. Based in sexuality, like that of many other Borzage couples, the religious and spiritual tie that will grow between the two is foreshadowed. The breaking down of emotional insularity that will follow is seen here when Julie cries, her first show of real and unguarded emotion.

Two of the groups meet at the shore and prepare to depart.
The second group, led by Flaubert, joins with this first when Telez
arrives, crawling over the sand. Flaubert earlier attempted to kill
Telez and left him to die in the jungle. Telez returns for revenge
and is only stopped by Cambreau, who not only saves his soul but
who cradles him and attempts to save his life as well. Cambreau
offers to suck the poison out of Telez's snake-bitten leg, telling Telez, "I hope it will help you." Hessler alone realizes that this was
a gesture only, and confronting Cambreau with this fact, is told that
"I had to show that someone cared." Cambreau, acting out his role
as spiritual savior, convinces Telez that a crucifix alone is not the
true sign of a belief in God and that one must open one's heart for
peace and salvation. In return, Telez confesses his sin to Cambreau--
his failure to share his bread with Flaubert--thus achieving earthly
and heavenly peace in the arms of Cambreau. Cambreau cradles
him in a Pietà-like pose and, when Telez dies, buries him under a
crucifix made of sticks.

Just as Telez dies Verne and Julie arrive, and Verne returns
the Bible to Cambreau, attempting by this action to regain his indiv-
idualism and to maintain his illusion of "wholeness" and oneness within himself. Cambreau undercuts this with his reading of a biblical
passage that refers to the human being as a "temple of God," implying once again that no one exists alone and that there are qualities of
God in all of us.

After Verne wins physical leadership of the group by defeating
Mall in a fight on the beach the group leaves for their journey to the
French coast. These seven inhabit the separated world of the sailboat that later becomes the arena of their initial individual conversions. Within this entity exist subunits: Verne and Julie; Mall and
Dufond, whose relationship takes on both father-son and subtle homo-
sexual overtones (in Mall's excessive tenderness toward the boy, in
his overprotectiveness, and in his later mourning, guilt, and sacrificial repentence); Flaubert, who exists alone; and Cambreau and
Hessler, who, as Christ and Satan figures, encompass all of good
and evil within their struggle. The journey takes on a symbolic and
biblical implication in its tie to the Israelites crossing the desert
after leaving the bondage of Egypt. This becomes especially apparent after Flaubert throws the remaining water cask over the side.
Realizing what he has done, he confesses his sins to Cambreau in a
litany ("I never trusted ... "), jumps overboard to regain the cask,
and is devoured by a shark. Dufond, the innocent, attempts to save
Flaubert but is accidentally killed by Mall, who knocks him out to
stop him. In return for his sin and after a soliloquy in which he
compares their relationship to that of Verne and Julie, Mall tests
the water in the cask for salt even though it is Verne who draws the
short straw. He, too, confesses his sins at this point and dies regenerated by his conversion.

The relationship of the four who remain takes on an allegorical and Edenic aspect, Verne and Julie acting as the Adam and Eve
figures, with Cambreau (God) and Hessler (Satan) fighting over pos-

Strange Cargo

session of the souls of these two mortals. Up on the deck, Julie
lies below Cambreau and asks him how he knows all that he knows.
She confesses her fears to him, refusing, however, to seek forgiveness, since she sees it as a sign of weakness. When Cambreau confronts her with the fact of her love for Verne, she is not so much
surprised as amused by his ability to see into her soul ("Your crys-
tal never misses a thing"). She confesses her inability to do anything for Verne, not even knowing how to pray properly. Cambreau,
comforting her through this series of confessions, tells her that
"you've been doing nothing else all this time." Converted, in truth,
Julie can now recognize and openly admit her love for Verne.

      The surviving four arrive on shore and quarter themselves in
a fisherman's hut. Hessler shaves and prepares to depart in search
of "a lonely lady with money." Before leaving he quotes Marcus
Aurelius, in contrast to Cambreau and Verne's quoting of the Bible,
reaffirming his secular belief in things of this world only. Refusing
to join Cambreau's flock, he leaves. Yet as he does so he undergoes one moment of regret and indecision. Gathering his will once
more, he says "no" to both Cambreau and to conversion, damning
himself eternally, and walks off into the night. While all of the
others are at least moving toward conversion, Hessler alone is not.
Leaving their Eden of the jungle and the sailboat, the group re-enters
life on earth, where both good and evil seek dominance. Hessler's
failure to convert to the goodness and spirituality of Cambreau's universe not only ensures the continued struggle humanity must undergo
within itself, but makes that struggle an individual one of greater

importance. Reaffirming free will and the ability to choose between good and evil, the film reaffirms a melodramatic view in which humanity's triumph is a temporary one only, yet no less important for being so.

Julie and Verne's realization of their love and their unity is visually underscored when he walks into her frame as he is admitting it. Yet their worldly problems are still unresolved. She refuses to live his carefree life, desiring a home and children in America, another Eden. Yet when she meets Monsieur Pig, a prison authority in the village, she is willing to sacrifice her own happiness for Verne's freedom. Thinking she has betrayed him, Verne confronts her and throws her over to Pig, a gesture revealing his unconverted state by both its violence and by his sense of possession. He does not yet understand interdependence. Not converted to a more spiritual ideal, Verne cannot and will not believe in Julie or in sacrifice. He refuses to listen to Cambreau (who realizes this, since in his state of grace he can "see" the truth) and, in a last attempt to maintain his illusion of wholeness, exits for the dock and for his attempt at escape from his spiritual awakening as well as to America. Yet Verne can escape neither the power of Cambreau and what he represents nor the power of Julie's love. He is finally forced by Cambreau to confront himself and the truth and, thereby, to be fully converted.

Cambreau brings about Verne's conversion when Verne realizes that Cambreau is divine, as a man made in God's image and as a Christ figure. This occurs when Cambreau dares Verne to throw him into a stormy sea "if you can do it." Verne does so and, standing upon the deck of the fisherman's boat, tells Cambreau that only a miracle can save him from drowning. The miracle is Verne's final conversion moment, which occurs after Verne tells Cambreau, "I'm the only God you can call on now" and, unconsciously recognizes and admits his own, and, by extension, humanity's divinity. Calling himself God, he realizes Cambreau's divine nature and, going through an actual baptism, jumps into the stormy sea and carries Cambreau out. Verne believes Cambreau to be dead, but Cambreau revives and the two hold each other, Verne now taking the mother role in their Pietà-like positioning. Verne saves Cambreau physically while Cambreau awakens Verne's soul.

The outward sign of Verne's final conversion is revealed when he gives himself up to the authorities and saves Julie (now dressed in stark black without make-up in contrast to her overly adorned appearance on the penal island) from giving herself to Pig. Verne, having "found something stronger," as the warden recognizes, is now able not only to admit his love for Julie but to act on it. The last shot of the two is of them walking together, transcendent in their love and joined by their mutual conversions. The final shot in the film is one of Cambreau, who, having once told Verne that he would go to others who need him, bids farewell to the fisherman (Peter) and disappears into the darkness.

Verne, having saved Cambreau, has saved himself. He and

Julie, transformed by their love, are reintegrated into the larger
physical and spiritual world. Thanks to Cambreau, they, and all of
the others except Hessler, are regenerated and brought into a new
spiritual state of grace through their conversions. Cambreau's presence allows all of the escapees to "accept their own mortality and to
understand their own divinity. He converts them to a spiritual system that helps them realize their quest for freedom."[115] Cambreau's
sensitivity to nature in his ability to lead them through the jungle and
across the sea and his identification with all of humankind give him
a sureness and a spirituality that is stronger than the selfish individualism of the others. The jungle, sea, and storms--and Hessler, by
extension--are as much a part of the spiritual system as Cambreau
and the calmness and goodness that he represents. Furthermore,
Cambreau's mysterious entrance into the film from within the jungle
and his easy disappearance into the darkness and the background at
the end of the film are symbolic of his oneness with nature.[116] Hessler shares some of this as well and, as representative of evil, shares
Cambreau's union with the supernatural.

In STRANGE CARGO Borzage fully and finally develops his
mystic sense. The major characters, and Verne and Julie especially, not only attain a spiritual awareness through a love relationship
but a deep sense of the spiritual and physical world around them.
Unlike the earlier films discussed in this section, the whole of this
film is an extended journey into awareness. The tripartite division
of the film becomes parallel to the stages of spiritual development.
Furthermore, the film uses, as a framework, not only a biblical
structure in the loss of Eden and the gain of knowledge but the struggle of good (Cambreau) and evil (Hessler). Cambreau, as Christ, is in
opposition to Hessler, as Satan. The two not only debate philosophical-
religious issues but their joint presence becomes symbolic of the dual
nature of humanity. The film is, then, a comment upon the melodramatic idea of the struggle of good and evil. And, as in literary
and stage melodrama, both exit into the darkness to work for their
own spiritual end. STRANGE CARGO works, therefore, on many
levels. It is one of the deepest expressions of Borzagean idealism,
concerning itself with love, transcendence, conversion, and the eternal struggle between good and evil. It not only becomes a final statement of Borzage's mysticism but "a significant expansion of the director's concerns and a deepening beauty of his art."[117]

NOTES

[1]John Belton, "Souls Made Great Through Love and Adversity, "
Focus! 9 (Spring-Summer 1973), p. 17.
  [2]John Belton, The Hollywood Professionals: Howard Hawks,
Frank Borzage and Edgar Ulmer vol. 3 (New York: Tantivity, 1974),
p. 128.
          [3]William K. Everson, "A Farewell to Arms, " New School
Program Notes (October 15, 1971), p. 2.
          [4]Ibid. , p. 2.

[5]Andrew Sarris, "First Takes, " Film Culture 25 (Summer 1962), p. 63.

[6]Belton, Hollywood Professionals, p. 87.

[7]Ibid. , p. 89.

[8]This shot is directly copied from the "War's Peace" still shot found in D. W. Griffith's BIRTH OF A NATION (1915).

[9]Belton, Hollywood Professionals, p. 87.

[10]Ibid.

[11]Ibid. , pp. 87-88.

[12]Everson, p. 2.

[13]Belton, Hollywood Professionals, p. 89.

[14]Ibid.

[15]Everson, p. 2.

[16]Lawrence J. Quirk, The Great Romantic Films (Secaucus, N. J. : Citadel, 1974), p. 32.

[17]Ibid. , p. 32.

[18]Ibid.

[19]Ibid.

[20]Belton, Hollywood Professionals, p. 125.

[21]Belton, "Souls Made Great, " p. 22.

[22]Ibid.

[23]Eric Sherman, Directing the Film: Film Directors on Their Art (Boston: Little, Brown, 1976), p. 242.

[24]Belton, Hollywood Professionals, p. 127.

[25]Ibid. , p. 128.

[26]Terry Curtis Fox, "Three Comrades, " Focus! 9 (Spring-Summer 1975), p. 32.

[27]Belton, Hollywood Professionals, p. 103.

[28]Ibid.

[29]Ibid.

[30]Ibid.

[31]Ibid. , pp. 103-104.

[32]Ibid. , p. 104.

[33]Belton, "Souls Made Great, " p. 19.

[34]Robert Smith, "The Films of Frank Borzage" (part 1), Bright Lights 1, 2 (Spring 1975), p. 17.

[35]Belton, Hollywood Professionals, p. 106.

[36]Ibid.

[37]Ibid. , p. 105.

[38]Ibid. , p. 108.

[39]Ibid.

[40]Ibid.

[41]Ibid. , p. 107.

[42]Ibid. , p. 108.

[43]Ibid.

[44]Ibid.

[45]Ibid. , p. 90.

[46]Fred Camper, "A Man's Castle, " Focus! 9 (Spring-Summer 1973), p. 37.

[47]THE BIG CITY (1937), also released as SKYSCRAPER WILDERNESS, is the story of Joe (Everyman) Benton and his foreign-born wife, Anna. The narrative centers on their struggle not so much against economic deprivation as their fight to stop Anna's de-

portation. Here the war between two opposing cab companies and the
actions of evil individuals becomes a microcosm for larger emotional
and worldly struggles. Joe's struggle to save his wife, like the
struggle undergone by other Borzage couples, eventually leads to their
reuniting and to their growth into a single entity.

Visually, the most striking aspect of the film is the use of
light and shadows. Anna is often shot in softly glowing light, such
as that produced by candles. When she is placed on board the ship
that will carry her back to Europe, the use of extreme close-ups and
of "over-hanging" shadows echoes her isolation and the unknown future
that she is facing. When Joe "saves" her the two are shot in these
same extreme close-ups and tight framing style and are isolated in
their own self-sustaining world.

As in LITTLE MAN, WHAT NOW?, the wife finds herself
pregnant at the end of the film. And as in MAN'S CASTLE, the
couple's unity and love are sealed in this creation.

[48]Camper, p. 37.
[49]Ibid.
[50]Ibid.
[51]Ibid.
[52]Belton, Hollywood Professionals, p. 91.
[53]Ibid., p. 92.
[54]Camper, p. 38.
[55]Belton, Hollywood Professionals, p. 92.
[56]Ibid.
[57]Camper, p. 39.
[58]Ibid., pp. 39-40.
[59]Ibid., p. 40.
[60]Ibid.
[61]Ibid., p. 51.
[62]Ibid.
[63]Belton, Hollywood Professionals, p. 93.
[64]Ibid., p. 95.
[65]Ibid.
[66]Ibid., p. 94.
[67]Ibid., p. 95.
[68]Ibid., p. 96.
[69]Ibid., p. 95.
[70]Ibid.
[71]Ibid., p. 96.
[72]Karyn Kay and Gerald Peary, eds., Women and the Cinema:
A Critical Anthology (New York: Dutton, 1977), pp. 68-69.
[73]Ibid., p. 69.
[74]Belton, "Souls Made Great," p. 20.
[75]Belton, Hollywood Professionals, p. 97.
[76]Ibid.
[77]Ibid., p. 118.
[78]Robert Smith, "The Films of Frank Borzage" (part 2),
Bright Lights 1, 3 (Summer 1975), p. 18.
[79]Belton, Hollywood Professionals, p. 76.
[80]Ibid.
[81]Richard Corliss, Talking Pictures: Screenwriters in the
American Cinema (New York: Penguin, 1975), p. 301.

[82]Michael Mahern, "History Is Made at Night," Focus! 9 (Spring-Summer 1973), p. 23.

[83]Ibid., p. 24.

[84]Smith, "The Films of Frank Borzage" (part 2), p. 17.

[85]Mahern, p. 25.

[86]Ibid.

[87]Ibid.

[88]Ibid.

[89]Ibid.

[90]Ibid.

[91]Belton, Hollywood Professionals, p. 97.

[92]Ibid.

[93]Fred Camper, "Disputed Passage," in Movies and Methods, ed. Bill Nichols (Berkeley: University of California Press, 1976), p. 339.

[94]Belton, Hollywood Professionals, p. 98.

[95]Smith, "The Films of Frank Borzage," (part 2), p. 7.

[96]Belton, Hollywood Professionals, p. 98.

[97]Camper, "Disputed Passage," pp. 342-343.

[98]Ibid., p. 340.

[99]Ibid.

[100]Ibid., p. 343.

[101]Ibid., p. 344.

[102]Ibid.

[103]Ibid., p. 339.

[104]Ibid., p. 343.

[105]Ibid., p. 341.

[106]Camper, "Disputed Passage," p. 341.

[107]Belton, Hollywood Professionals, p. 118.

[108]Fred Camper, "The Shining Hour," Harvard Film Studies (April 25, 1971), p. 4.

[109]Ibid., p. 6.

[110]Belton, Hollywood Professionals, p. 100.

[111]Ibid.

[112]Ibid., pp. 100-101.

[113]Ibid., p. 101.

[114]Ibid.

[115]Ibid., p. 102.

[116]Ibid.

[117]Ibid.

5. THE YEARS 1943-1949

Part One: Freelancing, 1943-1945

Between 1940 and 1945 Borzage's work took on a more eclectic and less ideologically recognizable quality.   From 1940 to 1942 he directed his last four M-G-M assignments: FLIGHT COMMAND (1940-41), SMILIN' THROUGH (1941), VANISHING VIRGINIAN (1942), and SEVEN SWEETHEARTS (1942).   Just as he left Fox in 1931 due to declining scripts, after 1942 he was again without a home base, freelancing for the most part at a number of less prestigious studios. This period of drift ended in 1945, when he signed a five-year/five-picture contract with Republic that gave him absolute control over the films he directed and, therefore, complete artistic freedom.   Borzage's popularity declined, however, as film styles changed to fit the war and postwar moods.   Whenever possible he worked out of his fundamental ideological framework, rarely attempting to change his basic stylistic and thematic conceptions to fit those of the film noir era.

Of the M-G-M films of this period FLIGHT COMMAND is the most interesting.   In its glorification of the Flying Tigers the film is similar to those earlier Warners' pictures that celebrated other branches of the armed services--the army in FLIRTATION WALK (1934) and Annapolis and the navy in SHIPMATES FOREVER (1935). And like these other films, the plot of FLIGHT COMMAND centered upon one man's attempt to win acceptance into a larger group, an acceptance achieved when the individual willingly sacrifices himself to something or someone outside of himself.   Here Alan Drake attempts to save his commander, "Dusty" Rhodes.   At the conclusion of the film Alan is united with the group, and the group itself is reunited after they grow beyond their internal struggles.   The final shot, a long low-angle shot of the squadron flying in formation through the sunny sky, is reminiscent of the doves flying across the sky in both MAN'S CASTLE and at the end of A FAREWELL TO ARMS. Here the formation of the planes signifies Drake's acceptance and the group's unification.   Unlike the single-plane shots of LIVING ON VELVET, THE SHINING HOUR, and the later CHINA DOLL (1958), there is no sense of isolation here, only a sense of unification and transcendence.

While freelancing at other studios Borzage made STAGE DOOR CANTEEN (United Artists, 1943), HIS BUTLER'S SISTER (Universal, 1943), TILL WE MEET AGAIN (Paramount, 1944), THE SPANISH MAIN (RKO, 1945), and MAGNIFICENT DOLL (Universal, 1946). STAGE DOOR CANTEEN was a star-filled extravaganza containing

recognizable Borzagean stylistic elements only in one of the final
scenes. Eileen, the self-centered actress who volunteers at the Canteen only in order to meet important stage and film personalities
and to get a part in a play, falls in love with Dakota, a soldier on
a short leave. Although it is against the rules, the two meet at her
apartment and spend the night on the roof, talking and planning their
future. Eileen's change is visually underscored by the coming of
dawn, symbolic not only of the new day but of her changed nature.
No longer the self-centered actress, she is willing to commit herself
to Dakota even though he is leaving to fight and, possibly, to die.
Eileen is given faith by her love and by her acceptance of the fact
that Dakota and millions like him are going off to serve humanity
and to make sure of "days without end. " Eileen is given courage
and transcends her baser nature, her love for Dakota having given
her an understanding of her partnership with society and of the necessity of a devotion to something more important than to the individual or to the self.

Perhaps the most underrated of this 1940-1945 freelance period is HIS BUTLER'S SISTER. Loosely patterned after MAN'S CAS-
TLE, the emphasis of the film is, however, more overtly romantic
and less spiritual ("This is a fable of the day before yesterday").
Borzage makes great use of tracking shots and overhead camera angles, and, if nothing else, the visual level of the film is masterful.
In the first shot of Ann Carter the camera follows behind her as she
"parts" the "waves" of men, catching their reactions in passing. This
same type of shot is used later when she and Charles Gerard, the
Broadway producer and song writer, fall in love. Here the extended
high-angle shot emphasizes their isolation in a world created out of
their love. This idea is metaphorically extended by the circle of
light they stand under, which separates them from the darkness and
the world outside of their newly created love unit. After framing
them from above the camera lowers to a medium level and follows
their meandering progress home, ending in a swirling shot that follows Ann as she falls on her back and onto her bed. This final picture of Ann, shot at an irregular angle, not only separates the sequence but visually ties her to Trina in MAN'S CASTLE, on the bed
after Bill leaves. A similar angle is used as she sang the Russian
medley just before she and Gerard left.

After numerous disagreements Gerard comes to find Ann at
the Butler's Ball. (An aspiring singer, she had been posing as a
maid in Gerard's apartment to get him to listen to her sing.) Her
first view of New York is visually like the view of the shantytown in
MAN'S CASTLE, the muted lighting softening the corners and edges
and the entire effect one that visually presents the city as Ann ro-
manticizes it. Gerard is refused entrance into the ball, in a reversal of class prejudice that emphasizes the slightly Marxist tone of
the film. He is neither poor nor of the working class, and only his
cook's claim that he is her brother gains him admittance. Once inside he looks for Ann, who soon after enters to sing. Ann's songs
had been used earlier to give fuller expression to events. When
first singing to a man on the train whom she believes to be Gerard

her song is "The Spirit of the Moment," which not only showcases
her vocal talent but emphasizes her nontranscendent nature and her
orientation toward the immediate.   The song and its implications are
undercut when it turns out that she is not singing to Gerard but to a
corset salesman who attempts to sell her his wares.   The song becomes a tie to Gerard, however, as he has not only written it but he
later sits at his piano and plays it in a melancholy manner.   In the
final "calling back" scene, much like the one in MAN'S CASTLE, Ann
sings Puccini's "The Prince."   As she sings she looks up, not forward, as if to God.   Her eyes filled with tears, the lyrics of the
song ("he'll be mine ... mine at last") and Ann's love for Gerard
seem to call Gerard to her.   Standing in the crowd, he slowly moves
forward, spiritually drawn to her in an almost magnetic manner.
Without knowing he is there or being told of his presence, she suddenly looks down and focuses directly on him, bridging any space that
exists between them.   She now directs her song to him and, descend-
ing from her lofty stage position, runs to him and into his arms.
The crowd seems to open before her, their faces dissolving as she
runs to Gerard.   Her love for him enables her to cross the separating space "with such ease that it would appear that her love had com-
pressed that separation into nothing."[1]

     This classic Borzage camera movement enhances the union of
these two by dissolving whatever stands between them.   The space
that separates them no longer has any meaning now that they have
transcended their immediate situation, its fixity disappearing during
Ann's easy movement.   This type of shot occurs in HEARTS DIVIDED
(1936) as well.   In this earlier film, when Betsy Patterson is reunited
with her love, Jerome Bonaparte, brother of Napoleon, a high-angle
shot is used to catch the two as they run along separate sides of a
wall to their reuniting.   The camera lowers to a medium shot as the
two meet and as Jerome crosses through the gate, the symbol of their
separation, and into Betsy's arms.

     HIS BUTLER'S SISTER is close to MAN'S CASTLE not only in
this last scene but in the visual romanticization of the landscape and
by the characters' slow movement into a transcendent union.   Gerard,
however, unlike Bill and numerous other Borzage "heroes," knows
himself to be incomplete.   He recognizes the fact that his being without love has made him unable to work since there is no emotional
source out of which his creativity can flow.   His joining with Ann
after numerous obstacles have been overturned takes place on her
territory.   Gerard must come to Ann and leave his past behind just
as Bill does when he and Trina leave for a new home.   Ann's life,
like Trina's, only begins when she comes to Gerard's home.   Both
have little or no past before they meet.   Ann and Gerard do not, like
Bill and Trina, dramatically set off for a new beginning, yet they do begin again in their interdependence.   Just as Trina and Bill transcend
the emotional space between them so Ann and Gerard bridge and transcend the physical and emotional space that separates them.

     During the rest of this transitional period Borzage worked on
a number of other films, most of which were far below his standard,

and the period itself is one of inconsistency in quality. While the
films contained Borzagean elements, except for TILL WE MEET
AGAIN they were not Borzagean in design or structure. THE SPAN-
ISH MAIN and MAGNIFICENT DOLL, two of the films that followed
HIS BUTLER'S SISTER, point this out best. Both of these films were
historical or period costume dramas, a genre Borzage had only worked
in once before, when he directed one of Marion Davies's last pictures,
HEARTS DIVIDED (1936), for Warner Brothers/Cosmopolitan. MAG-
NIFICENT DOLL is a weak and fanciful biography of Dolly Madison and
attempts to present an historical view of American political conflicts
in the early years of the nineteenth century by analyzing Dolly Madison's relationships with James Madison and with Aaron Burr. THE
SPANISH MAIN is a pirate adventure story like those made earlier
by such directors as Michael Curtiz (CAPTAIN BLOOD [1935] and
THE SEA HAWK [1940]) and Cecil B. De Mille (THE BUCCANEER
[1938]).

     In THE SPANISH MAIN, as in STRANGE CARGO, America
takes on Edenic symbolism. The ship bearing a group of peaceful
Dutch settlers led by Laurent Van Horn is wrecked off the coast of
a Caribbean island while the group is on its way to religious freedom
in America. The survivors are made slaves and prisoners by Don
Alvarado, the governor. America becomes symbolic of freedom not
so much as a commodity to be possessed but as an essential element
of the Borzagean universe. Van Horn's escape and his actions as a
pirate who plunders Spanish ships are not so much revenge as they
are a fight against the tyranny of the governor. When Van Horn cap-
tures a Spanish transport he finds Alvarado's bride-to-be, Francisca,
aboard and marries her out of spite as well as out of physical attraction. Yet Van Horn does not consummate the marriage, this action
being symbolic of his recognition of the divinity of love as well as
his understanding of the meaning of the marriage vows. When she
later helps him to escape from prison and gives him back his sword,
the sword being symbolic of his power and of his manhood, her action affirms a commitment to him not there before. When Van Horn
escapes the island he does so by dressing in a friar's gown, reaffirming his tie to God and allowing his earlier peaceful and religious nature to reassert itself. When Francisca joins him Van Horn gathers
her into his friar's robe. This action ties them as no words of the
marriage vow could. When the two sail off for their united life they
close a door behind them, leaving behind their past and ready to consummate their union. As they do so Don Alvarado, the defeated evil,
collapses and dies.

     When Francisca saved Van Horn, she wore a hooded cloak
that not only enabled her to hide her identity but gave her a nun-like
appearance. When Van Horn wears a friar's robe during the escape
the two are thus joined in their "taking on" of a spiritual nature.
His gathering her into his robe reinforces this idea of a spiritual
joining. Francisca leaves her worldly orientation and her past behind, therefore, as she finds and accepts love. This idea is a reversal of what occurs in TILL WE MEET AGAIN. In this film Sister Clothilde is forced to face the immediate world and to leave her

cloistered life and to test her faith. In doing so she finally transcends
"both the outside world and the cloister"[2] and emerges "into the death-
less and eternal realm of pure spirit. "[3]

The film of this period most like other Borzage works, TILL
WE MEET AGAIN, incorporates the director's ideas of spiritual transcendence into a more traditional religious mode. Yet here there is
less stress upon a love relationship, since Clothilde is a nun and
John is a happily married man. The film deals, rather, with Clothilde's physical and spiritual journey to a true understanding of religious love and humanist commitment. Clothilde not only transcends
the outside world, therefore, but transcends the insularity of her
personal and religious cloister. In learning of the beauty of her life
and commitment, she can make the ultimate sacrifice of her life,
thereby giving herself to something greater than her desire to shield
herself from reality. Clothilde's journey allows her to exorcise her
fears and her past and finally to find transcendence and inner peace.

Like A FAREWELL TO ARMS and THE MORTAL STORM, the
film opens with shots of a "placidly beautiful and peaceful landscape
on which war brutally intrudes. "[4] The camera moves from a high-
angle crane shot that isolates the village area, then lowers and tracks
slowly past a church belltower. The camera then follows alongside
a double line of children in medium shot, all in white and marching
to prayers at a convent shrine. This quiet, idyllic scene and the
children's prayers are interrupted by the off-screen sounds of what
turns out to be a double line of men being led away by dark-uniformed
Nazi soldiers. These two worlds, the convent and the larger political world in which it exists, are separate, and their contrast points
up Sister Clothilde's separation from both reality and from the place
of her faith in the larger immediate world, as well as her use of
the convent as an emotional hiding place. When shots interrupt the
children's prayers Clothilde refuses to recognize their presence:
"What was that noise, Sister Clothilde?" asks one of the children.
"I don't know ... I don't want to know, " answers the nun. Clothilde
refuses to face the exterior world, and her statement reflects upon
her attempt to shut out the war and the Nazi brutality that she knows
exists.

In contrast to Sister Clothilde is the Mother Superior, whose
faith is a far less contemplative one. She faces the fact of war, actively studying it--she recognizes the planes that fly overhead as
American--and accepting its reality. She faces and accepts the reality of war, claiming that her life has been punctuated by such ca-
tastrophes ever since she was born in 1870, the year of the Franco-
Prussian War. The Mother Superior actively supports the Resistance,
and her manner is both calm and controlled. She is saintly as well,
an idea reinforced when she sits below a portrait of the Virgin Mary,
posed in profile as Mary is. She can deal with Major Krupp, the
German commander who places German law above God's law, whereas Clothilde, like Elsa in THE MORTAL STORM, can only pale in
fright and drop her yarn nervously. Clothilde betrays both the Mother Superior's faith and her own weak sense of Catholicism when she

confesses what she knows of the downed flier because of her fear that Krupp will hurt one of her charges.

While Clothilde is proud that life has never touched her, the Mother Superior realizes the wrongness of this and recognizes Clothilde's flawed, untested faith. When the Germans shoot the door of the convent open it is their second violation of its sanctity, the first being the sound of Krupp's boots echoing as he crosses the convent floor and his uniformed presence seated below and between two religious paintings. When they accidentally kill the Mother Superior it is Clothilde's sense of her guilt and betrayal that forces her actions and eventually brings about her understanding of the essence of religion and, thereby, brings about her own spiritual transcendence. As the Mother Superior is dying Clothilde sits beside her and cradles her in a religious pose. When she dies an ascending-crane shot visually comments upon the older woman's saintliness and upon "the ascension of her spirit."[5]

Clothilde's guilt and her acknowledgment of her betrayal

> ...[draw] her closer to the Mother Superior's omniscient, experienced saintliness. In one sequence that prefigures Clothilde's subsequent identification with the Mother Superior, Borzage's cuts place Clothilde in the same position in the frame that the Mother Superior occupies in the preceding and succeeding shots, welding them, through fusion of image, into a single spiritual entity. [6]

Furthermore, this acknowledgment forces her action of penance--her helping John to escape to safety. After meeting John when he enters the convent through a basement trapdoor and after literally and figuratively turning her back on him, she finally decides that she must lead him to safety. The journey that the two undergo becomes more a rite of passage than simply a journey over physical space. Much like the journeys undergone in GREEN LIGHT, DISPUTED PASSAGE, and, especially, STRANGE CARGO, the journey leads to Clothilde's understanding and acceptance of the real world and allows for her transcendence into a realm of true spirituality. Clothilde's symbolic entrance into the immediate and secular world occurs when she looks into a mirror, an object used for much the same purpose as the Bible in STRANGE CARGO.

> Symbolised by the moment in which she sees herself for the first time in the mirror, Clothilde's initiation into the real world leads her to discoveries not only about others (e.g. John's quasi-sacred ideas about marriage, his ability to show her that God is everywhere in the world) but also about herself. Through her pretended "marriage" to John and their night together in a rustic cottage, she attains an understanding of secular spirituality. [7]

On the journey Clothilde listens to John's expressions of love for his wife and child, learning from him the beauty of the secular

world. He teaches her about realities, and, through his relationship
to his wife, she realizes the glory of earthly love.
John's idea that
talking about his wife makes him less lonely emphasizes the Borzagean idea that physical space has little importance. John's thoughts
bring his wife and son, symbolic of his worldly peace, close to him
in the same way that Clothilde learns to carry God with her always.
Her change is emphasized after she nurses John at the cabin during
his fever. The fever breaks at dawn and Clothilde's realizations occur at this same point in time. The dawn becomes symbolic of her
awakening, changing, and spiritual emergence as well as of his recovery. It is also at this point that she confesses her earlier "sins"--
her betrayal of a trust and her guilt over the death of the Mother Su-
perior--since John realizes that she is a nun after he sees her wash-
ing the cabin floor in the same way that she washed the basement
floor of the convent. She further confesses her reason for originally
going into the convent, her father's remarriage after her mother's
death. The two draw closer to each other as Clothilde's religious
beliefs and attitudes are humanized and as she begins to understand
John and his secular faith. John gives her advice that helps her to
lose her fear of the world ("God is everywhere, " "Marriage is a
sacrament, " "You mustn't fear life"). To him, home is as much a
haven as the convent is to her; in her creation of a home out of the
cabin, she begins to accept his ideas and, by implication, the world
itself. When they enter into the darkness of the night to continue on
their journey John leans on Clothilde for support and holds her hand,
an action symbolic of her change.

After they get to the railroad station they are recognized by
the Germans. Clothilde helps John to escape, refusing to tell him
of her own danger and claiming that where she will be going (i. e.,
heaven) she will be safe. John's exit is much like his entrance, exiting through a basement trapdoor. She kneels before him, holds his
hands and gives him a ring to give to his wife. This latter action
not only bestows a religious blessing on John's marriage but will keep
the memory of Clothilde's spirit alive. The action serves to tie the
body (John) and the spirit (Clothilde) in everlasting union. Confessing
how much she has learned from him, she tells him that while his
type of life is not what she desires, she finally understands it. Returning to her German captors, she makes a last confession of her
actions. They refuse to make her into a martyred heroine and decide to use her for sex instead, this punishment being much more
horrendous. Vitrey, the collaborator mayor, realizes the sinfulness
and sacrilegiousness of this and shoots Clothilde, thereby saving her
physical purity. The camera pulls close to her face in an overhead
shot as she thanks God. There follows a pan down her arm and to
her hand, in which she holds a crucifix. Her death, much like the
Mother Superior's, allows her to transcend the outside world she has
finally come to understand and to be incorporated into a greater universe realm. Like John, she has incorporated the real and the spiritual worlds into her being and becomes "whole" through the joining
of these two aspects into herself. Unlike John and other Borzage
characters, however, her unity is not expressed in her interdependence with another person. Clothilde becomes "whole" in her acceptance of the varied nature of human beings and in her ability to

devote herself to the tested faith that she loves best. She finally joins with Christ by sacrificing herself in her service to John and by learning what religious belief really is and what it means. Like the scientists in the conversion films, Clothilde no longer uses the "discipline" of something external or dogmatic, such as dogmatic religion here or scientific empiricism in the conversion films, to shield her from life[8] but accepts life and sacrifices herself to it much as Christ did.

Part Two: At Republic, 1946-1949

It is during the years that Borzage acted as an independent working through the Republic studio that his work moved out of a melodramatic framework and toward the theoretically tragic. This is particularly true because of the change in the nature of character redemption that takes place in these postwar films. In these works "the characters' happiness is thwarted less by the hostility of the environment"[9] and more by how that environment acts upon both forces within themselves, the personality of the character and the beliefs of that character. No longer is the source of that bitterness a war or economic or social depression; it is more a flaw within the character that influences his or her relationships. Also, no longer does the character perceive himself or herself as "whole," but recognizes the schisms that exist within and the need to heal these schisms. The spiritual transformation and transcendence "grows more out of themselves than out of the presence of an external agent, such as a lover or a religious figure."[10] In these films, I'VE ALWAYS LOVED YOU (1946), THAT'S MY MAN (1947), and MOONRISE (1949), the main characters must experience a spiritual regeneration that arises out of their own awareness and recognition of their flaws and out of their willingness to deal with their inner natures. In doing so, they do not so much make themselves "whole" as they accept their disparate parts. The redemptive mystical forces that operate within these films enable the characters to "conquer their own fears, despair, or cynicism and to work out their own salvation."[11]

The first of these postwar films, I'VE ALWAYS LOVED YOU is the story of Myra Hassman, a budding concert pianist, and her relationship with Leopold Goronoff, her teacher and a famous conductor, and George Sampter, the young farmhand who loves her. Myra is a part of both of these worlds, and they are actually blended in her blood. Her father, once a famous concert pianist, stopped playing when arthritis crippled his fingers. He then bought a farm and moved to it, raising his daughter there and teaching her to become a skilled musician. These two worlds--the concert hall and the farm--become representative of the two divergent strains within Myra that almost ruin her life: the love "triangle" that results is not so much one of two men and the one woman who must choose between them. Each of the men represents a different part of Myra, and these parts are in conflict. Unlike Olivia in THE SHINING HOUR, who must choose between the completely sensual or physical (David) and the spiritual (Henry), the choice here is not as clean. When Myra finally opts for the farm and George she does not, like

Olivia, become "whole" by joining spirit and body. She simply frees
herself from her netherland of drift and chooses a life that allows her
to join with another and to stop existing as a separate unit in a relationship. She does not so much choose between music and the farm
as she conquers one and can, thereby, accept the other.

The film opens in what John Belton terms the "coldly formal
world of statues and polished marble"[12] of a Philadelphia concert audition. This is the concert world in which Goronoff lives and thrives.

> Within the high-ceilinged, hollow-spaced foyer of the mansion,
> the camera pans from a close-up of an ornament on a wall
> to a medium shot of the hallway, revealing in the back-
> ground an interior room where a group is formally gathered
> around a piano. As the camera moves, objects--chandeliers,
> heads of statues--whip into the foreground, emphasizing the
> impersonal, surfacy nature of the room's decor, as if the
> camera were floating aimlessly, looking for something to
> latch onto. [13]

There is a preponderance of cold blue in the room, which contrasts
sharply with the softer blue-green of Myra's dress. Myra sits between the two men, Goronoff and her father, just as she later will
stand between Goronoff and George. Here, and in the scene on the
farm that follows, Myra's centrality and internal conflict are emphasized. In contrast to Myra and her father, who seem out of place
in this environment, Goronoff "seems to glide over and through the
room's smooth cultured surfaces"[14] and through this world itself.

Goronoff is attracted to Myra because of the feeling with which
she plays. Unlike the young man who misplays Bach, Myra's rendition of Beethoven's "Appassionata" is flawless and is filled with feeling. Myra alone is "at one" with her music,[15] and this allows her
to stand out from the others and from this highly glossed world of
appearances.

The cut to a long shot of the Hassman farm that follows is
followed by a tracking shot much like that which followed Goronoff
into the ballroom, yet here it is reversed, and the camera pans left
whereas earlier it panned right. As the camera tracks in it moves
over water and fields and past trees, all of which act as a contrast
to the cold unnatural setting of the audition salon. Again blue is the
prevailing color. The music that accompanies this first image acts
as a sign of Myra's integration here and of her integration with her
music as well. The direct cut into the interior of the farmhouse
that follows this movement through the landscape "suggests a greater
harmony of feeling and environment than we felt in the earlier recital
hall scene."[16] The homey interior of the farmhouse further acts as
a strong contrast to the hall. Goronoff's entrance into this scene
through an open window not only points up the informality of this
world but points up Goronoff's intrusion into it and into Myra's peace,
as well as his artificiality.

As Goronoff enters, Myra is seated at the piano, surrounded

I've Always Loved You

by both her father and George, dressed completely in blue, just as
Myra was earlier. Goronoff's entrance disrupts the scene, and while
Myra stands between these two it is Goronoff who commands everyone's attention. As Myra and Goronoff play, however, George slips
out, and when he rides by on his tractor the noise disrupts the mood
of these two, who are locked together by their music. This act and
these conflicting sounds again act to contrast the two worlds that Myra must choose between.

Goronoff is placed in visual opposition to both George and to
George's mother, the Hassman cook. When Goronoff tells Myra that
she will leave with him today her answer, "Yes, master," underscores her complete subservience to him. She visually breaks with
her family and with George when she leaves their frame and exits
left. Yet before she goes she asks George to "wish for me" and accepts the ring that he places upon her finger, a symbol serving much
the same purpose as the medals in SEVENTH HEAVEN. His answer,
"I wish, ..." is ambiguous and reflects George's fears of what will
follow.

Goronoff takes Myra around the world with him, and his the-
atrical gestures and manner are complemented by the artificial settings he inhabits.[17] He and Myra go to New York, Prague, London,
and Rio. Goronoff completely controls the naive and innocent Myra,
and "though they share a common ground in their music, the two

different worlds they come from separate them: Goronoff's egotism blinds him to Myra's love; Myra, possessed by an amour fou, refuses to see Goronoff's faults and seals herself into a one-way romantic relationship with him."[18] Myra becomes Goronoff's creation, and he not only teaches her music but dresses her as well, giving her a shawl, for example, and forcing her to wear it. When they play, their master-slave relationship is reinforced. Goronoff refuses to see her as a woman, telling her, "There is no woman in music" and making her accompany an overacted love scene he sets up, directs, and plays with another of his many beautiful and unquestioning lovers. Symbolic of her position in his life, Myra sits in the background in the living room, separated by a doorway. She finally undercuts one of these scenes when she drowns out Goronoff's words by playing louder and louder. Throughout their travels, however, Myra continues to do as Goronoff says, and Goronoff even goes so far as to call her his wife so that none of his other lovers can demand that he marry them. This act takes on a greater importance as well in that Goronoff's "use" of Myra undercuts the sacredness of her unquestioning love for him once again, this time with greater emphasis. Goronoff feels that Myra belongs to him and never recognizes her as anything more than an extension of himself. When he decides to let her do her first Carnegie Hall concert it is not so much because of Myra's readiness but because he wishes to "show them what Goronoff can make out of nothing."

The Carnegie Hall concert is shot much differently from the static concert scene of SONG O' MY HEART. When Myra and Goronoff stand backstage they are again separated by an arch, which symbolizes their lack of any true spiritual union. It is Goronoff who leads her onto the stage, again acting as master with Myra in the role of a child and slave. During the actual concert sequence numerous views and angles are used that tie Myra and Goronoff, echoing what he told her about ignoring the audience and watching only him, and that place them within the larger contexts of the orchestra and the audience. When Myra's performance steals the show from Goronoff he beats her down musically using the orchestra and "proves to her that he is her musical master."[19] Goronoff's power is too great for her. She gives up playing an extremely romantic Rachmaninoff piano concerto, stands, thereby breaking, at least temporarily, the hold of the music, and, by extension, of Goronoff, puts on George's ring, a gesture that foreshadows what is to follow, and leaves the stage and the concert world. She and Goronoff confront each other later at his apartment where she stands between two fully lit candelabra and he stands in the shadows of a dim lamp. Claiming that she has tried to steal his style and his fame, he berates her and sends her away. Only after she is gone does Goronoff admit to his wise and aged mother that Myra is greater than he is.

Though Myra returns to the farm and to George, she never resolves either the trauma that she has undergone or her break with Goronoff. She is still tied to Goronoff, playing a Chopin piece at the farm just at the same moment that he is playing it in concert in New York. The camera underscores this fact.

The camera tracks in on Myra through a window, then cuts
inside to a close shot of her as she starts to play. Borzage dissolves to a long-shot of Goronoff playing the same
piece in concert. Echoing the camera movement that closed
in on Myra, Borzage tracks in, along the aisle, on Goronoff. As the concert continues, Borzage cuts back and forth
from one to the other--the cutting and the continuous music
knitting the two together. [20]

Madame Goronoff, the maestro's mother, stands outside of the
farmhouse at this time and explains to George just how the music ties
the two in a mystical manner: "She talks with him. She says 'I'm
here, master. I sit beside you. I play as you play the things you
play.' The piano is her voice and he will hear her. What difference
if they are a hundred, a thousand miles apart? Walls cannot stop
that voice. Distance, time, nothing stops that."

George, admitting to Madame Goronoff that he has "always
loved her," runs into the house and stops Myra's playing ("I'm not
going to let you do it"). At the same moment that Myra stops and
walks away from the piano, Goronoff stops his playing, rises, and
walks off the concert stage, the movements of the one tied to those
of the other. George further berates Myra for falling in love with
a dream and for refusing to love something real. The two marry,
but Myra confesses to George that if Goronoff calls, she will go to
him.

Both characters, caught in the grip of unseen forces that
rob them of their individual will, move mechanically. Like
somnambulists, they appear possessed by some mysterious
presence within themselves that they cannot understand or
control. Their sudden paralysis, seen in Goronoff's loss
of the will to continue and in Myra's half-hearted marriage
to George, represents a capitulation to the self-destructive
elements within them. They lose the vital energy that earlier animated them, walling themselves off from those
around them in a tomb of lonely isolation and passively ac-
quiescent despondency. [21]

Myra's isolation from George continues unabated as the years
pass. George asks her to play for him and their daughter. As she
does so George looks out of a window, and there is a fade-in to another window before which Goronoff stands. Again reinforcing the
spiritual or mystical tie he and Myra share, Goronoff sits before the
piano and begins the piece that he was playing just before he stopped
for the last time. The time that has passed is, in this way, negated.
It is also at this point that he admits his love for Myra and that Madame Goronoff tells him of Myra and George's marriage. Goronoff's
reaction ("That's impossible. I created her. She's mine") is undercut by Madame Goronoff's statement that music is his only mistress,
since only music never grows old and only music "is sweet and fresh
and kindly to the years." Finally telling him this and making him
promise not to go after Myra, Madame Goronoff dies as she sits and

listens as her son plays. Her words and the mystical idea of the
holiness of her intuitive knowledge are reinforced by the thunder-
bursts that accompany her passing. Myra, also playing throughout
this time, stops when Madame Goronoff dies, claiming that she will
never play again. Just in the way that Goronoff faced the truth, Myra also faces the truth at this point. Telling her that he knows her
to be unhappy, George further tells her that "it's not what you have
that makes you happy; it's what you give." Myra has given him
everything except herself, and if George cannot have that he wants
nothing. George, with an intuitive understanding much like Madame
Goronoff's, tells Myra that she must stop fearing Goronoff. Myra
intellectually realizes this, and, as she plays George to sleep to the
same tune that Goronoff played to his mother, she prays to God, attempting to communicate without speech as she tried with Goronoff
during the Carnegie Hall sequence, that she will never see Goronoff
again, so that she will never "lose the things you've given me."

          "It is only through a ritualistic reenactment of an earlier,
crippling incident that Borzage's characters can free themselves from
the strange spirits that haunt them and recall themselves to life."[22]
Myra can free herself from Goronoff and make peace with herself
only by returning to the Carnegie Hall stage and by once again going
through a concert in which Goronoff is the conductor. Going to Goronoff ostensibly to have him test her daughter Porgy, she encounters
the master but refuses to let him kiss her and refuses to accept his
claim of superiority. While Porgy returns to George, who waits outside, Myra agrees to do another recital.

          The final concert is visually much like the first one and again
acts to negate time. By transporting Myra and Goronoff back into
the past, Borzage is suggesting that despite all external changes, the
two are inwardly the same and that, for them, time has stood still
even though actual years have separated them.[23] By returning to
the point at which time stopped Myra can free herself from Goronoff's
hold over her, can begin again with George, and can finally face the
world in which she lives.[24] Myra saves herself by facing Goronoff
and freeing herself from him. This is made almost inevitable by
Borzage's editing style.[25]

          Midway through the concert, Borzage cuts away from Car-
          negie Hall to Nicholas, the maestro's manager, listening
          to the concert on a radio in Goronoff's apartment. When
          he realizes that Myra and Goronoff are playing together
          again, he stands up and looks at a picture of Madame Gor-
          onoff, now dead, on the mantle. Borzage dollies into a
          close-up of Myra at the concert, integrating the dead wom-
          an's transcendent presence into the regenerative atmosphere
          at the concert and linking Myra's transcendence to hers.[26]

The cutting further integrates the different groups (Porgy/George,
Goronoff/Myra, Myra/Madame Goronoff, Myra/George/Porgy) into
a larger whole symbolized in the audience and creates the feeling
that a larger spiritual awakening is occurring.

> Borzage creates a rhythm that exists apart from the action,
> situation or characters. It has a life of its own, an out-
> growth more of a primitive religious mysticism than of any
> mundane logic or dramatic convention.... Borzage's [cut-
> ting] seems externally imposed, drawing his characters into
> an abstract, invisible spiritual state that exists outside the
> borders of the frame. As a result, Myra's discovery that
> she has always loved George is partly her own and partly
> one Borzage's editing thrusts upon her. Finally, Borzage's
> cutting rhythms instill a vitality and energy into his charac-
> ters that they had earlier lost, making their spirits sublime
> and immortal. [27]

Myra plays with, rather than for, Goronoff, and as Goronoff
admits in his thoughts that "there is a woman in music, " Myra rises
from the piano. Goronoff's spell broken, she first stares at and
then runs to George, telling him "I love you, George. I've always
loved you, always, " as the orchestral rendition of "Our Love" continues to rise and as George answers "And I've always known it. "
Goronoff looking on, George and Myra are united for the first time;
Myra's spiritual fears are at last exorcised, and she is regenerated.
She awakens to her love for George and Porgy, turning her back on
both Goronoff and the stage. Myra leaves the concert hall not confused, as she was after the first concert, but free and alive due to
her realization of the love that she has and to the inner healing that
this awakening has brought about.

What is essential is that Myra is internally healed. Unlike
earlier Borzage characters, but like those in the "conversion" films,
her spiritual regeneration and transformation is an internal one that
comes from the self. She does not find "wholeness" in interdependence so much as she only becomes interdependent and part of a love
relationship after she achieves an internal healing. Myra is, therefore, much like Newell Paige in GREEN LIGHT, John Beaven in
DISPUTED PASSAGE, and Olivia Riley in THE SHINING HOUR. Yet
she differs in the emphasis upon her increasingly internal transformation. A similar characteristic is recognized in the major characters in Borzage's remaining Republic films. Both Joe Grange in
THAT'S MY MAN and Danny Hawkins in MOONRISE must face and
transform themselves before they can accept their lives and move
into the future. Their transformations, like Myra Hassman's, do
not grow out of "the presence of an external agent, such as a lover
or a religious figure"[28] but out of their own awareness, acceptance,
and transformation. Love alone cannot surmount all of their pressures and tensions. [29]

THAT'S MY MAN, like LIVING ON VELVET and HISTORY IS
MADE AT NIGHT, is the story of an unsuccessful marriage. Here,
as in I'VE ALWAYS LOVED YOU, there is less emphasis on the
resolution of the couple's problems and more on one character's attempt to unify himself. Joe Grange is addicted to gambling. This
fault, close to the cynicism that characterizes other Borzage men
in earlier films, like Bill in MAN'S CASTLE and Beaven in DISPUTED

PASSAGE, for example, intrudes upon a yearning for peace. Joe and Ronnie reunite at the end of this film only when Joe's desire to gamble has been removed and only by Ronnie's bringing Gallant Man out of retirement to "save" Joe and to bring him back to her and to their son.

THAT'S MY MAN is set up in a flashback style reminiscent of the narration in the earlier Borzage film MAGNIFICENT DOLL. Toby Gleeton, a cab driver and friend of both Ronnie and Joe, tells to a cynical sports reporter the story of Gallant Man and of Joe's singular faith in the horse. Toby takes on the function of a conscience or Greek chorus as well, detailing Joe's sins and explaining how Joe's selfishness almost wrecked the marriage.

Joe's faith is immediately contrasted with the cynicism of the reporter, and while the two are introduced by similar shots and angles, Joe sits on the right side of the cab, in contrast to the reporter, who sits on the left. Stopping at a drugstore, Joe meets Ronnie, a fountain girl, and shares his cab with her. In the cab is his colt, Gallant Man, whom Joe refers to as "Baby" and with whom he shares a mystical communication. It is Joe's belief that Baby will grow up to be a great racehorse and will win because he loves and will listen to Joe. Joe believes this so strongly that he quit his job as an income-tax auditor and put all of his faith in life in the glory and possibility of the future.

In the cab Joe, Ronnie, and Baby are united within the frame and in a low-angle shot. When Joe leaves Baby at Ronnie's apartment after she agrees to watch the horse until morning, Baby reacts badly and Joe must return and stay with the newly created unit. The tie between the three is underscored by the reverse dolly shot that Borzage uses. When Ronnie is alone at the apartment the camera pulls back to include Baby in the frame. When Joe returns the camera follows a similar path, and the frame "grows" to include all three. This type of shot is used throughout the apartment scenes, and the fluid movement emphasizes the larger unit to which these three belong.

Ronnie admits that she never met anyone like Joe before, recognizing in Joe's not being quiet or ordinary a tie to herself. She too desires better things, claiming that she has always been unsatisfied with her existence. The two share their dreams, and Joe tells of his childhood wish of owning a horse. It is at this point that he confesses his belief that a horse will run fast "if it wants to," that is, if it is raised, cared for, and loved. Again the camera dollies back at this point to include all three in the frame.

The two confess that they feel as if they have known each other for much longer than one evening, reinforcing the Borzagean idea of the immediate tie created by love. When the lights are shut off the two sleep head to head, Joe on the couch and Ronnie on the Murphy bed. As Borzage cuts between the two lying at opposing angles Joe talks of the rain and of this "funny, wonderful world" while

Ronnie confesses how much she likes him and agrees with his assess-
ment. Joe's final words, "and everything in it [the world] is perfect ...
perfect ... " indirectly verbalizes the recognition of their love.

At the racetrack Borzage again uses a dolly shot to tie Joe,
Ronnie, and Baby together and to separate them within the world they
have created. It is only at this point that Joe's obsession with gambling is mentioned, and Ronnie takes on the roles of conscience and
reason. When Joe shows her the money he won betting and tells her
that they can now marry, she refuses, claiming that "cheap, grubby
money" is not the proper foundation for their "clean" love. Joe agrees,
and the two promise to marry the day of Gallant Man's first race.
When Borzage immediately fades-in to this the camera reverses and
pulls in on Joe and the horse, tying them together tightly. Later
Ronnie joins the group and again becomes part of the unit.

Gallant Man wins the race and Joe and Ronnie marry. The
two go to an amusement park to celebrate when Joe meets Ramsey,
his racing rival. The two groups (Joe and Ronnie; Ramsey and his
girl) stand in opposition to each other. Ramsey further tells Joe of
some gambling that will take place at Joe's hotel that night, thereby
tempting Joe and indirectly testing his will against Ronnie's. Joe's
answer and his freeing of the two doves that he won earlier reinforces
Ronnie's faith in him, the free doves paralleling both of their aspirations, Joe's renewed sense of faith and Ronnie's happiness and relief.

When the two return to their hotel room they walk through a
set of Moorish arches and into the air as they talk of their dream
house. Like the doves, they soar above reality and find escape in
each other. The room, though shoddy, has an almost fantasy design
to it, as recognized in not only the arches but by the fact of the
amusement park that is outside. As in both LILIOM and MANNE-
QUIN, however, the continually flashing lights undercut the dreamlike
happiness while serving as a symbol of Joe's double nature, loving
husband and devoted gambler. This image, and the larger use of
contrasting lines of black and white throughout the film, symbolizes
the differing desires of the two. Outside of their love for each other
what ties them together is the love that they share for Gallant Man.

Ronnie's fears about Joe's gambling continue to plague her.
When she stands on the balcony outside of the room and above the
street, much like the garret in SEVENTH HEAVEN, she is trapped
between the amusement park below her, viewed from a high angle,
and the gambling noises and voices above. She runs into the room
and locks the windows, attempting to lock that world out and to separate herself and Joe from their problems. When Joe returns and
opens the windows she makes as much noise as is discretely possible
in an attempt to cover up the gambling sounds. His eyes look upward and he realizes what is above him. While momentarily torn,
he realizes the desperation in Ronnie's attempts to save him. Refusing to give in to temptation, he stays with her, and, in recognition of their union, tells her that he has placed the ownership of Gallant Man, the symbol of their dreams and hopes, in her name as well.

As the years pass Joe's wealth increases, as does Gallant Man's success. Yet as Toby says in his narration, "A man can't be tops at two things at once," implying that Joe and Ronnie's marriage is failing as Joe's gambling mania increases. Joe fails to show up at a New Year's Eve party, the significance of the event implying not only their separation but the fact that things will not be better in the near future. Like Hennessey in MANNEQUIN, as Joe moves up economically he temporarily loses his spirituality and he and Ronnie grow apart. Their large and cold apartment only serves to emphasize this and to undercut both the significance of Ronnie's promise not to leave her from this moment on. As Toby tells us in his narration, this promise, like all of the others, was broken, and it is Toby who later accompanies Ronnie to the hospital when the child is due, since Joe cannot be found. He is, we learn later, once again out gambling.

Joe's visit to Ronnie after the birth of their son establishes her as a more spiritual character. The camera moves in to an overhead shot much like that of Lammchen after the birth of her child at the close of LITTLE MAN, WHAT NOW? This is also a comment to the adjoining overhead shots of Joe and Ronnie that were used when Joe stayed in Ronnie's apartment. Now in the darkened room, the low-angle shot of Joe acts as an ironic contrast to his "lower" position. His opening of the blinds and the shadows of the bars on the wall that result once again create the dark-light or flashing-light effect that reflects his dual nature. His gift to Ronnie--a jar of earth--reinforces the idea of her essential goodness and her role as earth mother. Only after he tells her of the new house he has bought for them and promises her once again to "be there" does she agree to a reconciliation. It is only at this point, as well, that he speaks to his son in the same tones and manner that he addressed Baby, telling the boy that he is, indeed, his father.

The new house that Joe brings his family to is high above the city, overlooking the hills from every window. It is a starkly modern abode, one that is almost cold. Throughout are the parallel dark-light lines, both in the stairwell and in the black-and-white floor. Only Ronnie's happiness warms the house, and she runs to Joe across a number of large windows, joining him within his space. This is much like their honeymoon scene, when the two kissed beneath the Moorish arch of the window of their hotel room.

Things really never change; Joe continues to be absent at important times. He misses Christmas and Ronnie falls asleep alone under the tree. It is also during this time that Joe retires Gallant Man from racing, telling the horse of his love for him, and thanking him for his greatness. During this scene a rooster, like Marsden's crow in THE RIVER, oversees the scene, and his call foreshadows the doom soon to follow. When Joe returns home he stands outside the dining room arch and looks in upon his wife, surrounded by candles, and son having dinner. His son is seated at the head of the table, thereby symbolically taking Joe's place of importance in Ronnie's world. After reprimanding his son Joe and Ronnie argue, and

Ronnie stands before a large fireplace that surrounds her like a halo,
much like the shot through the chandelier after Moonyean's death in
SMILIN' THROUGH, with Joe conspicuously out of the circle.   When
he offers to leave she agrees and tells him to go quickly so that
Richard, their son, will forget.   Joe leaves, but not before he visits
his sleeping son, kisses his forehead, and apologizes for being a bad
father.   His method of communication, much like that with Gallant
Man, is a clue to Richard's later actions.

Without Ronnie and Gallant Man, Joe loses all of the wealth
that he previously gained.   He further learns from Toby that Richard
is seriously ill with pneumonia.   The bedside scene that follows reinforces Joe's ties to his son and the power of his love.   Richard,
on a white bed, requests that his father recite a poem, "The Little
Tin Soldier, " as he had done in days past.   Intercutting between the
father, son, and mother ties the three into a family unit just as a
similar set of cuts tied David, Olivia, and Henry during the marriage
scene of THE SHINING HOUR and as Pat, Otto, Gottfried, and Erich
were tied during the marriage ceremony of THREE COMRADES.   The
boy falls asleep to the poem as Joe begins to cry.   As the sun rises
the next morning Ronnie awakens to Joe's singing to Richard.   Standing at the archway of the bedroom door, she watches the father and
son.   She enters the room and kneels before the boy.   Joe, about to
join the group, realizes he doesn't belong there any longer and leaves.

It seems as if the potential loss of his son and his realization
of his negligence cure Joe of his gambling habit.   He is next found
in Florida, where he works for a construction firm and refuses to
bet on the Gold Cup race.   Learning that Ronnie has brought Gallant
Man out to race, he returns to California to stop her.   Refusing to
realize why Ronnie has done this, and refusing to recognize that Gallant Man symbolizes their own union, Joe's only response is anger.
Ronnie sees that Gallant Man has made her life with Joe possible and
that this act is the only way to bring Joe back.   When the horse wins
the race Joe does not join Ronnie in the winner's circle.   Instead,
he goes to Gallant Man's stable and realizes just how wrong he was
and, by implication, how much he misjudged and mistreated Ronnie.
His admission ("She had the faith, you had the heart") is the sign of
his redemption.   Now able to become "whole" because of his willingness to see his own faults and selfishness, he can return to Ronnie
and to their life together.   When she comes to him and asks him to
return home the two share what they began with--Gallant Man and
their love.   Their other "winnings"--the $100,000 for the race and
their home--are unimportant compared to the love that they have re-
captured.   Ronnie crosses the space that separates them and enters
Joe's frame.   Gallant Man pushes his head into the frame as well,
and the three are once again united.

Like Myra, Joe must first come to understand his own divided nature and must finally heal himself of his obsession.   Only then
can he and Ronnie live happily.   Just as Myra exorcises Goronoff
and can accept George and the love she can share with him, so Joe
exorcises his need to gamble and can accept life and love with Ron-

nie. In both films the characters become "whole" not so much by
joining with another as by their ability to heal their own internal divisions. In both films the love relationship that follows this act is
the reward that they achieve. [30] In Borzage's last Republic film,
MOONRISE, this is even more strongly echoed, and the film becomes
a metaphor for Danny Hawkins's journey out of the swamp (i. e., confusion and fear) and into the light (i. e., acceptance of self and inner
healing).

Whenever later critics write about Borzage they concentrate
upon what are recognized as his major works: SEVENTH HEAVEN
(1927), STREET ANGEL (1928), MAN'S CASTLE (1933), THE MOR-
TAL STORM (1940), and MOONRISE (1949). This last film is unique
and perhaps most interesting because of its emphasis, the mise-en-
scêne and the landscape in particular "gradually developing over the
course of the film as a reflection of the changing state of the mind of
the single character. "[31] Danny's journey, the movement of the film,
is from the self-centered "I" to the community "We"[32] not so much
after the simple "dissolution of the first person singular"[33] as after
the individual returns to his source, faces his divisions, and integrates his own self into a sharable whole.

MOONRISE is Borzage's most "noir" film; its progression,
paralleling Danny's awakening, leads to a final shot of sunlight and
clear skies. Here the physical surroundings, and especially the
swamp where Danny murders Jerry Sykes, completely reflects Danny's own dark and confused mental state. Like earlier Borzage films,
however, the conclusion, on both the visual and the narrative levels,
reflects the Borzagean idea of ego transformation. Here this is due
not so much to love alone as to the unification of the self and of that
self with a previously submerged soul.

Not only is Danny's instability and tension reflected in the
overriding blackness of the physical landscape and by the "disturbing
and entrapping shadows, "[34] but Danny is continually trapped within
the frame either in high-angle shots, as in the prologue, or in his
being viewed through windows (the hardware store scene) or under
arches of light (at the amusement park). This latter image not only
gives the viewer the sense of Danny's entrapment but allows us to
view him as a Christian martyr as well, his head surrounded by a
halo and his suffering arising not only from his own sins but from
those of others. Throughout, the focal changes shift all of the pressure on to Danny and emphasize the weight of guilt and persecution
that he feels. [35]

Borzage's change of thematic focus, from his emphasis upon
spirit and soul in his earlier works to the psychological emphasis
here, is marked by the dynamic stylistic aspects of the film.

> The psychological intensity of Borzage's images, seen in
> his constant use of foreground-background interaction, rack
> focus, tight close-ups of parts of bodies (especially feet
> and hands), shadows and off-axis, angled shooting, seems

Moonrise

> to weigh oppressively on the film's characters, to constrict
> their actions and to prevent their spiritual liberation from
> the crazy forces that imprison them. [36]

In all, however, he completely negates the fatalistic philosophy of literary and cinematic naturalists and once again commits himself to
the idea of ultimate salvation. In this way the film becomes "the
summing up and reaffirmation of past work, [and] the final statement,
or testament, of a man"[37] all of whose films express a belief in
transcendence and regeneration.

In the shadowy opening a clear pond is disrupted by the ripples
of waves and the reflections seen upon the water. The camera pans
to the feet of three men walking past the pond and, once they reach
their destination, pulls back to reveal a gallows. What follows is not
seen directly, but as shadows upon the wall. A noose is placed around
a man's neck, and we see the shadowed form of the executioner in a
sudden camera movement left, pulling the lever. The cut that immediately follows, like the flat cut at the end of SEVENTH HEAVEN when
Chico returns from the dead, is to what appears to be the shadow of
the hanged man "cast over a crying baby's crib; as the camera moves
back, it becomes evident that it is the shadow of a toy. "[38] The presence of the shadow parallels the shadow that covers Danny throughout
most of his life.

> The shadows take on a supernatural quality, becoming de-
> monic, deathless presences that, like the shadows on the

wall of Plato's cave, have a ghostly, abstract reality of
their own, a reality ultimately independent of the concrete
reality of their source. As the trap springs, hanging Danny's father, Borzage cuts from a shadow of the execution
to that of a doll suspended by a string over a baby's crib,
transferring the spirits conjured up in the first scene into
the next where they haunt the dead man's son. [39]

A time montage follows that depicts Danny's growth, his persecution by his schoolmates, and an undercut reprise of his father's
execution. The hold of the past over the present is shown not only
through this reprise but in the high-angle shots that pin Danny down
during a fight as much as the other boys do and that, along with the
accompanying shadows, create the feeling of mental torture that Danny feels. This sequence ends with a cut to Danny's legs, similar to
the shot of his father's before the hanging, as Danny walks through
the woods "towards his own spiritual 'execution': he accidentally
kills Jerry Sykes, his chief tormentor, and tries to conceal the
crime. "[40] The enigmatic quality of the scenes indicates the subjec-
tivity of what we have seen and creates the feeling that what we are
viewing is what Danny feels. This also gives the viewer the sense
of what Danny defines as the causes and conditions of his life and
his "curse. "[41] Danny is sure of his own doom due to the "curse"
of his father's deed, and the second execution becomes "Danny's vision of his own death. "[42] Danny's murder of Sykes, preceded by a
pan up from the swamp like the one from the puddle, is made to appear a fated act. Unlike traditional Freudian imagery, the water of
the swamp and the muddy water of the puddle are not symbols of rebirth but of confusion, destruction, and death.

Danny truly believes in his curse and allows himself to give
his life over to the negative forces of this self-fulfilling prophesy. A
positive force that acts counter to this is his love for Gilly, the woman who offers him understanding as well as redemption and salvation.
The conflict of these two forces, echoing the split within Danny, becomes symbolic of the struggle that he undergoes during the rest of
the film. Danny can neither accept life nor completely reject it.

When he returns from the killing, Danny stops a group of men
from teasing Billy Scripture, a deaf mute who is in a position like
that of Danny. Billy, with the mind of a child, is an outcast from
the immediate world in which he lives. He and Danny are very much
alike in that both are still caught up in the past and cannot face or
deal with the future effectively. When Danny returns to the dance
hall to clean up he stands before three mirrors. Unlike a similar
scene in LITTLE MAN, WHAT NOW?, Danny has little sense of himself, and the mirrors reflect his internal division rather than reiterate a positive spiritual nature.

As he is driving Gilly home from the dance Gilly talks of a
little boy in her class who is unhappy and has been hurt by the other
children. This becomes her view of Danny as well, and as her love
for him grows she will help him to reach adulthood. Danny's re-

mark to the other boy in the car, who watches Danny's suicidal speed-
ing and whose father owns the car, "don't worry about your old man, "
is more telling in its obvious implications. Danny's suicidal crash
is an attempt not only to escape his "old man" but to escape life itself. Seeing Sykes's face in the windshield, Danny loses control of
the car, as he did his temper when he killed Sykes. When he crashes and sees Gilly's unconscious body his conflict is crystalized: "his
death will mean the end of his unhappiness, but it will also mean
losing Gilly"[43] and any chance for a positive internal healing.

Danny's sense of entrapment is further symbolized in the gold-
fish bowl on his aunt's mantel in the next scene and his continual
placement under arcs of light throughout. This is first seen as Danny wanders through the dance after the murder. While the triple
mirror symbolizes the disunity within his personality, his position
under the arc of lights symbolizes both his entrapment and his potential spiritual regeneration.

When Danny later confesses his love to Gilly she at first rejects his aggressiveness ("This is all I want"). Only later does she
admit her love for him. The simpleness of this is undercut by the
larger situation that surrounds them: Danny's instability and his act
of murder. This is visually underscored in the web-like shadows of
the twigs that fall upon his face during their embrace. This symbol
is later expanded, and when Danny meets Gilly in the woods the swamp
is in the background. While Gilly's love is the first completely positive thing that has happened in Danny's life, his guilt and what he is
hiding continually halt the regenerative growth that their closeness
could bring about.

Danny's "rigid self-containment"[44] continually "walls him off
from the characters who try to help him."[45] Like Mose, the brake-
man, Danny has withdrawn from the world and has moved into one he
has created for himself. Yet Mose's isolation is partially a transcendence of the immediate world[46] while Danny's is a complete rejection of all that can help him because of his own blindness and fear.
Mose respects all men and all creatures, addressing all animals as
"Mister" and realizing that to live without the human race is the
worst crime of all. He instructs Danny, telling him that loneliness
is a crime and that a man needs to be with others, especially with
a woman. The low-angle shots of Mose and Danny's position at his
feet act to reinforce his transcendence and spirituality and give his
words a meaning far beyond the immediate.

Danny follows his meeting with Mose by one with Gilly at the
deserted Blackwater plantation, the name itself taking on implications
of the swamp and of Danny's murky consciousness. The two escape
their present reality, and Danny retreats from his aggressive treatment of Gilly. Gilly pretends to be Mrs. Blackwater giving a dance
for Confederate officers and, for an instant as they dance and kiss,
they are one and all of their separations are gone.

As she and Danny dance around the room, after he reluc-

tantly gives in to her fantasy, the camera elevates to a
point beyond where we would imagine the ceiling to be, and
then descends, tracking in on them as they stop and kiss
by a window in silhouette. The scene makes Danny aware
of the possibility of escaping time. His fatalism causes
him to see time as a repeating cycle of events in which he
is trapped. His love for Gilly can take him out of this
cycle; at the beginning of the scene he remarks that "time
goes slowly--it seems like all the clocks in Virginia stopped
this afternoon. At night they hurry and we haven't enough
time."[47]

The portrait of Mrs. Blackwater that hangs above them reiterates
both their dreams of escape and the influence of the past. As the
camera ascends Danny and Gilly's transcendence is expressed as is
their freedom from all of time and space. Yet this transcendence
is only temporary, and the camera descends and moves in to a shot
of the lovers kissing in the shadows. Their images are so dark as
to appear almost black. This reflects Danny's continued desire not
only to "negate the relationship"[48] but to disappear from life (i. e.,
his continued thoughts of suicide).

Danny's entrapment is further symbolizes in the coon-hunting
scene that follows. As Danny climbs a tree to get the coon he looks
at the swamp pond where he committed Sykes's murder. The cross-
cutting within the scene aligns Danny with the coon, and when the
coon falls and is attacked by the dogs Danny's possible destruction
is implied as well. The dissolve used to move from Danny to the
coon links these two through their entrapment. This same entrapment image occurs in the following scene when Danny is in the hardware store and Sykes's body is brought into town.

Borzage pulls focus from the sheriff looking out the window in the background to Danny as he steps into the shot
in the near foreground. The sudden focal change shifts
all the pressure onto Danny, alone in the foreground. [49]

During the conversation that follows this Danny "impatiently smashes
a fly the sheriff has been toying with on the table."[50] This does not
so much reflect a death wish[51] as it does Danny's nervousness and
his sense of the smallness of his selfhood.

The most powerful presentment of Danny's sense of entrapment
takes place during the ferris-wheel sequence that occurs soon after.
Not only do the amusement-park crowds push against Danny and Gilly,
but Danny's attempt to escape on the wheel fails as well. Up on the
wheel, and again surrounded in a halo made up of lights, Danny tells
Gilly about his father and of the murder of a doctor he commited after the doctor's negligence caused his wife's death. The wheel and
its unending circular motion reflect Danny's inability to escape his
past and to transcend, therefore, his internal divisions.

Borzage's camera rises and falls with the turning of the

wheel, the longer shots intercut with close-ups of Danny
beginning to panic and the sheriff glowering down. Here,
Borzage makes Danny's fatalism totally concrete--the turning of the wheel becomes the turning of time. As a passive
rider on the wheel, Danny is unable to escape the sheriff,
yet the sheriff is unable to catch up with him. Danny half
resents and half welcomes death in the form of the sheriff,
and, finding that the turning of the wheel will not resolve
the conflict within him, suicidally jumps from the top. [52]

Danny leaps from the wheel, and, as in the Sykes murder sequence,
a subjective camera is used. This creates a sense of immediacy and
forces the viewer "to be" Danny and to feel the entrapment Danny
feels. This sequence does not, as David Kehr states, so much dem-
onstrate "that Danny's only way out is by taking decisive action himself"[53] as it demonstrates the continued negative pattern of action he
has followed throughout.

        Danny's return to Mose reinforces the sense that more posi-
tive action must be undertaken. Earlier Mose expressed his ideas
that "there isn't enough dignity in the world" and that "blood is red,
it keeps you alive. It doesn't tell you what you have to do." Now
he reinforces this latter idea by telling Danny that he must take positive action by himself and, as Danny sits at his feet, tells him that
he must stop killing the "dead over and over." Mose attempts to
"make Danny aware of the ignominy of being 'shoved around'"[54] and
to make him resist his deterministic ideology. Mose is, however,
too closely associated with the darkness and the isolation of the swamp,
and Danny must choose to act positively and on his own[55] and cannot
simply do as Mose tells him without first facing his disunity and accepting it.

        Danny continues his negative course of action, savagely beat-
ing Billy Scripture when he finds that Billy has the knife he lost during the murder. Billy, like Danny, has no sense of time--he cannot
understand why his feet no longer fit into the footsteps he made in
cement as a child--and is tied to Danny throughout, such as when
his face is seen in the mirror with Danny's after the murder. Danny's beating of Billy becomes another self-destructive act, since
there is so much of the mute in himself.

        When Danny finally runs away from the pursuing sheriff and
posse he leaves with the knowledge that both the sheriff and Gilly believe in his essential innocence. These two know that Danny must
return of his own accord, accept his punishment, and, thereby, be
able to live the rest of his life as a human being. Danny's journey
becomes a trip back into time, and the posse's dogs that follow him
become symbolic of his haunting memories. Danny runs through the
water, deeper and deeper into the swamp. Finally he returns to his
grandmother's house in the mountains, where he is forced to face
the truth of his past. His return to his birthplace is recognized by
the crib seen originally in the prologue.

The old lady gives Danny "a human conception of his father,
a conception which Danny is at first unable to accept, still holding to
his view of his father as a monster."[56] She echoes Mose's words
and confronts Danny as he is sneaking out at dawn ("You want to hate
your pa"). As he flees, however, Danny comes upon the graves of
his parents, at which point he frees himself "from his isolation in
the present and his claustrophobic self-containment" by placing his
rifle upright against the grave markers. His deeds echo his grandmother's idea--that only a coward blames others for his own actions;
Danny is tied to his father now because, like his father, he finds the
answers he seeks by honest thought. Apologizing to his father, he
finally believes he can attain the peace he seeks. Borzage emphasizes Danny's transcendence by his cut to a low-angle shot that places
Danny against a bright sky for the first time. Released from the
"curse" of his past, he is no longer framed in the "dark-edged, heavy,
claustrophobic" manner of the earlier portions of the film. When he
gives himself up he walks through the forest and into a brightly lit
clearing to "rejoin the human race." He hugs one of the dogs that
had been tracking him and awaits the arrival of the sheriff and the
posse. When Gilly emerges from the forest "the intercut tracking
shots melt the movement of Danny walking towards Gilly with that of
her walking towards him" and slowly reduces the symbolic and physical distance that previously separated them. Although less abrupt
than the same type of ending found in HIS BUTLER'S SISTER, the
meaning is the same. The pair finally join, the editing giving them
an equality of weight and making Gilly more the reward than the
means for Danny's redemption.[57] The concluding extreme long shot
places these two in harmony with nature and the environment and reinforces the transcendent nature of their love. Danny's isolation and
division now gone, he is integrated with Gilly and the two are integrated into the larger universe through "a timeless and weightless
romantic union."[58]

While MOONRISE is considered by many to be Borzage's greatest sound film, this is an overstatement. The film is an important
work, but it does not exist alone, separated from the director's
other films. Discussing Borzage, for instance, as an "auteur" pre-
sumes that any of his individual works grow out of the stylistic and
thematic concerns of his earlier films. Therefore, when studying
these three films, and MOONRISE in particular, we must remember
that these works are complete films in themselves, but also that their
meaning is made clearer by what has already been discovered in
earlier works.

These three films come at the end of a thirty-five-year period in which Borzage was consistently at work. After these works
Borzage left Republic and directing, avoiding the field for ten years
and working either in television or not at all. While theories for
this hiatus range from alcoholism to trouble with the House Un-American
Activities Committee, the most probable reason was Borzage's growing dislike for changing film conditions and tastes. I'VE ALWAYS
LOVED YOU, THAT'S MY MAN, and MOONRISE were all financial
failures, and Borzage probably realized that the ideals and beliefs

he puts into his films were no longer popular with the public. The pessimism of postwar American society affected film styles very sharply. Borzagean lyricism and romanticism, seen even as late as MOONRISE, lost vogue with the rise of film noir and its essentially pessimistic outlook.

Not primarily a search for a place within society, these films concerned themselves almost exclusively with the conflicts and neuroses that divided the individual, and that individual's struggle for internal unity. Danny, like Myra in I'VE ALWAYS LOVED YOU and like Joe in THAT'S MY MAN, must come to terms with his internal conflicts so that he can escape his physical and emotional entrapment and move into the future. The films become a journey for each of these characters just as in earlier films, such as GREEN LIGHT, DISPUTED PASSAGE, and STRANGE CARGO, the major characters undertake an immense physical journey that leads to a spiritual transcendence and ideological conversion. In these later films, however, the hardships of the physical journey are completely downplayed, whereas the mental and emotional conflicts are first recognized and then positively acted upon. The resultant transcendence is, therefore, not so much an entrance into some larger spiritual state or belief system as it is an individual healing and, through that healing, the achievement of internal peace. It is only after each of these characters finds this internal peace that he or she can join with another and become interdependent. This is what ties and separates these characters to earlier Borzage protagonists. In these later films the "wholeness" that the characters achieve is not one that comes through love and their joining with another. Here the "wholeness" is achieved only after a clash of internal oppositions occurs and after a state of internal harmony is created. These characters become "whole" before they become interdependent and do not become interdependent to find or achieve "wholeness." These later films concentrate almost exclusively upon the individual, downplaying the importance of the love relationship and making it, as previously stated, more a reward for redemption than the cause of it. By exorcising their self-destructive conflicts in an almost primitive or mystical manner, [59] these characters are reborn.

NOTES

[1]Fred Camper, "Disputed Passage," in Movies and Methods. Ed. Bill Nichols (Berkeley: University of California Press, 1976), p. 339.

[2]John Belton, The Hollywood Professionals: Howard Hawks, Frank Borzage and Edgar Ulmer vol. 3 (New York: Tantivity, 1974), p. 112.

[3]Belton, Hollywood Professionals, p. 112.

[4]Ibid., p. 109.

[5]Ibid., p. 111.

[6]Ibid.

[7]Ibid.

[8]Robert Smith, "The Films of Frank Borzage" (part 1), Bright Lights 1, 2 (Spring 1975), p. 113.

[9]John Belton, "I've Always Loved You," Focus! 9 (Spring-Summer 1973), p. 42.

[10]Belton, "I've Always Loved You," p. 42.

[11]Ibid.

[12]Ibid.

[13]Ibid.

[14]Ibid.

[15]Ibid.

[16]Ibid., p. 43.

[17]Ibid.

[18]Ibid., p. 42.

[19]Ibid.

[20]Ibid.

[21]Ibid.

[22]Ibid.

[23]Ibid., p. 44.

[24]Ibid.

[25]Ibid.

[26]Ibid.

[27]Ibid.

[28]Ibid., p. 42.

[29]Robert Smith, "The Films of Frank Borzage" (part 2), Bright Lights 1, 3 (Summer 1975), p. 18.

[30]Belton, Hollywood Professionals, p. 117.

[31]David Kehr, "Moonrise," Focus! 9 (Spring-Summer 1973), p. 26.

[32]Kehr, p. 27.

[33]Ibid.

[34]Smith, "The Films of Frank Borzage" (part 2), p. 19.

[35]Belton, Hollywood Professionals, p. 115.

[30]Ibid., p. 112.

[37]Kehr, p. 26.

[38]Ibid., p. 27.

[39]Belton, Hollywood Professionals, p. 113.

[40]Ibid.

[41]Kehr, p. 27.

[42]Ibid.

[43]Ibid., p. 28.

[44]Belton, Hollywood Professionals, p. 114.

[45]Ibid.

[46]Ibid.

[47]Kehr, p. 28.

[48]Ibid.

[49]Belton, Hollywood Professionals, p. 115.

[50]Kehr, p. 27.

[51]Ibid.

[52]Ibid., p. 30.

[53]Ibid.

[54]Ibid.

[55]Ibid.

[56]Ibid.
[57]Belton, <u>Hollywood Professionals</u>, p. 117.
[58]Ibid.
[59]Ibid., p. 118.

6.   TWO FINAL FILMS

After a ten-year absence Borzage returned to direct two final films.   It is fitting that the ostensible subjects of these works were of tremendous importance throughout Borzage's career: war, in CHINA DOLL (1958), and religion, in THE BIG FISHERMAN (1959).

In the first of these films there is a significant shift.   The war itself becomes even less important as a potential force of spiritual destruction than it was in SEVENTH HEAVEN or A FAREWELL TO ARMS.   Cliff Brandon's "bitter loneliness and hate have no specific source,"[1] and the war zone that he inhabits becomes, like the swamp in MOONRISE, a reflection of his emotional turmoil.   Cliff's death becomes, therefore, not only an implied spiritual transcendence but a metaphoric transcendence out of his own conflict and into the peace of eternity.   CHINA DOLL becomes, in this way, a fully developed synthesis of Borzagean ideas, drawing from various earlier films in both ideology and actual construction.   The film meshes the lyricism of SEVENTH HEAVEN with the sensuality of THE RIVER, alludes to the conversion films of 1937-1940 and to DISPUTED PASSAGE, in particular, as well as to the personal exorcism idea stressed in the Republic films of 1946-1949.   This film differs from these latter works in that love in CHINA DOLL becomes a central part of Cliff's redemption and not simply his reward for this.   Cliff and Shu-Jen's child becomes a stronger symbol of this regeneration, being far more than the symbol of unity and spiritual rebirth that it is at the end of MAN'S CASTLE and LITTLE MAN, WHAT NOW?   The child in the later film not only becomes symbolic of this and of the marriage bond that existed between the two parents but joins both spirit, in Cliff's sacrifice and transcendence, and body in a far more natural and lasting manner than through a marriage bond.

CHINA DOLL, like LIVING ON VELVET and THE SHINING HOUR, opens with a shot of an airplane flying through the sky.   Yet unlike these earlier films, the varied views of the airplane through both close, medium and long shots give us a greater symbolic sense of the drift that Cliff Brandon is in the midst of.   The association is made stronger by the fade-in from the plane as it moves toward the camera to Cliff within the plane.   Also, like the movement of the plane, which is from right to left, Cliff moves from right to left as well.   Cliff's bitterness and cynicism is due as much to his loneliness and drifting as to the war itself.[2]   He is alienated from his men, as seen in various frame compositions in which Cliff stands alone while the others are grouped, his only friend being Father Cairns.   His close friendship with the priest and the priest's ability

184

to see beyond Cliff's brutish nature makes it clear that Cliff's soul
is only waiting to be tapped.   Yet the priest and what he offers are
not enough, and Cliff continues his on-the-ground life of drunken loneliness.

Cliff spends his ground time at Sadie's, a drinking club fre-
quented by prostitutes.   He stands alone at the bar, separated from
the men clustered at a table in the foreground, turning down their
company as he does that of a prostitute.   Exactly what Cliff is "trying to drown" is unclear, but in doing so, he isolates himself from
himself and from the others.

> Like Joe Grange's gambling fever in THAT'S MY MAN,
> Brandon's drunkenness drives him further into himself: in
> attempting to escape the war he shuts out involvement with his
> men.   As he leaves Sadie's, one of his men stops him and says
> innocently: "Hello, Captain. You're leaving early, aren't
> you?"   Brandon gruffly snaps back, "I got here early."[3]

As he is leaving Sadie's, Cliff meets an aged Chinese man
who offers to sell him his daughter.   In lighting a lighter to stare
at her, Cliff underscores her basic purity and the light that she will
bring to him.   While he refuses the offer, he gives the old man money, telling him to "keep her" and turning away.   The father's pride
will not allow for this, and Shu-Jen follows Cliff home, where she
becomes his house servant.   While it is not clear whether or not
she loves him or acts out of duty, Shu-Jen transforms Cliff's quar-
ters into a home, much as Diane did for Chico in SEVENTH HEAV-
EN, as Trina did for Bill in MAN'S CASTLE, and as Pat did for
Erich, Otto, and Gottfried in THREE COMRADES. [4]   And while Cliff
continues his excursions to Sadie's and still gets drunk, a change
does slowly occur.   Cliff and Shu-Jen, along with Ellington, Cliff's
Chinese houseboy, become a pseudo family.   Their functions shift
throughout, Shu-Jen acting as mother to both Cliff and Ellington,
Cliff acting as surrogate father to these two, and Ellington acting
as chaperone.   Just as Cliff changes (e.g., he is seen drinking
coffee at the bar), Shu-Jen changes as well.   She is soon seen out-
fitted in a Chinese silk gown, her hair cut and styled by one of the
Red Cross women.   This act becomes a rite of passage, because
from this time on both Cliff and the viewer see her as a woman and
not just as a child.   A change in their relationship is seen as well.
While at first Shu-Jen covered Cliff with a blanket while he slept, he
now gives her his trenchcoat to protect her from the rain.   While he
refuses fully to acknowledge her importance, he at least acknowledges
her presence.   His change and his admission of affection for Shu-Jen
are most clearly noted when returning home drunk one night from Sadie's.   Cliff removes his shoes so as not to mess the floor, staggers
over to Shu-Jen's bed, looks at her, smiles, and enters to cover her.
This action, the first positive one from Cliff, ties the two and reflects their growing love.   Cliff's relationship with Shu-Jen remains
in a state of limbo since he cannot consciously admit and accept his
love for her.   Yet the fact that he is home for supper and not at Sadie's and that he is wearing his bedroom slippers and not muddy

boots when the priest enters tells all that he cannot admit.   Cliff's
tenderness is noted in his changed attitude toward the men as well.
When he goes off on a mission later he explains his anger to them
and joins them as they are grouped at a table.

When Cliff is next seen on his plane no external shots of the
flying plane are used, an omission that reflects Cliff's change.   When
he returns to Shu-Jen after this mission with a recurrence of his ma-
laria the restorative and regenerative nature of their relationship is
clearly recognized and their love is sealed by a sexual consummation.
In a scene that draws upon scenes from both THE RIVER and from
DISPUTED PASSAGE Cliff returns to the house and climbs into his
bed shivering.   Shu-Jen covers him tightly with blankets and holds
him to her much as Rosalee did to the frozen Allen John in THE
RIVER, attempting to infuse his body with her own warmth and so
revive him.   He in turn calls for her in his delirium, and the overhead shot that is used echoes his growing spiritual regeneration as
he admits his love for her.   As she hugs him the camera rises up
to a window, out of which we see the lightning and storm and which
ties their sexual consummation to greater spiritual and universal
forces.   After this upward pan there is a fade-in to a bright, clear
dawn, and the camera pulls down to reveal Cliff revived, his fever
broken.   As in a similar scene at the end of DISPUTED PASSAGE,
Cliff and Shu-Jen, like Beaven and Audrey, are integrated into a
higher order, the male's physical recovery symbolic of his spiritual
healing as well.   Shu-Jen's kneeling before Cliff and the touch that
they share when she gives him a cup of coffee echo the spiritual nature of their love as words cannot.   Shu-Jen's touching of the brooch
that he has given her and that she wears over her heart echoes her
feelings for him.   The brooch, like the medals in SEVENTH HEAV-
EN, becomes a signifier of this love.

Cliff's guilt is assuaged by the priest ("What happened is nothing compared to what could have happened without you"), yet Cliff
still cannot understand and deal with Shu-Jen's totally giving nature
("All she wants to do is give").   When he later learns that Shu-Jen
is pregnant and has run away in fear he finds her, pins the brooch
over her heart again, covers her with his coat, and carries her
home.   Admitting that he has "spent my whole life shutting myself
off from people, " Cliff realizes just how much Shu-Jen has done for
him.   The two marry in a combination Chinese-Christian ceremony,
this act symbolizing not only their commitment to each other but a
cultural fusing as well.   Their integration into the larger immediate
sphere is reflected by their being surrounded by all of the other men
and women who live at the base.   Cliff's regeneration, it should be
noted, reflects a larger group transformation as well.   While earlier
the men only flirted with the Red Cross women, their love deepens
as does their sense of commitment.   As in the Borzagean films of
the 1937-1940 period, the regeneration of a central individual is
echoed in a group regeneration.   There is the sense of there being
some larger spiritual forces at work.   This is reflected in the fare-
wells that occur the next day at the airfields as the men go off on
another mission.   There are separate shots of each of the couples

saying goodbye, as well as one of Cliff, Shu-Jen, and Ellington, Cliff's family, embracing.

It is important to note that Cliff names his plane "Shu-Jen," representative of the fact that she is always with him. When they are reunited later it is as if they have never been separated at all. Shu-Jen moves to the base with Ellington and Cliff's child, a girl. It is this child who symbolizes Cliff's rebirth, and while he and Shu-Jen die in air raids later, the child lives on as "a living symbol of her parents' regeneration."[5]

When the crew return from a raid Cliff finds Shu-Jen dead in the wreckage of the base, and the child missing. While he sends his men off, he remains behind, covering Shu-Jen's body with his coat as he did earlier, and laying the body out in the sunshine as if under the eye of God. When Cliff finds the infant safe under Ellington's body, he lifts the child in a high-angle shot and carries it to safety under a truck, where he places his dogtags around her neck. This act is significant, since by doing so, Cliff symbolically gives over his identity and his spirit to the child.

> In the midst of a tremendously chaotic action sequence with the camera now in the air with the enemy; now on the ground with Brandon, Borzage cuts back and forth from Brandon, machine-gunning enemy planes, to the baby he is fighting to protect. As the action grows more frenetic, the pace of the cutting between Cliff and his child quickens, binding the two together and achieving Cliff's rebirth not in his own body but in that of his child. [6]

In the final shot the camera pulls back to incorporate Cliff and the truck the child is under into the larger landscape and thereby into the larger universe as well. Neither Cliff's nor Shu-Jen's death is followed by an ascending crane shot, yet the spirituality of the two is linked in the overhead and high-angle shots used previously and in their deaths under the sunny sky. Cliff has found, as Sergeant Forster said earlier, happiness in death. While it may be said that Cliff is essentially irredeemable because his anger and hate have no actual source, [7] he does exorcise these negative spirits in his relationship with Shu-Jen. His death is more a sacrificial one, since in dying he gives life to his child. Cliff is not so much doomed, therefore, as his spirit is triumphant through his actions.

The film's epilogue echoes Cliff's sacrifice and his "triumph over time, space and mortality"[8] as well as the group transcendence that has occurred. The crew gathers at Los Angeles airport to meet Cliff and Shu-Jen's child, found by Father Cairns in a Hong King orphanage. She has never removed the dogtags, which are now as much a part of her own identity as they are symbolic of Cliff's spirit, which exists within her. She exits the plane, shot at a low angle (which echoes her spiritual nature), and, as the camera pulls back, she holds up her dogtags. The group gathers around her, incorporating her into their midst, as they did Shu-Jen and Cliff after their wed-

ding. As they do so the camera ascends to a high-angle shot that
isolates the group and reflects their own rebirth. The spirituality
of the moment is further underscored in the hymn that rises throughout. The child, like Cliff and Shu-Jen, "is at one with a larger,
divine and eternal order that watches over all human achievement
and gives it meaning."[9]

CHINA DOLL is, of sorts, a culmination of Borzage's work.
It not only incorporates the ideas of earlier films but joins together
the ideas of regeneration, rebirth, transcendence, and conversion
more completely than any other single work. Through the child and
in what she symbolizes, not only is the love and regeneration of
Cliff Brandon and Shu-Jen realized, but so is Cliff's sacrifice and
change as well as the changes in those around them. The child becomes an extension of Cliff and Shu-Jen, as did the children or the
expectation of children in MAN'S CASTLE and LITTLE MAN, WHAT
NOW?, yet here the child becomes representative of Borzage's belief
in the joint and continuing nature of spiritual transcendence. The
girl's radiance arises from the souls that exist within her. Cliff
and Shu-Jen's souls exist not only outside of the immediate world
after their deaths, therefore, but within the world as well. This
joins the two different spiritual spheres into a greater continuum and
makes Cliff's sacrifice one that is close to that of Christ himself.
By extension, the child becomes not only a symbol of the living souls
of Cliff and Shu-Jen, but a symbol of procreation and one of transcendence over the seeming finality of death.

Borzage's concern with transcendence always took on spiritual
and religious overtones, yet it is only in his last film, THE BIG
FISHERMAN, that he concerns himself with an actual biblical tale
and not a religious or symbolic allegory. Perhaps it is this factor
that harms the film most. Unlike earlier Borzage films, such as
SEVENTH HEAVEN, THE RIVER, THE SHINING HOUR, and STRANGE
CARGO, that integrate the spiritual and the secular, Borzage attempts
to create an overriding sense of holiness in THE BIG FISHERMAN that
excludes any sensual relationships between characters. While there are
provocative and interesting moments in the film, these moments are
few, and the film is on the whole lacking in feeling. Whereas in the
films mentioned earlier Borzage infused both characters and situations with an underlying sense of holiness or spirituality, the overtly
religious sense created here is strained and hollow. In the earlier
film THE RIVER the water imagery evokes Christian images of salvation, rebirth, and baptism. Here, words take the place of images
and this creates both a visual and narrative lack.

Like GREEN LIGHT and DISPUTED PASSAGE, THE BIG FISH-
ERMAN is based on a novel by Lloyd C. Douglas. Borzage's making
of THE BIG FISHERMAN coincides with a film trend of the 1950s and
1960s. Throughout this period a number of directors turned to the
Bible and used biblical incidents for film stories. De Mille, who
had done this in the 1920s when he produced and directed THE TEN
COMMANDMENTS (1923) and KING OF KINGS (1927), returned to the
genre with SAMSON AND DELILAH (1949) and a successful remake

of THE TEN COMMANDMENTS (1956).   Other biblical films of this
period include QUO VADIS? (1951), a remake of the 1912 spectacle;
THE ROBE (1953); SALOME (1953); LAND OF THE PHARAOHS (1955);
BEN HUR (1959), a remake of Fred Niblo's 1926 film; THE GREAT-
EST STORY EVER TOLD (1965); and THE BIBLE (1966).

The focus of Borzage's film is the conversion of Simon-Peter.
Intermingled with this, however, is the story of the Arabian Princess
Fara and her quest for revenge against the father who deserted her,
Herod-Antipas.   The movement of these two characters toward reli-
gious conversion joins them as searchers and as believers.   Their
progress is not only paralleled, but the end finds Peter, and the
Christianity that he symbolizes, replacing Herod and the decadent
secularity he represents, as Fara's father figure.   This process re-
sults in Fara's internal healing and, like Danny Hawkins in MOON-
RISE, in her ability to forget the past and to move into the future.

There are some very "traditional" Borzage devices that occur
throughout the film and that give it moments of life.   The opening
track shot is one such example.   As a shepherd approaches and passes, the camera follows his movements through a dark tunnel and into
the light of the valley.   As he reaches this dividing line the camera
halts, and as the shepherd continues his movement his form grows
smaller and smaller against the landscape.   This tracking shot is
used not only to give the viewer a sense of the movement and of the
area through which the shepherd walks, but by stopping where it does,
gives the viewer the sense of isolation in which the Arabian community exists.   The separation of dark and light exemplifies this further,
the light of the valley being representative of the happiness-in-isolation
of those within it.   When Fara and Voldi, the man she loves, return
there at the end of the film Fara realizes that she no longer belongs
there, since she has accepted the greater vision of Christ.   While
the two have returned from the darkness of the larger foreign world
Fara's acceptance of Christianity and her resulting internal healing
temporarily separate her from Voldi until he too is converted and
can join her ("I'll come to you someday").   It is only fitting that
the last shot of Fara and Peter be of them on a boat, floating down
the river, the voice of Christ leading them and exhorting them to
"love God with all thy heart, soul, strength and thy neighbor as thy
self. "

Other "splits" are presented and resolved throughout the film
as well.   Not only is there a continuing dark-light contrast, but space
itself serves as an indication of distance and difference.   Fara's mother and father live in warring nations, she in Arabia and he in Judea.
Their physical separation reflects their ideological one as well.   Fara's
mother, Princess Arnon, is a faithful and devoted woman whose isolation is due to her break with her husband.   In returning to Arabia
she returns to her past and creates a romantic dream world for Fara
in which everyone lives "happily ever after. "   In contrast, Fara's
father, Herod-Antipas, is a total hedonist.   He lives in a depraved
world where passion is recognized as love and where flesh and blood
and not spirit are central.   While Arnon could not defeat or conquer
Herod, Christ's coming into this community ensures Herod's defeat.

These two split strains that coexist within Fara cause her to seek revenge. Her dual nature, earlier recognized when she looks into a pond and sees her reflection, torments her. The physical journey that she undertakes, while ostensibly one of revenge, becomes a spiritual journey in which she finds "wholeness" through salvation. John the Baptist sees this internal split when he meets her in the desert, just as Christ later recognizes the split in Simon. It is the spiritual side of Fara that is strongest, as Hannah, Simon's mother-in-law, sees, yet she must first root out her desire for revenge before this side of her nature can triumph. Whereas Simon's conversion to Christ comes after he sees a blind child cured (symbolic of his own situation), Fara's is not so easily achieved.

Fara's dual nature comes out most clearly after the murder of John the Baptist. Awakening from a troubled sleep, she hears the voices of Christ ("Thou shalt not kill") and Voldi ("I love you"). She rises and, almost without understanding, goes to the palace where she witnesses the execution of John the Baptist, shot in shadow through a curtain. She then witnesses the wrath of God as Herod's temple is wrecked and his crown symbolically blown off and crushed. When she later comes to kill Herod, and after he warns her that the consequences of her action will be eternal guilt, she admits to hearing the voice of Christ but of being more strongly driven by her hatred. This she claims to be her inheritance from Herod, and this division not only reflects her own schism but the dual nature of human beings. As she quotes both men, she finally realizes the greatness of Christ and of his words, her conversion visually underscored by the low-angle shot of her that follows. Simon then enters and tells her that "you have won." She agrees, and her words reflect her internal healing: "I am free, Esther [the name she had been using] is gone from me. I am no longer an outcast. I am Judean, Galilean, Egyptian, Roman, Greek, all of them." Herod's answering statement, "I am only what I have always been," serves only to invest her words with greater meaning. Fara and Peter stand above the dazed Herod and leave him to suffer alone.

Both Simon-Peter and Fara are converted by Christ and join his service. Simon-Peter joins the other Apostles to spread Christ's word, his physical rebuilding of the temple he earlier defaced representative of the faith he is to help to spread. When Christ calls Peter to him he must first walk through a fog on the seashore, which is symbolic of his own confusion, before he can reach the mountain Christ stands upon. This is directly contrasted to the final shot, in which Fara and Peter leave Arabia. Here the two stand in a boat under a clear sky. Christ's holiness is fully exemplified as well in that, whereas he earlier exists as a man, and we see his arm or foot but never all of him, he now exists only as "the word."

While THE BIG FISHERMAN lacks the power of most of Borzage's work and while it is not as well constructed as CHINA DOLL, the film does have interesting threads running through it. The idea of regeneration and transcendence through love is changed to that of regeneration and transcendence through Christianity. Christ not only replaces the worldly lover but becomes the source of healing as well. Like Newell Paige in GREEN LIGHT and John Beaven in DISPUTED PASSAGE, Fara embarks upon a physical journey that becomes a metaphor for her spiritual change. Also, like Myra Hassman in I'VE ALWAYS LOVED YOU and Danny Hawkins in MOONRISE, she returns to the source of her division so as to undergo an internal reunification. Fara joins within herself both the spiritual and the physical in her ability to love both Christ and a single man, Voldi. Her resulting "wholeness" makes her a more spiritual character and forces her to leave Voldi until such time as he is converted as well. In joining with Christ she, like Clothilde at the end of TILL WE MEET AGAIN, finds happiness in service to all of mankind. This is an extension of Borzage's belief in interdependence and the healing and wholeness it brings. Fara's joining with Christ connects her to Voldi and to all humanity. And, as in CHINA DOLL, all spiritual states are joined into a greater continuum.

NOTES

[1]John Belton, The Hollywood Professionals: Howard Hawks, Frank Borgage and Edgar Ulmer vol. 3 (New York: Tantivity, 1974), p. 121.

[2]Ibid., p. 118.
[3]Ibid., p. 119.
[4]Ibid.
[5]Ibid., p. 122.
[6]Ibid., p. 121.
[7]Ibid.
[8]Ibid., p. 122.
[9]Ibid.

CONCLUSION

It has been written that Borzage remade the same film through-out his career, never varying in theme or in style. While it is true that he maintained a singular and unwavering belief in the efficacy of spiritual love, his films are not the same, but rather dependent upon each other. Borzage did not so much choose melodrama as his way of viewing the world as he seemed innately to accept it. Each of his films is, therefore, structured in such a way that Good is opposed to Evil and the end of the film finds Evil at least temporarily van-quished, locked out of the safety zone created by the interdependence of the united couple or exorcised from an internally united individual. It is through this crisis situation, which is so basic to melodrama, that the individual or the couple finds peace. While Griffith relied upon melodrama as a way of presenting the conflict between the in-dividual and the external world, Borzage used the form to explain the unification possible within an individual or between individuals.

What we find within the Borzage corpus are lines of thematic and stylistic development that create a sense of continuity and growth. To fully understand the later films, therefore, it is necessary to study the earlier ones and to understand the development of the particular Borzagean attitude presented. The idea of transcendence, of almost unconsciously moving out of the self-centered and into the sphere of spiritual and physical interdependence, is a larger idea that is, either overtly or in an understated manner, in almost all of his films. In the 1915-1926 period love implies religious transcendence. With SEVENTH HEAVEN and STREET ANGEL secular love is fused with religious and spiritual growth. With THE RIVER this is fused with sexual love as well. The later films draw upon this and do not so much copy the earlier works as they refine the ideas stressed earli-er. In SEVENTH HEAVEN Chico and Diane are united under a gleam-ing white light that signifies their new spirituality. In A FAREWELL TO ARMS Frederick gives the body of the dead Catherine up to the sun, thereby signifying her union with the elements and his acceptance of her physical parting. In THREE COMRADES not only does Erich hold Pat up in a similar manner, but in the following scene as he and Otto leave the graveyard, they are accompanied by the spirits of both Pat and Gottfried, their two dead comrades. This same type of growth pattern is found in other related films as well. Basic visual and thematic ties can be found in BAD GIRL, MAN'S CASTLE, LITTLE MAN, WHAT NOW?, MANNEQUIN, and HIS BUTLER'S SISTER. Sim-ilar ties exist between such films as DOCTOR'S WIVES, GREEN LIGHT, and DISPUTED PASSAGE. There are also individual ties be-tween one or two films that create this same sense of continuity. In all, we recognize a number of strains tied together by such larger thematic ideas as transcendence and conversion due to the acceptance of the spiritual and healing nature of love.

The distinction between "fact" and "feeling" stated within the body of the thesis is crucial for understanding what is stated above and for understanding Borzage's work itself. In understanding this distinction we can understand how while the settings and primary narratives of the films may change, the basic ideology develops but remains relatively consistent throughout. Borzage is not so much concerned with the "real" or immediate level as it exists on a tactile level as with the infusion of mood or feeling around and into a situation. The "fact" of economic hardship, deprivation, loss of aspirations, and impoverishment is the signifier of these feelings. Setting a film within the midst of some larger social crisis, Borzage creates a sense of mood without relying upon the crisis itself. By creating this "free-floating" mood Borzage strives to create a sense of the timelessness of the ideas as well. Emphasizing the facts would center the narrative too closely upon a particular conflict or time period. Borzage is striving for a universality of both time and place. This is true in his use of economic hardship, war, Fascism, and even traditional religion. The particular time period is not stressed, nor are dogmatic elements emphasized. All of these larger "facts" are placed within a larger humanistic framework.

The same confusion often seems to occur in attempting to understand Borzage's images. Borzage often strives to invest his images and symbols with several different and, possibly, opposing meanings at once. The problem here, as with that of differentiating such terms as transcendence and conversion and of attempting to specify the religiosity of these conflicts, is that at times this overuse of nuance can sap the strength of the image. This is true, however, only to a small degree, and Borzage's important images--the medals in SEVENTH HEAVEN, the painting in STREET ANGEL, the stove in MAN'S CASTLE, the dressing table in LITTLE MAN, WHAT NOW?, the flashing light in MANNEQUIN, and the Bible in STRANGE CARGO are examples--are well used and often help to crystalize pictorially what is happening within the narrative yet what the characters cannot yet understand. There are points at which Borzage's striving for complexity causes problems. Bill's tie to an anchored barge in MAN'S CASTLE is too ambiguous a sign, as is the sandwich board he wears, which ties him to a world of exchange in which he cannot afford to participate. Yet the images, for all of the confusion that they may seem to create, do not detract from the films in any essential way, and in understanding their complexity we get a sense of Borzage's multifaceted ideology.

What makes Borzage such an important figure is not only his work itself but the time span during which he worked. Borzage's career spans cinematic history from its earliest period until the era of independent production and the decline of the studio system. The increasing complexity of his films reflects both a general mastery of film techniques and the recognition that film was no longer an inconsequential toy. Most important is Borzage's devotion to the cinema as an art form, as a means of expression, and as a way of express-ing and redefining a melodramatic world view. Working out of the framework and conceptions of melodrama, Borzage helped to change melodrama by giving it a subtlety and beauty previously undeveloped and unrecognized. It is in this way that he "opened the field" for and influenced such later directors as Max Ophuls, Douglas Sirk, and Vincente Minnelli. The beauty and finesse of Borzage's work helped to rescue melodrama from its clichéd and simplistic outlook. The genre moved away from being one reflecting immediate cultural and social concerns. The timelessness of Borzage's work grew out of a romanticism that the genre had never had before. His visual style, his use of images, and his devotion to a particular ideology renewed both the artistic vitality and validity of this much-maligned concept.

DIRECTORIAL FILMOGRAPHY

Material in this filmography is based on information found in The Hollywood Professionals: Howard Hawks, Frank Borzage and Edgar Ulmer (vol. 3), by John Belton, and by information supplied by the American Film Institute.

Asterisk (*) denotes a film that is considered lost or that could not be found by the author.

THE PITCH O' CHANCE (1915)
   With: Frank Borzage

THAT GAL OF BURKE'S (1916)*
   With: Anna Little, Frank Borzage

MAMMY'S ROSE (1916)*
   With: Frank Borzage, Neva Gerber, Antrim Short
Co-Director: James Douglass
Screenplay: James Douglass

LIFE'S HARMONY (1916)
   With: Vivian Rich, Alfred Vosburgh, Frank Borzage, Antrim
   Short
Co-director: Lorimer Johnston
Screenplay: Lorimer Johnston
Released by American Mutual

THE SILKEN SPIDER (1916)*
   With: Vivian Rich, Frank Borzage

THE CODE OF HONOR (1916)*
   With: Estella Allan, Frank Borzage

NELL DALE'S MEN FOLKS (1916)*
   With: Anna Little, Frank Borzage
Released by American Mutual

THE FORGOTTEN PRAYER (1916)*
   With: Anna Little, Frank Borzage

THE COURTIN' OF CALLIOPE CLEW (1916)*
   With: Anna Little, Frank Borzage

NUGGET JIM'S PARDNER (1916)

With: Anna Little, Frank Borzage, Jack Farrell, Dick La Reno
Released by American Mutual on two reels

THE DEMON OF FEAR (1916)*
With: Anna Little, Frank Borzage
Released by American Mutual on two reels

LAND O' LIZARDS (1916)*
With: Frank Borzage
Released by American Mutual, 4600 feet
Reissued in 1922 as SILENT SHELBY

IMMEDIATE LEE (1916)*
With: Frank Borzage, Anna Little, Chick Morrison, Jack Richardson
Released by American Mutual, 4600 feet
Reissued in 1922 as HAIR TRIGGER CASEY

ENCHANTMENT (1916)*
With: Vivian Rich, Alfred Vosburgh, Frank Borzage, Antrim Short
Screenplay: Frank Borzage
Released by American Mutual

THE PRIDE AND THE MAN (1916)*
With: William Russell, Gertrude Short, Antrim Short, Frank Borzage
Screenplay: Frank Borzage
Released by American Mutual

DOLLARS OF DROSS (1916)*
With: Vivian Rich, Alfred Vosburgh, Louise Lester, George Periolat
Screenplay: Frank Borzage
Released by American Mutual

WEE LADY BETTY (1917)*
With: Bessie Love, Frank Borzage, Charles K. French, Walt Whitman, Aggie Herring
Co-director: Charles Miller
Screenplay: Catherine Carr
Camera: Pliny Horne
Producer: Allan Dwan for Triangle Corporation

FLYING COLORS (1917)*
With: William Desmond, Alma Rubens, J. Barney Sherry, Joseph King
Screenplay: Monte S. Katterjohn
Camera: Pliny Horne
Released by Triangle Corporation

UNTIL THEY GET ME (1917)
With: Jack Curtis, Joe King, Wilbur Higbee, Pauline Stark, Walter Perry

Screenplay: Monte S. Katterjohn
Camera: C. H. Wales
Producer: Allan Dwan for Triangle Corporation

THE ATOM (1918)*
 With: Pauline Stark, Harry Mestayer, Belle Bennett, Tom Buck-
 ingham, Frank Borzage
Screenplay: Catherine Carr
Camera: Pliny Horne
Producer: Allan Dwan for Triangle Corporation

THE GUN WOMAN (1918)
 With: Texas Guinan, Darrell Foss, Francis McDonald, Frank
 Borzage
Screenplay: Monte S. Katterjohn
Camera: Pliny Horne
Producer: Allan Dwan for Triangle Corporation

SHOES THAT DANCED (1918)*
 With: Pauline Stark, Anna Dodge, Lydia Yeamans Titus, Wallace
 MacDonald, Dick Rosson
Screenplay: Jack Cunningham (from a story by John A. Morosco)
Camera: Pliny Horne
Producer: Allan Dwan for Triangle Corporation

INNOCENT'S PROGRESS (1918)*
 With: Pauline Stark, Lillian West, Alice Knowland, Jack Living-
 ston, Charles Dorian, Graham Pett
Screenplay; Catherine Carr (from a story by Frances Quinlan)
Camera: Pliny Horne
Producer: Allan Dwan for Triangle Corporation

AN HONEST MAN (1918)*
 With: William Desmond, Mary Warren, Claire Anderson, William
 Franey, Charles K. French
Screenplay: Monte S. Katterjohn
Camera: Pliny Horne
Producer: Allan Dwan for Triangle Corporation

SOCIETY FOR SALE (1918)*
 With: William Desmond, Gloria Swanson, Herbert Prior, Lillian
 Langdon, Charles Dorian, Lillian West, Claire Anderson
Screenplay: Monte S. Katterjohn
Camera: Pliny Horne
Producer: Allan Dwan for Triangle Corporation

WHO IS TO BLAME? (1918)*
 With: Jack Abbe, Jack Livingston, Lillian West, Maud Wayne,
 Lillian Langdon
Screenplay: Monte S. Katterjohn (from a story by E. M. Ingleton)
Camera: Pliny Horne
Released by Triangle Corporation

THE GHOST FLOWER (1918)*

With: Alma Rubens, Charles West, Francis McDonald, Dick
Rosson, Emory Hohnson, Naida Lessing, Tote Ducrow
Screenplay: Monte S. Katterjohn and Catherine Carr

THE CURSE OF IKU (1918)*
    With: Frank Borzage, Tsuru Aoki
Screenplay: Catherine Carr
Released by Essanay, seven reels

TOTON (1919)*
    With: Olive Thomas, Norman Kerry, Francis McDonald, Jack
    Perrin
Screenplay: Catherine Carr
Camera: Jack MacKenzie
Released by Triangle Corporation, six reels

PRUDENCE OF BROADWAY (1919)*
    With: Olive Thomas
Screenplay: Catherine Carr
Camera: Pliny Horne

WHOM THE GODS DESTROY (1919)*
    With: Pauline Stark, Kathryn Adams, Jack Mulhall
Screenplay: Catherine Carr (from a story by Cyrus T. Brady)
Released by First National

ASHES OF DESIRE (1919)*
    With: Alma Rubens, Walter McGrail
Screenplay: Sam Small, Jr.
Released by Essanay, six reels

HUMORESQUE (1920)*
    With: Alma Rubens, Vera Gordon, Dore Davidson, Gaston Glass,
    Bobby Connelly, Sidney Carlyle, Helen Connelly, Ann Wallick,
    Joseph Cooper, Maurice Levigne, Alfred Goldberg, Edward Stan-
    ton, Miriam Battista
Screenplay: Frances Marion (from a story by Fanny Hurst)
Camera: Gilbert Warrenton
A Cosmopolitan Production--released by Paramount, six reels

THE DUKE OF CHIMNEY BUTTE (1921)*
    With: Fred Stone, Vola Vale, Josie Sedgwick, Chick Morrison,
    Buck Connors, Harry Dunkinson
Screenplay: Marian Ainslee (from a story by George W. Ogden)
Producer: Andrew J. Callaghan for Fred Stone Productions, 4600
    feet

GET-RICH-QUICK WALLINGFORD (1921)*
    With: Sam Hardy, Norman Kerry, Doris Kenyon, Diana Allen,
    Edgar Nelson, Billie Dove, Mrs. Charles Willard, Eugene Keith,
    William Carr, William Robyns, Theodore Westman, Jr., Patter-
    son Dial, Jerry Sinclair, Benny One
Screenplay: Luther Reed (from a play by George M. Cohan based

on George Randolph Chester's Willingford stories)
Camera: Chester Lyons
Art Director: Joseph Urban
Released by Paramount Pictures, 7381 feet

BACK PAY (1922)*
    With: Seena Owen, Matt Moore, J. Barney Sherry, Ethel Duray,
    Charles Criag, Jerry Sinclair
Screenplay: Frances Marion (from a story by Fannie Hurst)
Camera: Chester Lyons
Art director: Joseph Urban
A Cosmopolitan Production--released by Paramount Pictures, 6460
    feet

BILLY JIM (1922)*
    With: Fred Stone, Millicent Fisher, George Hernandez, William
    Bletcher, Marian Skinner, Frank Thorne
Screenplay: Frank Howard Clark (from a story by Jackson Gregory)
Producer: Andrew J. Callaghan for Fred Stone Productions, 4900 feet

THE GOOD PROVIDER (1922)*
    With: Vera Gordon, Dore Davidson, Miriam Battista, Vivienne
    Osborne, William Collier, Jr., John Roche, Ora Jones, Edward
    Phillips, Muriel Martin, James Devine, Blanche Craig, Margaret
    Severn
Screenplay: John Lynch (from a story by Fannie Hurst)
Camera: Chester Lyons
A Cosmopolitan Production--released by Paramount Pictures, 7753 feet

VALLEY OF SILENT MEN (1922)*
    With: Alma Rubens, Lew Cody, Joseph King, Mario Majeroni,
    George Nash, J. W. Johnston
Screenplay: John Lynch (from a story by James O. Curwood)
Camera: Chester Lyons
A Cosmopolitan Production--released by Paramount Pictures, 6500
    feet

THE PRIDE OF PALOMAR (1922)*
    With: Forrest Stanley, Marjorie Daw, Tote Ducrow, James Bar-
    rows, Joseph Dowling, Alfred Allen, George Nichols, Warner
    Oland, Mrs. Jessie Hebbard, Percy Williams, Mrs. George Her-
    nandez, Edward Brady, Carmen Arselle
Screenplay: Grant Carpenter and John Lynch (from a story by Peter
    Bernard Kyne)
Camera: Chester Lyons
A Cosmopolitan Production--released by Paramount Pictures, 7494
    feet

THE Nth COMMANDMENT (1923)
    With: Coleen Moore, James Morrison, Eddie Phillips, Charlotte
    Merriam, George Cooper
Screenplay: Frances Marion (from a story by Fannie Hurst)
Camera: Chester Lyons

Producer: Frances Marion for Cosmopolitan--released by Paramount
Pictures, 7339 feet

CHILDREN OF DUST (1923)*
With: Bert Woodruff, Johnnie Walker, Frankie Lee, Pauline Garon,
Josephine, Lloyd Hughes, Newton Hall, George Nichols
Screenplay: Agnes Christine Johnson and Frank Dazey (story by
Tristram Tupper)
Camera: Chester Lyons
Art Director: Frank Ormston
Editor: H. P. Bretherton
Producer: Arthur H. Jacobs for First National Pictures.   6, 228 feet

AGE OF DESIRE (1923)*
With: Joseph Swickard, William Collier, Jr., Frank Truesdell,
Bruce Guerin, Frankie Lee, J. Farrell MacDonald, Mary Jane Ir-
ving, Myrtle Stedman, Aggie Herring, Mary Philbin, Edithe Yorke
Screenplay: Mary O'Hara, Lenore Coffee and Dixie Wilson
Camera: Chester Lyons
Art Director: Frank Ormston
Producer: Arthur H. Jacobs for First National Pictures.   5, 174 feet

SECRETS (1924)
With: Norma Talmadge, Eugene O'Brien, Patterson Dial, Emily
Fitzroy, Claire McDowell, George Nichols, Harvey Clark, Charles
Ogle, Francis Feeny
Screenplay: Frances Marion (from a play by Rudolph Besier and May
Edington)
Camera: Tony Gaudio
Producer: Joseph M. Schenck for First National.   8, 363 feet

Film exists in fragments with Yugoslavian subtitles.

THE LADY (1925)*
With: Norma Talmadge, Wallace MacDonald, Brandon Hurst, Alf
Goulding, Doris Lloyd, Walter Long, George Hackathorne, Marc
MacDermott, Emily Fitzroy
Screenplay: Frances Marion (from a story by Martin Brown)
Camera: Tony Gaudio
Producer: Joseph M. Schenck for Norma Talmadge Productions.
7, 357 feet

DADDY'S GONE A-HUNTING (1925)*
With: Alice Joyce, Percy Marmont, Virginia Marshall, Helena
D'Algy, Ford Sterling, Holmes Herbert, Edythe Chapman
Screenplay: Kenneth B. Clarke (from a novel by Zoe Akins)
Camera: Chester Lyons
Art Director: Cedric Gibbons
Editor: Frank Sullivan
Producer: Louis B. Mayer for Metro-Goldwyn Pictures.   5, 851 feet

WAGES FOR WIVES (1925)*
With: Jacqueline Logan, Creighton Hale, Earle Fox, Zasu Pitts,

Claude Gillingwater, David Butler, Margaret Seddon, Margaret Liv-
ingston, Dan Mason, Tom Ricketts
Screenplay: Kenneth B. Clarke (from a play by Guy Bolton and
Winchell Smith)
Camera: Ernest G. Palmer
Producer: William Fox for Fox Film Corporation, 6650 feet

LAZYBONES (1925)
With: Buck Jones, Madge Bellamy, Virginia Marshall, Edythe
Chapman, Leslie Fenton, Jane Novak, Emily Fitzroy, Zasu Pitts,
William Norton Bailey
Screenplay: Frances Marion (from a story by Owen Davis)
Camera: Glen MacWilliams and George Schneiderman
Producer: William Fox for Fox Film Corporation, 7234 feet

THE CIRCLE (1925)
With: Eleanor Boardman, Malcolm McGregor, Alec Francis, Eu-
genie Besserer, George Fawcett, Creighton Hale, Otto Hoffman,
Eulalie Jensen
Screenplay: Kenneth B. Clarke (from a play by W. Somerset Maugham)
Camera: Chester Lyons
Art director: Cedric Gibbons and James Basevi
Released by M-G-M Pictures, 5511 feet

THE FIRST YEAR (1926)
With: Matt Moore, Kathryn Perry, John Patrick, Frank Currier,
Frank Cooley, Virginia Madison, Carolynne Snowden, J. Farrell
MacDonald
Screenplay: Frances Marion (from a play by Frank Craven)
Camera: Chester Lyons
Producer: William Fox for Fox Film Corporation, 5126 feet

EARLY TO WED (1926)*
With: Matt Moore, Kathryn Perry, Albert Gran, Julia Swayne
Gordon, Arthur Housman, Rodney Hildebrand, Zasu Pitts, Belva
McKay, Ross McCutcheon, Harry Bailey
Screenplay: Kenneth B. Clarke (from a story by Evelyn Campbell)
Camera: Ernest G. Palmer
Producer: William Fox for Fox Film Corporation, 5912 feet

"MARRIAGE LICENSE?" (1926)*
With: Alma Rubens, Walter McGrail, Richard Walling, Walter
Pidgeon, Charles Lane, Emily Fitzroy, Langhorne Burton, Edgar
Norton, George Cowl
Screenplay: Bradley King (from a play by F. Tennyson Jesse and
Harold Marsh Harwood)
Camera: Ernest Palmer
Producer: William Fox for Fox Film Corporation, 7168 feet

SEVENTH HEAVEN (1927)
With: Janet Gaynor, Charles Farrell, Ben Bard, David Butler,
Marie Mosquini, Albert Gran, Gladys Brockwell, Emile Chautard,
George Stone, Jessie Haslett, Brandon Hurst, Lillian West

Screenplay: Benjamin Glazer, Katherine Hilliker and H. H. Caldwell
    (from a story by Austin Strong)
Camera: Ernest Palmer
Art director: Harry Oliver
Editor: Katherine Hilliker and H. H. Caldwell
Producer: William Fox for Fox Film Corporation, 8500 feet

Released both silent and with sound (musical score and sound effects).

Frank Borzage won the Academy Award for best director, and Janet
Gaynor won the award for best actress for this and for STREET AN-
GEL at the first Academy Awards.

STREET ANGEL (1928)
    With: Janet Gaynor, Charles Farrell, Alberto Rabagliati, Gino
    Conti, Guido Trento, Henry Armetta, Louis Liggett, Natalie King-
    ston, Milton Dickinson, Helena Herman, David Kashner, Jennie
    Bruno
Screenplay: Marion Orth, Katherine Hilliker, H. H. Caldwell, Philip
    Klein and Henry Roberts Symonds (from a play by Monckton Hoffe)
Camera: Ernest Palmer and Paul Ivano
Editor: Barney Wolf
Producer: William Fox for Fox Film Corporation, 9221 feet

Released both silent and with sound (talking sequences, musical score
    and sound effects).

THE RIVER (1928)
    With: Charles Farrell, Mary Duncan, Ivan Linow, Margaret Mann,
    Alfred Sabato, Bert Woodruff
Screenplay: Philip Klein, Dwight Cummins and John Hopper Booth
    (from a story by Tristram Tupper)
Camera: Ernest Palmer
Art director: Barney Wolf
Music: Maurice Baron and Erno Rapee
Producer: William Fox for Fox Film Corporation, 7704 feet (silent)
    and 6536 (sound)

Released both silent and with sound (talking sequences and musical
    score).

LUCKY STAR (1929)*
    With: Charles Farrell, Janet Gaynor, Big Boy Williams, Paul
    Fix, Hedwig Reicher, Gloria Grey, Hector V. Sarno
Screenplay: Sonia Levien, John Hunter Booth, Katherine Hilliker and
    H. H. Caldwell (from a story by Tristram Tupper)
Camera: Chester Lyons and William Cooper Smith
Art director: Harry Oliver
Editor: Katherine Hilliker and H. H. Caldwell
Producer: William Fox for Fox Film Corporation, 8784 feet

Released both silent and with sound (talking sequences, musical score,
    and sound effects).

Sound Films

THEY HAD TO SEE PARIS (1929)
   With: Will Rogers, Irene Rich, Owen Davis, Jr., Marguerite
   Churchill, Fifi Dorsay, Rex Bell, Ivan Lebedeff, Edgar Kennedy,
   Bob Kerr, Christine Yves, Marcelle Corday, Marcia Manon, An-
   dre Cheron, Gregory Gaye
Screenplay: Sonia Levien, Owen Davis and Wilbur Morse, Jr. (from
   a story by Homer Croy)
Camera: Chester Lyons and Al Brick
Art director: Harry Oliver
Editor: Margaret V. Clancey
Producer: William Fox for Fox Film Corporation, 96 minutes

SONG O' MY HEART (1930)
   With: John McCormack, Alice Joyce, Maureen O'Sullivan, Tom
   Clifford, J. J. Kerrigan, John Gerrick, Edwin Schneider, J. Far-
   rell MacDonald, Effie Ellser, Emily Fitzroy, Andres De Segurola,
   Edward Martindel
Screenplay: Sonia Levien and Tom Barry (from a story by Tom
   Barry and J. J. McCarthy)
Camera: Chester Lyons, Al Brick and J. O. Taylor
Art director: Harry Oliver
Music: Charles Glover, William Kernell, James Hanley, Albert
   Malotte, C. Mordaunt Spencer
Editor: Margaret V. Clancey
Producer: William Fox for Fox Film Corporation, 85 minutes

LILIOM (1930)
   With: Charles Farrell, Rose Hobart, Estelle Taylor, Lee Tracy,
   James Marcus, Walter Abel, Mildren Van Dorn, Guinn Williams,
   Lilian Elliot, Bert Roach, H. B. Warner, Dawn O'Day
Screenplay: S. N. Behrman and Sonia Levien (from a play by Ferenc
   Molnár)
Camera: Chester Lyons
Art director: Harry Oliver
Editor: Margaret Clancey
Music: Richard Fall and Marcella Gardner
Producer: William Fox for Fox Film Corporation, 90 minutes

AS YOUNG AS YOU FEEL (1931)
   With: Will Rogers, Fifi Dorsay, Lucien Littlefield, Donald Dilla-
   way, Terrance Ray, Lucille Brown, Rosalie Roy, C. Henry Gor-
   don, John T. Murray, Brandon Hurst, Marcia Harris, Gregory
   Gaye
Screenplay: Edwin Burke (from a play by George Ade)
Camera: Chester Lyons
Art director: Jack Schultze
Editor: Margaret Clancey
Released by Fox Film Corporation, 75 minutes

DOCTORS' WIVES (1931)
   With: Warner Baxter, Joan Bennett, Victor Varconi, Helene Mil-

lard, Paul Porcasi, Nancy Gardner, John St. Polis, Cecilia Lof-
tus, Violet Dunn, Ruth Warren, Luise Mackintosh, William Mad-
dox
Screenplay: Maurine Watkins and Henry and Sylvia Lieferant
Camera: Arthur Edeson
Editor: Jack Dennis
Released by Fox Film Corporation, 80 minutes

BAD GIRL (1931)
    With: James Dunn, Sally Eilers, Minna Gombell, Frank Darien,
    William Pawley
Screenplay: Edwin Burke (from a novel by Vina Delmar and a play
    by Vina Delmar and Brian Marlowe)
Camera: Chester Lyons
Editor: Margaret Clancey
Released by Fox Film Corporation, 88 minutes

Borzage won an Academy Award as best director.

AFTER TOMORROW (1932)
    With: Charles Farrell, Marian Nixon, Minna Gombell, William
    Collier, Sr., Josephine Hull, William Pawley, Greta Granstedt,
    Ferdinand Munier, Nora Lane
Screenplay: Sonia Levien (from a play by Hugh S. Strange and John
    Golden)
Camera: James Wong Howe
Art director: William Darling
Editor: Margaret Clancey
Music: James Hanley
Released by Fox Film Corporation, 79 minutes

YOUNG AMERICA (1932)
    With: Spencer Tracy, Doris Kenyon, Tommy Conlon, Ralph Bella-
    my, Beryl Mercer, Sarah Padden, Robert Homans, Raymond Bor-
    zage, Dawn O'Day, Betty Jane Graham, Louise Beavers, Spec
    O'Donnell, William Pawley, Eddie Sturgis
Screenplay: William Conselman (from a play by John F. Ballard)
Camera: George Schneiderman
Art director: Duncan Cramer
Editor: Margaret Clancey
Released by Fox Film Corporation, 71 minutes

A FAREWELL TO ARMS (1932)
    With: Gary Cooper, Helen Hayes, Adolphe Menjou, Mary Phillips,
    Jack La Rue, Blanche Frederici, Henry Armetta, George Humbert,
    Fred Malatesta, Mary Forbes, Tom Ricketts, Robert Cautero,
    Gilbert Emery
Screenplay: Benjamin Glazer and Oliver H. P. Garrett (from a nov-
    el by Ernest Hemingway)
Camera: Charles Lang
Art director: Roland Anderson and Hans Dreier
Editor: Otho Lovering
Released by Paramount Pictures, 90 minutes

Borzage was nominated for an Academy Award but lost to Edmund
Goulding, who won for GRAND HOTEL.

SECRETS (1933)
  With: Mary Pickford, Leslie Howard, C. Aubrey Smith, Blanche
  Frederici, Doris Lloyd, Herbert Evans, Ned Sparks, Allan Sears,
  Mona Maris, Lyman Williams, Virginia Grey, Ellen Johnson, Ran-
  dolph Connelley, Huntley Gordon, Ethel Clayton, Bessie Barris-
  cale, Theodore von Eltz
Screenplay: Frances Marion, Salisbury Field and Leonard Praskins
  (from a play by Rudolf Besier and May Edington)
Camera: Ray June
Editor: Hugh Bennett
Released by United Artists, 85 minutes

This is a remake of Borzage's 1924 film of the same name.

MAN'S CASTLE (1933)
  With: Spencer Tracy, Loretta Young, Glenda Farrell, Walter Con-
  nolly, Arthur Hohl, Marjorie Rambeau, Dickie Moore
Screenplay: Jo Swerling (from a story by Lawrence Hazard)
Camera: Joseph August
Editor: Viola Lawrence
Music: Frank Harling and Bakaleinikoff
Released by Columbia Pictures, 75 minutes

LITTLE MAN, WHAT NOW? (1934)
  With: Margaret Sullavan, Douglass Montgomery, Alan Hale,
  Catherine Doucet, Alan Mowbray, Christian Rubb, Fred Kohler,
  Mae Marsh, De Witt Jennings, Muriel Kirkland, G. P. Huntley,
  Jr., Etienne Girardot, Hedda Hopper, Sarah Padden, George
  Meeker, Donald Haines, Bodil Rosing, Paul Fix
Screenplay: William Anthony McGuire (from a novel by Hans Fallada)
Camera: Norbert Brodine
Art director: Charles D. Hall
Editor: Milton Carruth
Music: Arthur Kay
Producer: Carl Laemmle, Jr., for Universal Pictures, 90 minutes

NO GREATER GLORY (1934)
  With: George Breakston, Jimmy Butler, Jackie Searle, Frankie
  Darro, Donald Haines, Rolf Ernest, Christian Rubb, Ralph Mor-
  gan, Lois Wilson, Egon Brecher, Julius Molnar, Wesley Giraud,
  Beaudine Anderson, Samuel Hinds
Screenplay: Jo Swerling (from a novel by Ferenc Molnár)
Camera: Joseph August
Editor: Viola Lawrence
Music: Louis Silvers
Released by Columbia Pictures, 78 minutes

FLIRTATION WALK (1934)
  With: Dick Powell, Ruby Keeler, Pat O'Brien, Ross Alexander,
  John Arledge, John Eldredge, Henry O'Neill, Guinn Williams,

Frederick Burton, John Darrow, Glen Boles, Col. Tim Lonergan,
Gertrude Keeler, Tyrone Power
Screenplay: Delmer Daves (from a story by Delmer Daves and Lou
Edelman)
Camera: Sol Polito and George Barnes
Art director: Jack Okey
Editor: William Holmes
Music: Ellie Wrubel and Mort Dixon
Dance direction: Bobby Connolly
Producer: Frank Borzage for Warner Brothers-First National, 97
minutes

LIVING ON VELVET (1935)
With: George Brent, Kay Francis, Warren William, Russell Hicks,
Maud Turner, Sam Hinds, Martha Merrill, Helen Lowell, Henry
O'Neill, Edgar Kennedy
Screenplay: Jerry Wald and Julius Epstein
Camera: Sid Hickox
Art director: William Holmes
Music: Leo F. Forbstein
Producer: Edward Chodorov for Warner Brothers-First National, 80
minutes

STRANDED (1935)
With: Kay Francis, George Brent, Patricia Ellis, Donald Woods,
Robert Barrat, Barton MacLane, John Wray, Florence Fair,
Frankie Darro, Ann Shoemaker, Mae Busch, Henry O'Neill, Joan
Gay, Gavin Gordon
Screenplay: Delmer Daves and Carl Erickson (from a story by Frank
Wead and Ferdinand Reyher)
Camera: Sid Hickox
Art director: Anton Grot and Hugh Reticker
Editor: William Holmes
Released by Warner Brothers-First National

SHIPMATES FOREVER (1935)
With: Dick Powell, Ruby Keeler, Lewis Stone, Ross Alexander,
Eddie Acuff, Dick Foran, John Arledge, Robert Light
Screenplay: Delmer Daves
Camera: Sol Polito
Art director: Robert Haas
Editor: William Holmes
Music: Leo F. Forbstein (songs by Harry Warren and Al Dubin)
A Cosmopolitan Production--released by Warner Brothers-First Na-
tional, 124 minutes

DESIRE (1936)
With: Marlene Dietrich, Gary Cooper, John Halliday, William
Frawley, Ernest Cossart, Alan Mowbray, Effie Tilbury, Akim
Tamiroff, Enrique Acosta, Alice Feliz
Screenplay: Edwin Justus Mayer, Waldemar Young and Samuel Hoff-
enstein (from a play by Hans Szekely and R. A. Stemmle)
Camera: Charles Lang

Art director: Hans Dreier and Robert Usher
Editor: William Shea
Music: Frederick Hollander and Leo Robbin
Producer: Ernst Lubitsch for Paramount Pictures, 99 minutes

HEARTS DIVIDED (1936)
   With: Marion Davies, Dick Powell, Charlie Ruggles, Claude Rains,
   Edward Everett Horton, Arthur Treacher, Henry Stephenson, Clara
   Blandick, Halliwell Hobbes, John Larkin, Walter Kingsford, Eti-
   enne Girardot, Hattie McDaniels
Screenplay: Laird Doyle and Casey Robinson (from a play by Rida
   Johnson Young)
Camera: George Folsey
Art director: Robert Haas
Editor: William Holmes
Music: Harry Warren and Al Dubin
Producer: Harry Joe Brown for Cosmopolitan Productions--released
   by Warner Brothers-First National, 76 minutes (18 minutes were
   cut from the film between its Hollywood and New York previews)

GREEN LIGHT (1937)
   With: Errol Flynn, Anita Louise, Margaret Lindsay, Sir Cedric
   Hardwick, Walter Abel, Henry O'Neill, Spring Byington, Erin
   O'Brien-Moore, Henry Kolker, Pierre Watkins, Granville Bates,
   Russell Simpson, Myrtle Stedman
Screenplay: Milton Krims (from a novel by Lloyd C. Douglas)
Camera: Byron Haskins
Art director: Max Parker
Editor: James Gibbons
Music: Max Steiner (conducted by Leo F. Forbstein)
Producer: Hal B. Wallis for Cosmopolitan Productions--released by
   Warner Brothers, 85 minutes

HISTORY IS MADE AT NIGHT (1937)
   With: Charles Boyer, Jean Arthur, Colin Clive, Leo Carrillo,
   Ivan Lebedeff, George Meeker, Lucian Prival, Georges Renavent,
   George Davies, Adele St. Mauer
Screenplay: Gene Towne and Graham Baker
Camera: Gregg Toland
Editor: Margaret Clancey
Producer: Walter Wanger for United Artists, 97 minutes

THE BIG CITY (1937)
   With: Spencer Tracy, Luise Rainer, Charlie Grapewin, Janet
   Beecher, Eddie Quillan, Victor Varconi, Oscar O'Shea, Helen
   Troy, William Demarest, John Arledge, Irving Bacon, Guinn Willi-
   ams, Regis Toomey, Edgar Dearing, Paul Harvey, Grace Ford,
   Alice White, Clem Beavens, Jack Dempsey, Jim Jeffries, Maxine
   Rosenbloom, Jim Thorpe
Screenplay: Dore Schary and Hugo Butler (from a story by Norman
   Krasna)
Camera: Joseph Ruttenberg
Art director: Cedric Gibbons

208   The Film Work of Frank Borzage

Editor: Frederick Y. Smith
Music: Dr. William Axt
Producer: Norman Krasna for M-G-M, 80 minutes

Retitled THE SKYSCRAPER WILDERNESS.

THREE COMRADES (1938)
    With: Robert Taylor, Margaret Sullavan, Franchot Tone, Robert
    Young, Guy Kibbee, Lionel Atwill, Henry Hull, George Zucco,
    Charlie Grapewin, Monty Woolley, Spencer Charters, Sarah Pad-
    den
Screenplay: F. Scott Fitzgerald and Edward E. Paramore (from a
    novel by Erich Maria Remarque)
Camera: Joseph Ruttenberg
Art director: Cedric Gibbons
Editor: Frank Sullivan
Music: Franz Waxman
Producer: Joseph L. Mankiewicz for M-G-M, 100 minutes

THE SHINING HOUR (1938)
    With: Joan Crawford, Margaret Sullavan, Robert Young, Melvyn
    Douglas, Fay Bainter, Allyn Joslyn, Hattie McDaniel, Oscar
    O'Shea, Frank Albertson, Harry Barris
Screenplay: Jane Murfin and Ogden Nash (from a play by Keith Win-
    ter)
Camera: George Folsey
Art director: Cedric Gibbons
Editor: Frank E. Hull
Music: Franz Waxman
Producer: Joseph L. Mankiewicz for M-G-M, 76 minutes

MANNEQUIN (1938)
    With: Joan Crawford, Spencer Tracy, Alan Curtis, Ralph Morgan,
    Mary Phillips, Oscar O'Shea, Elizabeth Risdon, Leo Gorcy
Screenplay: Lawrence Hazard (from a story by Katherine Brush)
Camera: George Folsey
Editor: Frederick Y. Smith
Music: Edward Ward
Producer: Joseph L. Mankiewicz for M-G-M, 94 minutes

DISPUTED PASSAGE (1939)
    With: Dorothy Lamour, Akim Tamiroff, John Howard, Judith
    Barrett, William Collier, Sr., Victor Varoni, Gordon Jones,
    Keye Luke, Elizabeth Risdon, Gordon Pendleton, Billy Cook,
    William Pawley
Screenplay: Arthur Vellier and Sheridan Gibney (from a novel by
    Lloyd C. Douglas)
Camera: William C. Mellor
Art director: Hans Dreier and Roland Anderson
Editor: James Smith
Music: Frederick Hollander and John Liepold
Producer: Frank Borzage and Harlan Thompson for Paramount Pic-
    tures, 90 minutes

I TAKE THIS WOMAN (1940) (NEW YORK CINDERELLA)
    With: Hedy Lamarr, Spencer Tracy, Ina Claire, Kent Taylor,
    Mona Barrie, Louis Calhern
Screenplay: Charles MacArthur and James Kevin McGuinness
Camera: Harold Rosson
Art director: Cedric Gibbons and Paul Groesse
Music: Bronislau Kaper and Arthur Guttman
Released by M-G-M, 94 minutes

The film was begun by Josef von Sternberg (eighteen days) and was
completed by Frank Borzage in 1938. It was then reshot by W. S.
Van Dyke, who received full directorial credit when the film was released.

STRANGE CARGO (1940)
    With: Joan Crawford, Clark Gable, Ian Hunter, Peter Lorre,
    Paul Lukas, Albert Dekker, J. Edward Bromberg, Eduardo Cian-
    nelli, John Arledge, Victor Varoni, Frederic Worlock
Screenplay: Lawrence Hazard (from a novel by Richard Sale)
Camera: Robert Planck
Art director: Cedric Gibbons
Editor: Robert J. Kern
Music: Franz Waxman
Producer: Joseph L. Mankiewicz for M-G-M, 113 minutes

The film was given a "C" rating by the Legion of Decency and was
condemned for its "irreverent use of Sacred Scriptures" and for the
"lustful implications in dialogue and situation."

THE MORTAL STORM (1940)
    With: Margaret Sullavan, James Stewart, Robert Young, Frank
    Morgan, Robert Stack, Bonita Granville, Irene Rich, William T.
    Orr, Maria Ouspenskaya, Gene Reynolds, Russell Hicks, William
    Edmonds, Esther Dale, Dan Dailey, Granville Bates, Thomas
    Ross, Ward Bond
Screenplay: Claudine West, Anderson Ellis, and George Froeschel
    (from a novel by Phyllis Bottome)
Camera: William Daniels
Art director: Cedric Gibbons
Editor: Elmo Veron
Music: Edward Kane
Producer: Frank Borzage and Victor Saville (uncredited)--released
    by M-G-M, 100 minutes

FLIGHT COMMAND (1940-41)
    With: Robert Taylor, Ruth Hussey, Walter Pidgeon, Sheppard
    Strudwick, Red Skelton, Nat Pendleton, Dick Purcell, William
    Tannen, William Stelling, Stanley Smith, Addison Richards, Don-
    ald Douglas, Pat Flaherty, Marsha Hunt
Screenplay: Wells Root and Com. Harvey Haislip (from a story by
    Com. Haislip and John Sutherland)
Camera: Harold Rosson
Editor: Robert J. Kern

Music: Franz Waxman
Producer: J. Walter Ruben for M-G-M, 113 minutes

SMILIN' THROUGH (1941)
   With: Jeanette MacDonald, Brian Aherne, Gene Raymond, Ian
   Hunter, Frances Robinson, Patrick O'Moore, Eric Lonsdale,
   Jackie Horner, David Clyde, Frances Carson, Ruth Rickaby
Screenplay: Donald Ogden Stewart and John Balderson (from a play
   by Jane Cowl and Jane Murfin)
Camera: Leonard Smith (technicolor)
Art director: Cedric Gibbons
Editor: Frank Sullivan
Music: Herbert Stothart
Producer: Victor Saville for M-G-M, 100 minutes

VANISHING VIRGINIAN (1942)*
   With: Frank Morgan, Kathryn Grayson, Spring Byington, Natalie
   Thompson, Douglass Newland, Mark Daniels, Elizabeth Patterson,
   Juanita Quigley, Scotty Beckett, Dickie Jones, Leigh Whipper,
   Louise Beavers, J. M. Kerrigan
Screenplay: Jan Fortune (from a novel by Rebecca Yancey Williams)
Camera: Charles Lawton
Art director: Cedric Gibbons
Editor: James M. Newcom
Music: David Snell and Lennie Hayton
Producer: Edwin Knopf for M-G-M, 97 minutes

SEVEN SWEETHEARTS (1942)*
   With: Kathryn Grayson, Van Heflin, Marsha Hunt, Cecelia Park-
   er, Peggy Moran, Mrs. Nugent, S. Z. Sakall, Dorothy Morris,
   Frances Rafferty, Frances Raeburn, Carl Esmond, Michael But-
   ler, Cliff Danielson, Donald Meek, Louise Beavers, William Rob-
   erts
Screenplay: Walter Reisch and Leo Townscend
Camera: George Folsey
Art director: Cedric Gibbons
Editor: Blanche Sewell
Music: Franz Waxman (songs by Walter Jurman, Paul Francis Web-
   ster, Burton Land, and Ralph Field)
Producer: Joe Pasternak for M-G-M, 98 minutes

STAGE DOOR CANTEEN (1943)
   With: Cheryl Walker, William Terry, Marjorie Riordan, Lon
   McCallister, Margaret Early, "Sunset Carson" Harrison, Dorothea
   Kent, Fred Brady, Marion Shockley, Patrick O'Moore, Ruth Ro-
   man and a variety of guest stars including Tallulah Bankhead,
   Katharine Hepburn, George Jessel and Aline MacMahon
Screenplay: Delmer Daves
Camera: Harry Wild
Art director: Hans Peters
Editor: Hal Kern
Music: C. Bakaleinikoff
Producer: Sol Lesser for United Artists, 132 minutes

HIS BUTLER'S SISTER (1943)
  With: Deanna Durbin, Franchot Tone, Pat O'Brien, Akim Tamir-
  off, Alan Mowbray, Walter Catlett, Elsa Janssen, Evelyn Ankers,
  Frank Jenks, Sig Arno, Hans Conreid, Florence Bates, Andrew
  Tombes
Screenplay: Samuel Hoffenstein and Betty Reinhardt
Camera: Woody Bredell
Art director: John B. Goodman and Martin Obzina
Music: Charles Previn
Producer: Frank Borzage and Frank Shaw for Universal Pictures,
  93 minutes

TILL WE MEET AGAIN (1944)
  With: Ray Milland, Barbara Britton, Walter Slezak, Lucille Wat-
  son, Konstantin Shayne, Vladimir Sokoloff, Marguerite D'Alvarez,
  Mona Freeman, William Edmunds, George Davis, Peter Helmess,
  John Wengraf
Screenplay: Lenore Coffee (from a play by Alfred Maury)
Camera: Theodor Sparkuhl
Art director: Hans Dreier and Robert Usher
Editor: Elmo Veron
Music: David Buttolph
Producer: Frank Borzage for Paramount Pictures, 88 minutes

THE SPANISH MAIN (1945)
  With: Paul Henreid, Maureen O'Hara, Walter Slezak, Binnie
  Barnes, John Emergy, Barton MacLane, J. M. Kerrigan, Fritz
  Leiber, Nancy Gates, Jack La Rue, Mike Mazurki, Ian Keith,
  Victor Kilian, Curt Bois
Screenplay: George Worthing Yates, Herman Mankiewicz and Aeneas
  Mackenzie (from a story by Aeneas MacKenzie)
Camera: George Barnes (technicolor)
Art director: Al D'Agostino
Editor: Ralph Dawson
Music: Hanns Eisler and C. Bakaleinikoff
Producer: Robert Fellows for RKO-Radio Pictures, 101 minutes

MAGNIFICENT DOLL (1946)
  With: Ginger Rogers, David Niven, Burgess Meredith, Horace
  McNally, Peggy Wood, Frances Williams, Robert Barrat, Gran-
  don Rhodes
Screenplay: Irving Stone
Camera: Joseph Valentine
Editor: Ted J. Kent
Music: H. J. Salter
Producer: Jack H. Skirball and Bruce Manning for Hallmark Pro-
  ductions--released by Universal Pictures, 95 minutes

I'VE ALWAYS LOVED YOU (1946)
  With: Philip Dorn, Catherine McLeod, William Carter, Maria
  Ouspenskaya, Felix Bressart, Fritz Feld, Elizabeth Patterson,
  Vanessa Brown, Lewis Howard, Adele Mara, Gloria Donovan,
  Cora Witherspoon

Screenplay: Borden Chase (from a story by Borden Chase)
Camera: Tony Gaudio (technicolor)
Art director: Howard E. Johnson, John McCarthy, Jr., and Leanora
    Pierotti
Editor: Richard L. Van Enger
Music: Walter Scharf (piano recordings by Arthur Rubinstein)
Producer: Frank Borzage for Republic Pictures, 117 minutes

This was Republic's first technicolor film.

THAT'S MY MAN (1947)
    With: Don Ameche, Catherine McLeod, Roscoe Karns, John Ridge-
    ly, Kitty Irish, Joe Frisco, Gregory Marshall, Dorothy Adams,
    Frankie Darro, Hampton J. Scott, William B. Davidson, Joe Her-
    nandez, Gallant Man
Screenplay: Steve Fisher and Bradley King
Camera: Tony Gaudio
Art director: James Sullivan
Editor: Richard L. Van Enger
Music: Hans Salter and Cy Feuer
Producer: Frank Borzage for Republic Pictures, 104 minutes

MOONRISE (1949)
    With: Dane Clark, Gail Russell, Ethel Barrymore, Allyn Joslyn,
    Rex Ingram, Henry Morgan, David Street, Selena Royale, Harry
    Carey, Jr., Irving Bacon, Lloyd Bridges, Phil Brown, Clem Bev-
    ens, Lila Leeds
Screenplay: Charles Haas (from a novel by Theodore Straus)
Camera: John L. Russell
Art director: John McCarthy, Jr., and George Sawley
Editor: Harry Keller
Music: William Lava ("The Moonrise Song" by Harry Tobias and
    William Lava)
Producer: Charles Haas for Republic Pictures, 90 minutes

CHINA DOLL (1958)
    With: Victor Mature, Li Li Hua, Ward Bond, Bob Mathias, Stu-
    art Whitman, Johnny Desmond, Ken Perry, Don Barry, Danny
    Chang, Steve Mitchell, Elaine Curtis, Ann McCrea, Ann Paige,
    Denver Pyle
Screenplay: Kitty Buhler (from a story by James Benson Nablo and
    Thomas F. Kelly)
Camera: William H. Clothier
Art director: Howard Richmond
Editor: Jack Murray
Music: Henry Vars
Producer: Frank Borzage for Romina Productions--released by Uni-
    ted Artists

THE BIG FISHERMAN (1959)
    With: Howard Keel, Susan Kohner, John Saxon, Martha Hyer,
    Herbert Lom, Ray Stricklyn, Marian Seldes, Alexander Scourby,
    Beulah Bondi, Jay Barney, Charlotte Fletcher, Mark Dana, Rhodes

Reason, Henry Brandon, Brian Hutton
Screenplay: Howard Estabrook and Rowland V. Lee (from a novel by
   Lloyd C. Douglas)
Camera: Lee Garmes (Panavision and technicolor)
Art director: Julia Heron
Editor: Paul Weatherwax
Music: Albert Ray Malotte and Joseph Gershenson
Producer: Rowland V. Lee for Centurion Films--released by Buena
   Vista, 180 minutes

Abbott, Jere, et al. Hound and Horn: Essays on Cinema. New York: Arno, 1972.

Abel, Lionel, ed. Moderns on Tragedy: An Anthology of Modern and Relevant Opinions on the Substance and Meaning of Tragedy. Greenwich, Conn.: Fawcett, 1967.

Agee, James. Agee on Film. 2 vols. New York: Grosset and Dunlap, 1969.

Agel, Henri, and Henry, Michael. "Frank Borzage." Anthologie du Cinema. 21 vols. (1973), 243-291.

Aherne, Brian. A Proper Job. Boston: Houghton Mifflin, 1969.

Alpert, Hollis. The Barrymores. New York: Dial, 1964.

_____. The Dreams and the Dreamers. New York: Macmillan, 1962.

Andrew, J. Dudley. The Major Film Theories: An Introduction. London: Oxford University Press, 1976.

Annenkov, Georges. Max Ophuls. Paris: Le Terrain Vague, 1962.

Appel, Alfred, Jr. Nabokov's Dark Cinema. New York: Oxford University Press, 1974.

Arnheim, Rudolf. Film as Art. Berkeley: University of California Press, 1957.

Ballio, Tino, ed. The American Film Industry. Madison: University of Wisconsin Press, 1976.

Bare, Richard L. The Film Director: A Practical Guide to Motion Picture and Television Techniques. New York: Macmillan, 1971.

Barrymore, Ethel. Memories, An Autobiography. New York: Harper and Brothers, 1955.

Barrymore, Lionel, with Cameron Shipp. We Barrymores. New York: Appleton-Century-Crofts, 1951.

Basinger, Jeanine. "Ten That Got Away," in Women and the Cine-
    ma: A Critical Anthology, ed. Karyn Kay and Gerald Peary. New
    York: Dutton, 1977.

Bazin, Andre. What Is Cinema? 2 vols. Berkeley: University of
    California Press, 1967.

Belton, John. "I've Always Loved You." Focus! 9 (Spring-Summer
    1973), 42-44.

_____. "Souls Made Great Through Love and Adversity." Focus!
    9 (Spring-Summer 1973), 16-22.

_____. The Hollywood Professionals: Howard Hawks, Frank Bor-
    zage and Edgar Ulmer. vol. 3. New York: Tantivity, 1974.

Bennett, Joan, and Kibbee, Lois. The Bennett Playbill. New York:
    Holt, Rinehart and Winston, 1970.

Bentley, Eric. "Melodrama," in The Life of Drama. New York:
    Atheneum, 1964.

Bergman, Andrew. We're in the Money. New York: Harper and
    Row, 1971.

Biereton, Gregory. Principles of Tragedy: A Rational Examination
    of the Tragic Concept in Life and Literature. Coral Gables, Fla.:
    University of Miami Press, 1968.

Bluestone, George. Novels into Film: The Metamorphosis of Fic-
    tion into Cinema. Berkeley: University of California Press,
    1973.

Bobker, Lee. Elements of Film. New York: Harcourt, Brace &
    World, 1969.

Bodeen, Dewitt. From Hollywood: The Careers of Fifteen Great
    American Stars. New York: Barnes, 1976.

Bogdanovich, Peter. Pieces of Time: Peter Bogdanovich on the
    Movies. New York: Arbor House, 1973.

Booth, Michael R. English Melodrama. London: Herbert Jenkins,
    1965.

Bourget, Jean-Loup. "Seventh Heaven." Monogram 4 (1972), 24-
    25.

Brooks, Cleanth, ed. Tragic Themes in Western Literature. New
    Haven: Yale University Press, 1960.

Brooks, Peter. The Melodramatic Imagination. New Haven: Yale
    University Press, 1976.

Brown, Karl. Adventures with D. W. Griffith. New York: Farrar, Straus, and Giroux, 1973.

Brownlow, Kevin. The Parade's Gone By. New York: Knopf, 1969.

_____. The War, the West and the Wilderness. New York: Knopf, 1979.

Bruccoli, Matthew J., ed. F. Scott Fitzgerald's Screenplay for THREE COMRADES by Erich Maria Remarque. Carbondale and Edwardsville: Southern Illinois University Press, 1978.

Brunel, Adrian. Filmcraft. London: George Newkes, 1935.

Bruno, Michael. Venus in Hollywood: The Continental Enchantress from Garbo to Loren. New York: Lyle Stuart, 1970.

Calarco, N. Joseph. Tragic Being: Apollo and Dionysis in Western Drama. Minneapolis: University of Minnesota Press, 1969.

Camper, Fred. "A Man's Castle." Focus! 9 (Spring-Summer 1973), 37-41, 51-54.

_____. "Disputed Passage," in Movies and Methods, ed. Bill Nichols. Berkeley: University of California Press, 1976.

_____. "The Shining Hour." Harvard Film Studies (1975), 1-8.

Capra, Frank. The Name Above the Title. New York: Macmillan, 1971.

Cawkwell, Tun, and Smith, John M., eds. The World Encyclopedia of the Film. New York: Galahad, 1972.

Clair, Rene. Cinema Yesterday and Today. New York: Dover, 1972.

Cooper, John C., and Skrade, Carl. Celluloid and Symbols. Philadelphia: Fortress, 1970.

Corliss, Richard. Talking Pictures: Screenwriters in the American Cinema. New York: Penguin, 1974.

Corrigan, Robert W. Laurel British Drama: The Twentieth Century. New York: Dell, 1972.

_____, ed. Tragedy: Vision and Form. San Francisco: Chandler, 1965.

Courtney, W. L. The Idea of Tragedy in Ancient and Modern Drama. New York: Russell and Russell, 1900.

Crist, Judith. The Private Eye, the Cowboy and the Very Naked Girl. Chicago: Holt, Rinehart and Winston, 1968.

Crowther, Bosley. Hollywood Rajah. New York: Holt, Rinehart and Winston, 1960.

Curtiss, Thomas Quinn. Von Stroheim. New York: Farrar, Straus, and Giroux, 1971.

Dardis, Tom. Some Time in the Sun: The Hollywood Years of Fitz-gerald, Faulkner, Nathanael West, Aldoux Huxley and James Agee. New York: Scribner's, 1976.

Davies, Marion. The Times We Had: Life with William Randolph Hearst, ed. Pamela Pfau and Kenneth Marx. New York: Bobbs-Merrill, 1975.

Davy, Charles, ed. Footnotes to the Film. London: Lovat Dickson, 1938.

Day, Donald. Will Rogers: A Biography. New York: McKay, 1963.

De Mille, Cecil. The Autobiography of Cecil B. De Mille. Englewood Cliffs, N. J.: Prentice-Hall, 1959.

Disher, Maurice. Blood and Thunder: Mid-Victorian Melodrama and Its Origins. London: Frederick Muller, 1949.

Drinkwater, John. The Life and Adventures of Carl Laemmle. New York: Putnam's, 1931.

Dunne, John Gregory. The Studio. New York: Farrar, Straus, and Giroux, 1969.

Durgnat, Raymond. Films and Feelings. Cambridge, Mass.: M. I. T. Press, 1967.

_____. The Crazy Mirror: Hollywood Comedy and the American Image. London: Faber and Faber, 1969.

Early, Steven C. An Introduction to American Movies. New York: New American Library, 1978.

Eels, George. Ginger, Loretta and Irene Who?. New York: Pocket Books, 1976.

Elsaesser, Thomas. "Tales of Sound and Fury: Observations on the Family Melodrama." Monogram 4 (1972), 2-15.

Ernst, Morris, and Lorentz, Pare. Censored: The Private Life of the Movies. New York: Jonathan Cape and Harrison Smith, 1930.

Everson, William K. A Pictorial History of the Western Film. Secaucus, N. J.: Citadel, 1969.

_____. "A Farewell to Arms." The New School Program Notes (October 15, 1971), 1-2.

_____ . American Silent Film. New York: Oxford University Press, 1978.

Eyles, Allen. The Western. New York: Barnes, 1975.

Fanin, George N. , and Everson, William K. The Western: From the Silents to the Seventies. New York: Grossman, 1973.

Farber, Manny. Movies. New York: Hillstone, 1971.

Fell, John L. Film and the Narrative Tradition. Norman: University of Oklahoma Press, 1970.

Fernett, Gene. Poverty Row. Satellite Beach, Fla.: Coral Reef, 1973.

Finler, Joel W. Stroheim. Berkeley: University of California Press, 1968.

Flynn, Errol. My Wicked, Wicked Ways. New York: Putnam's, 1959.

Fox, Terry Curtis. "Three Comrades." Focus! 9 (Spring-Summer 1973), 31-33.

French, Philip. The Movie Moguls: An Informal History of the Hollywood Tycoons. London: Weidenfeld and Nicolson, 1969.

_____ . Westerns: Aspects of Movie Genre. New York: Oxford University Press, 1977.

Froug, William. A Screenwriter Looks at Screenwriting. New York: Macmillan, 1972.

Frye, Northrop. Anatomy of Criticism: Four Essays. Princeton, N.J.: Princeton University Press, 1973.

Garbicz, Adam, and Klinowski, Jacek. Cinema, the Magic Vehicle: A Guide to Its Achievement. Metuchen, N.J.: Scarecrow, 1975.

Garnett, Tay. Lite Your Torches and Pull Up Your Tights. New Rochelle, N.Y.: Arlington House, 1973.

Geduld, Harry. The Birth of the Talkies: From Edison to Jolson. Bloomington: Indiana University Press, 1975.

Geduld, Harry M. , and Gottesman, Ronald. An Illustrated Glossary of Film Terms. New York: Holt, Rinehart and Winston, 1973.

Getlein, Frank, and Gardiner, S. J. Movies, Morals and Art. New York: Sheed and Ward, 1961.

Giannetti, Louis D. Understanding Movies, second edition. Englewood Cliffs, N.J.: Prentice-Hall, 1976.

Gissner, Robert. Moving Image: A Guide to Cinematic Literacy.
New York: Dutton, 1968.

Glatzer, Richard, and Raeburn, John, eds. Frank Capra: The Man
and His Films. Ann Arbor: University of Michigan Press, 1975.

Grant, Barry K. , ed. Film Genre: Theory and Criticism. Metuch-
en, N. J. : Scarecrow, 1977.

Greenberg, Harvey R. The Movies on Your Mind. New York: Dutton, 1975.

Greene, Graham. Graham Greene on Film: Collected Film Criticism, 1935-1940. New York: Simon and Schuster, 1972.

Griffith, Richard, and Mayer, Arthur. The Movies. New York:
Simon and Schuster, 1970.

Grimsted, David. Melodrama Unveiled: American Theater and Culture, 1800-1850. Chicago: University of Chicago Press, 1968.

Guiles, Fred Lawrence. Marion Davies. New York: McGraw-Hill,
1972.

Harris, Mark. The Case for Tragedy: Being a Challenge to Those
Who Deny the Possibilities of a Tragic Spirit in the Modern
World. New York: Putnam's, 1932.

Haskell, Molly. From Reverence to Rape: The Treatment of Wom-
en in the Movies. New York: Holt, Rinehart and Winston, 1973.

Haskins, Harrison. "The Photoplay of the Proletariat. " Motion
Picture Classic. XI, 1 (September 1920), 18, 88-90.

Hayes, Helen, with Louis Funke. A Gift of Joy. New York: Evans,
1965.

_____, with Sandford Dody. On Reflection: An Autobiography.
New York: Evans, 1968.

Heilman, Robert Bechtold. The Iceman, the Arsonist and the Troubled Agent: Tragedy and Melodrama on the Modern Stage. Seattle: University of Washington Press, 1973.

Henderson, Robert. D. W. Griffith: The Years at Biograph. New
York: Farrar, Straus, and Giroux, 1970.

Henn, T. R. The Harvest of Tragedy. London: Methuen, 1955.

Higham, Charles. The Art of the American Film. Garden City,
N. Y. : Anchor, 1974.

_____. Warner Brothers. New York: Scribner's, 1975.

Higham, Charles, and Greenberg, Joel. The Celluloid Muse: Holly-
    wood Directors Speak. New York: New American Library, 1969.

Hochman, Stanley, ed. American Film Directors: A Library of
    Film Criticism. New York: Ungar, 1974.

Horrigan, William. "Dying Without Death: Borzage's A FAREWELL
    TO ARMS, " in The Classic American Novel and the Movies, eds.
    Gerald Peary and Roger Shatzkin. New York: Ungar, 1977.

Huaco, George. The Sociology of Film Art. New York: Basic
    Books, 1965.

Huss, Roy, and Silverstein, Norman. The Film Experience: Ele-
    ments of Motion Picture Art. New York: Harper & Row, 1968.

Jacobs, Louis. The Rise of the American Film: A Critical History.
    New York: Teachers College Press, 1948.

_____. Introduction to the Art of the Movies. New York: Noon-
    day, 1960.

_____. The Emergence of Film Art: The Evolution and Develop-
    ment of the Motion Picture as an Art, from 1900 to the Present.
    New York: Hopkinson and Blake, 1969.

_____. The Movies as Medium. New York: Farrar, Straus, and
    Giroux, 1970.

Jarvie, I. C. Movies as Social Criticism: Aspects of Their Psy-
    chology. Metuchen, N. J. : Scarecrow, 1978.

Johnson, Lincoln F. Film: Space, Time, Light and Sound. New
    York: Holt, Rinehart and Winston, 1974.

Kael, Pauline. I Lost It at the Movies. Boston: Little, Brown,
    1965.

_____. Kiss Kiss, Bang Bang. Boston: Little, Brown, 1968.

_____. Going Steady. Boston: Little, Brown, 1970.

_____. Deeper into Movies. New York: Bantam, 1974.

Kaminsky, Stuart. American Film Genres: Approaches to a Critical
    Theory of Popular Film. New York: Dell, 1974.

Kantor, Bernard, et al. Directors at Work: Interviews with Ameri-
    can Film Makers. New York: Funk and Wagnalls, 1970.

Kauffmann, Stanley. A World on Film: Criticism and Comment.
    New York: Harper & Row, 1966.

_____. Figures of Light: Film Criticism and Comment. New York: Harper & Row, 1971.

_____. Living Images. New York: Harper & Row, 1975.

_____, and Henstell, Bruce. American Film Criticism: From the Beginnings to Citizen Kane. New York: Liveright, 1972.

Kaufman, Walter. Tragedy and Philosophy. New York: Doubleday, 1968.

Kay, Karyn, and Peary, Gerald, eds. Women and the Cinema: A Critical Anthology. New York: Dutton, 1977.

Kehr, David. "Moonrise." Focus! 9 (Spring-Summer 1973), 26-30.

Kitses, Jim. Horizons West. Bloomington: Indiana University Press, 1969.

Knight, Arthur. The Liveliest Art. New York: New American Library, 1959.

Koenigil, Mark. Movies in Society: Sex, Crime and Censorship. New York: Robert Speller, 1962.

Koszarski, Richard. Hollywood Directors, 1914-1940. London: Oxford University Press, 1976.

Kracauer, Siegfried. Theory on Film: The Redemption of Physical Reality. New York: Oxford University Press, 1960.

Krook, Dorothea. Elements of Tragedy. New Haven: Yale University Press, 1969.

Laeska, Michael. The Voice of Tragedy. New York: Robert Speller, 1963.

Lahue, Kalton C. Dreams for Sale: The Rise and Fall of the Triangle Film Corporation. New York: Barnes, 1971.

Latham, Aaron. Crazy Sundays: F. Scott Fitzgerald in Hollywood. London: Secker and Warburg, 1971.

Lawson, John Howard. Film in the Battle of Ideas. New York: Masses and Mainstream, 1953.

Leech, Clifford. Tragedy. London: Methuen, 1969.

Levy, Leo B. Versions of Melodrama: A Study of the Fiction and Drama of Henry James, 1865-1897. Berkeley: University of California Press, 1957.

Lorentz, Pare. Pare Lorentz on Film: Movies, 1927-1941. New
York: Hopkinson and Blake, 1975.

Lucas, F. L. Tragedy: Serious Drama in Relation to Aristotle's
Poetics. New York: Collier, 1962.

MacCann, Richard. Film: A Montage of Theories. New York:
Dutton, 1966.

McCollom, William G. Tragedy. New York: Macmillan, 1957.

McConnell, Frank D. The Spoken Seen: Film and the Romantic
Imagination. Baltimore: Johns Hopkins University Press, 1975.

MacDonald, Dwight. Dwight MacDonald on Movies. Englewood
Cliffs, N. J.: Prentice-Hall, 1969.

McMurtry, Larry. "Cowboys, Movies, Myths and Cadillacs: Realism
in the Western, " in Man and the Movies, ed. W. R. Robinson.
Baton Rouge: Louisiana State University Press, 1967.

Madsen, Axel. Billy Wilder. Bloomington: Indiana University
Press, 1969.

Mahern, Michael. "History Is Made at Night." Focus! 9 (Spring-
Summer 1973), 23-25.

Mandel, Oscar. A Definition of Tragedy. New York: New York
University Press, 1961.

Manoogian, Haig P. The Film-Maker's Art. New York: Basic
Books, 1966.

Manville, Roger. What Is a Film? London: MacDonald, 1965.

Marx, Samuel. Mayer and Thalberg: The Make-Believe Saints.
New York: Random House, 1975.

Mast, Gerald, and Cohen, Marshall, eds. Film Theory and Criticism. New York: Oxford University Press, 1974.

Maynard, Richard A. The American West on Film: Myth and Reality. Rochelle Park, N. J.: Hayden, 1974.

Michel, Lawrence, and Sewell, Richard B., eds. Tragedy: Modern
Essays in Criticism. Englewood Cliffs, N. J.: Prentice-Hall,
1963.

Milne, Peter. Motion Picture Directing: The Facts and the Theories of the Newest Art. New York: Falk, 1922.

Milne, Tom. Rouben Mamoulian. Bloomington: Indiana University
Press, 1969.

Minnelli, Vincente. I Remember It Well. Garden City, N.Y.:
Doubleday, 1974.

Mizener, Arthur. The Far Side of Paradise: A Biography of F.
Scott Fitzgerald. Cambridge, Mass.: The Riverside Press, 1951.

Montgomery, John. Comedy Films: 1894-1954. London: Allen and
Unwin, 1954.

Morse, David. "Aspects of Melodrama." Monogram 4 (1972), 16-
17.

Nachbar, Jack, ed. Focus On: The Western. Englewood Cliffs,
N.J.: Prentice-Hall, 1974.

Naumberg, Nancy. We Make the Movies. New York: Norton, 1937.

Nichols, Bill, ed. Movies and Methods. Berkeley: University of
California Press, 1976.

Noble, Peter. Hollywood Scapegoat: The Biography of Erich von
Stroheim. New York: Arno, 1972.

Parish, James Robert, and Bowers, Ronald L. The MGM Stock
Company: The Golden Era. New York: Bonanza, 1972.

Parish, James Robert, and Pitts, Michael R. The Great Western
Pictures. Metuchen, N.J.: Scarecrow, 1976.

Patterson, Frances. Cinema Craftsmanship. New York: Harcourt,
Brace and Howe, 1920.

Perkins, V. F. Film as Film: Understanding and Judging Movies.
Baltimore: Penguin, 1972.

Pickford, Mary. Sunshine and Shadow. Garden City, N.Y.: Doubleday, 1955.

Piper, Henry Dan. F. Scott Fitzgerald: A Critical Portrait. New
York: Holt, Rinehart and Winston, 1965.

Powdermaker, Hortense. Hollywood the Dream Factory: An Anthro-
pologist Looks at the Movie-Makers. Boston: Little, Brown,
1950.

Pratt, George. Spellbound in Darkness. New York: New York
Graphic Society, 1966.

_____. "In Search of 'Natural': An Interview with Frank Bor-
zage." Image 20, 3-4 (September-December 1977), 34-43.

Quirk, Lawrence. The Great Romantic Films. Secaucus, N.J.:
Citadel, 1974.

Rahill, Frank.   The World of Melodrama.   University Park: Pennsylvania State University Press, 1967.

Ramsaye, Terry.   A Million and One Nights: A History of the Motion Picture.   2 vols.   New York: Simon and Schuster, 1926.

Raphael, D. D.   The Paradox of Tragedy.   Bloomington: Indiana University Press, 1960.

Rhode, Eric.   A History of the Cinema from Its Origins to 1970. New York: Hill and Wang, 1976.

Rogers, Will.   The Autobiography of Will Rogers.   Boston: Houghton Mifflin, 1949.

Rosen, Marjorie,   Popcorn Venus: Women, Movies and the American Dream.   New York: Coward, McCann and Geoghegan, 1973.

Rosen, Philip.   "Difference and Displacement in SEVENTH HEAVEN, " Screen, 18, 2 (Summer 1977), 89-105.

Rosenberg, James L.   "Melodrama, " in The Context and Craft of Drama, eds. Robert W. Corrigan and James L. Rosenberg.   San Francisco: Chandler, 1964.

Rotha, Paul.   The Film Till Now: A Survey of the Cinema.   New York: Jonathan Cape and Harrison Smith, 1931.

Roud, Richard.   Max Ophuls.   London: British Film Institute, 1958.

Sarris, Andrew.   "First Takes. "   Film Culture 25 (Summer, 1962), 33-36.

_____.   The Films of Josef von Sternberg.   New York: Doubleday, 1966.

_____.   The American Cinema: Directors and Directions, 1929-1968.   New York: Dutton, 1968.

_____.   Confessions of a Cultist: On the Cinema, 1955-1969. New York: Simon and Schuster, 1969.

_____.   The Primal Screen: Essays on Film and Related Subjects.   New York: Simon and Schuster, 1973.

Scholes, Robert, et al.   Elements of Literature.   New York: Oxford University Press, 1978.

Seldes, Gilbert.   The Great Audience.   New York: Viking, 1950.

_____.   An Hour with the Movies and the Talkies.   New York: Arno, 1973.

Shales, Tom, et al. The American Film Heritage: Impressions
    From the American Film Institute Archives. Washington: Acrop-
    olis, 1973.

Shapiro, Burt. "Desire, Gun Woman, Stage Door Canteen." Focus!
    9 (Spring-Summer 1973), 34-36.

Sherman, Eric. Directing the Film: Film Directors on Their Art.
    Boston: Little, Brown, 1976.

Sherman, Eric, and Rubin, Martin, eds. The Director and the
    Event. New York: Atheneum, 1970.

Sinclair, Upton. Upton Sinclair Presents William Fox. Los An-
    geles: Upton Sinclair, 1933.

Sklar, Robert. Movie-Made America: A Cultural History of Ameri-
    can Movies. New York: Vintage, 1975.

Slide, Anthony. Aspects of Film History Prior to 1920. Metuchen,
    N. J.: Scarecrow, 1976.

_____. The Big V: A History of the Vitagraph Company. Me-
    tuchen, N. J.: Scarecrow, 1976.

Smith, James L. Melodrama. London: Methuen, 1973.

_____, ed. Victorian Melodrama: Seven English, French and
    American Melodramas. London: Methuen, 1976.

Smith, Robert. "The Films of Frank Borzage" (part 1). Bright
    Lights 1, 2 (Spring 1975), 4-13.

_____. "The Films of Frank Borzage" (part 2). Bright Lights
    1, 3 (Summer 1975), 15-21.

Suid, Lawrence H. Guts and Glory: Great American War Movies.
    Reading, Mass.: Addison-Wesley, 1978.

Taylor, John Russell. Cinema Eye, Cinema Ear: Some Key Film-
    makers of the Sixties. New York: Hill and Wang, 1964.

_____. Directors and Directing. New York: Hill and Wang,
    1975.

Thomas, Bob. Thalberg: Life and Legend. Garden City, N. Y.:
    Doubleday, 1969.

_____, ed. Directors in Action. Indianapolis: Bobbs-Merrill,
    1973.

Thomson, David. Movie Man. New York: Stein and Day, 1967.

Trent, Paul. Those Fabulous Movie Years: The Thirties. Barre,
   Mass.: Barre, 1975.

Tuska, Jon, ed. Close-up: The Contract Director. Metuchen, N. J.:
   Scarecrow, 1976.

_____, ed. Close-up: The Hollywood Director. Metuchen, N. J.:
   Scarecrow, 1978.

Vidor, King. A Tree Is a Tree. New York: Harcourt, Brace,
   1953.

Wagenkecht, Edward. The Movies in the Age of Innocence. Norman: University of Oklahoma Press, 1962.

Wagner, Geoffrey. The Novel and the Cinema. Rutherford, N. J.:
   Fairleigh Dickinson University Press, 1975.

Walker, Alexander. Stardom. New York: Stein and Day, 1970.

Ward, J. A. The Imagination of Disaster: Evil in the Fiction of
   Henry James. Lincoln: University of Nebraska Press, 1961.

Watt, Harry. Don't Look at the Camera. New York: St. Martin's,
   1974.

Weinberg, Herman. Josef von Sternberg: A Critical Study. New
   York: Dutton, 1967.

_____. The Lubitsch Touch. New York: Dutton, 1968.

Wilcox, Herbert. Twenty Five Thousand Sunsets: The Autobiography
   of Herbert Wilcox. London: The Bodley Head, 1967.

Williams, Raymond. Modern Tragedy. Stanford, Calif.: Stanford
   University Press, 1966.

Wilson, Robert, ed. The Film Criticism of Otis Ferguson. Philadelphia: Temple University Press, 1971.

Wood, Leslie. The Romance of the Movies. London: Heinemann,
   1937.

Wright, Basil. The Long View. New York: Knopf, 1974.

Zinman, David. Fifty Classic Motion Pictures: The Stuff That
   Dreams Are Made Of. New York: Bonanza, 1970.